The French Theatre of To-day

An English View

by

HAROLD HOBSON

BENJAMIN BLOM
New York

Printed in U.S.A. by
NOBLE OFFSET PRINTERS, INC.
NEW YORK 3, N. Y.

To
My Dear Mother
who loves French restaurants and French theatres
as much as I do

Preface

THE object of this book is less to provide an encyclopædic survey of the French theatre than to give an Englishman's estimate of the work of its principal living masters. This aim excludes from consideration, on the one hand, the amusing plays of such writers as Roger Ferdinand, and, on the other, the productions of the late Jean Giraudoux. It has led me to concentrate, after attempting to give a general picture of the Parisian stage, on Sartre, Montherlant, Salacrou, and Anouilh. With Anouilh I have dealt less fully than with the other three, because his work is well known in this country, and has already been the subject of much critical discussion. The translations, except where otherwise stated, are my own, and I must bear responsibility for any imperfections in them.

H. H.

Contents

I

The Theatres of Paris

PARIS is almost wholly a capital; London is liberally endowed with capital things. Any city in the world might be proud of the Mall, of Westminster Abbey and Hall, of Brompton Square, or Hyde Park, or of the Haymarket Theatre seen at night across St James's Square, when its twinkling lights make it as gay, as brightly coloured, and as brittle as a pleasure pavilion in a revue of Charles Cochran's.

But these things do not make London look like a capital city. A capital city, to my mind, should resume in itself the spirit and splendour of the nation of which it ought to be the chief glory, and to do that it must be a conscious unity, an achievement of art, not, as London is, a ramshackle conglomeration of many towns and villages consisting of pretentious, coy, and gimcrack buildings and dirty streets, even though, in this sprawling and unattractive muddle, there occur isolated, rewarding delights.

Paris, on the other hand, is everywhere visibly the civic expression of a great nation. Its enormous *places*, its great boulevards, nearly all completed and closed by some grandiose piece of architecture, do not look as though they had just happened; they have an air of design; an air of being designed, moreover, in relation to each other. One does not need in Paris, as one does in London, to seek out some historic landmark before one feels in the midst of a truly great city. In the considerable distance separating the Arc de Triomphe in the west, by way of the Champs-Élysées, the Place de la Concorde, the Palais-Royal, the Louvre, and Notre-Dame, from the Place de la Bastille in the east; in the distance, almost equally great, between the white mass of the Sacré-Cœur on its hill in the north and the Luxembourg Gardens in the south, passing by the outer boulevards, the Opéra, the Tuileries, the *caves* of Saint-Germain-des-Prés, the Odéon, and the Sorbonne, there is hardly a square yard of pavement, hardly a hotel, café, bookstore, or antique shop, that does not bear the impress of a capital city. Paris is the thought-out product of ordered mind, where London is a gigantic accident, sometimes magnificent, but often distressing.

The area of Paris, then, that properly belongs to a capital city is much larger than the corresponding area of London; but London is considerably the bigger place. The population of London is over eight millions; the population of Paris is rather less than five. Yet the number of seats in the theatres of the two cities is very nearly the same. There are roughly forty-four thousand seats in the forty principal theatres of London. In the fifty-odd theatres of Paris, for a city not much more than half London's size, there are about forty-six thousand seats—that is, ten extra theatres (to say nothing of *chansonniers* and a couple of circuses), two thousand extra seats, for three and half million fewer people.

Paris is plainly a theatre-going city; yet it is a city in which theatre-going is not made easy. It is in fact accompanied by several small but irritating frustrations. In London one buys a ticket either at the theatre box-office or at an agency. In either case, provided with the ticket, one's admittance to one's seat is simple and direct. In Paris the short passage from the taxi at the door to the reserved but unnumbered seat in the stalls is beset with dangers. First of all, there is the *Contrôle* to be negotiated. At a high desk in the centre of the foyer, surrounded by a crowd of people waving tickets in the air, sit three gentle-

men in evening-dress. One of them is the manager of the
theatre. A second represents the State, and collects the
appropriate tax. The third represents the Société des
Auteurs et Compositeurs Dramatiques; he is there to see
that the author duly receives his twelve and a half per
cent. royalty. Before one can penetrate farther the ticket
one has bought must be surrendered, and another obtained in its place; and this operation must be performed
while one is being jostled, good-humouredly but with
vigour, by thirty or forty other people all bent on the
same purpose. Why the crowd round the *Contrôle*, in the
smallest and the largest theatres, should at any given
time always be about twoscore, why it should not, for
example, be four or four hundred, is something I have
never understood.

Then the programme has to be obtained. It is sold in
the foyer, which in Paris, as in every other city, is a place
of shoving and pushing, instead of in the comparative
quiet and leisure of the auditorium. English people (and
Americans used to free programmes) are annoyed that
London programmes cost sixpence. But the theatre-goer
does at least know what the cost will be, and can come
provided with the proper silver coin. In Paris, however,
this cost varies infuriatingly. It may be a shilling; it may
be one-and-six; it may, as at the Hébertot, be three
shillings. On top of this the programme-seller has to be
tipped sixpence or ninepence. On the other side of the
account is the fact that Parisian programmes are elaborate and informative documents, charmingly designed and
printed, giving photographs of the company and theatre
manager, biographies, artistic appreciations, introductions
to the plot of the play, and an agreeably scented leaflet
telling the audience what it could have seen that night if
it had gone to any other theatre than the one it has
chosen.

The price of seats in Paris theatres is high by London,
though not by New York, standards. For straight plays

stalls vary between sixteen shillings and just over a pound. The best seats at the Folies-Bergère or the Casino de Paris are sold at thirty-eight shillings each. In addition to this, and to the toll levied by the sellers of programmes, further money has to be given to the girl who finally shows one to one's seat. The first essential of theatre-going in Paris, therefore, is to remember that one must set out with one's pocket full of small change.

Some of the Parisian theatres, like the Atelier, in its pleasantly melancholy little tree-shaded square on the southern slopes of Montmartre, or the red-and-gold Marigny by the side of the open-air stamp-market in the Champs-Élysées, are very agreeable to the eye. But when all the doors are shut during the performance Parisian theatres are extraordinarily airless. These doors seem to be hermetically sealed, just as those in a London play-house wave about in the wind. If the characteristic danger of a West End auditorium is an icy draught, that of a Paris theatre is asphyxiation. But the peril is miti-gated by the fact that Parisian theatres, like those in New York, follow the civilized rule of no smoking.

The entrance halls of the bigger Paris theatres are extremely spacious. That of the Théâtre de Paris seems to be almost as big as the theatre itself. Like the foyer of the Comédie des Champs-Élysées, it has an admirable bookstall as well as a bar. There is a sizable art exhibi-tion in the entrance hall of the Folies-Bergère, as well as various sideshows of a curious nature. The exact pur-poses of these large halls might well repay a social investigator. They are probably made possible by the lowness of rents in comparison with those of London.

Paris eats dear, but sleeps cheap. One of the most successful of contemporary French dramatists lives in a large apartment in the Avenue Foch, the most fashionable of the streets that radiate outward from the Arc de Triomphe. The Avenue Foch, between the Champs-Élysées and the Bois, is in the sixteenth arrondissement,

which André Siegfried has recently pronounced to be the
most exclusive area in Paris. Is it not the home of nine
Academicians and seventeen dukes? Does not the
widow of the Baron Édouard-Alphonse-James de Rothschild, who was head of the eldest branch of the French
Rothschilds, live at Number 19 in the Avenue Foch, and
the Baron Guy de Rothschild, head of the Rothschild
bank, at Number 21? This dramatist's flat would, in
London, be rented at £1000 or £1200 a year, while the
Paris rent is, or was recently, less than a tenth of the
latter sum.

The lowness of rents and the spaciousness of the Parisian foyers would lead one to expect the Parisian theatres
to be large and cavernous places; and, indeed, some of
them are. The Palais de Chaillot, on the site of the old
Trocadéro, is the biggest theatre in Europe. It seats 700
more people than Drury Lane, and 600 more than the
Palladium; it is twice the size of the Old Vic, and three
times as big as the Haymarket. Its stage is huge enough
to accommodate five hundred chorus-girls. The other
large Parisian theatres—the Gaîté-Lyrique, the Mogador,
the Casino, the Folies-Bergère, and the Grand Théâtre
des Champs-Élysées—are about the size of the Winter
Garden, and they devote themselves industriously, along
with the Châtelet, which is as big as Drury Lane, to
monster musicals with elaborate stage effects, and spectacular revues. There you can see a stage-coach crash
from a broken bridge into a ravine between the mountains: the whole thing is made of cardboard, but it will
fill the entire proscenium opening. Or a carriageful of
romantically tipsy young people of the nineties will drive
up the long, steep hill of Montmartre from the bottom to
the top, revellers, horses, and carriage being got into the
theatre by means of a panorama. For if the Paris musical
stage is more ambitious than the London in its spectacular effects, it is also more naïve in its methods of
achieving them. Many are designed to astonish the

citizens of the future: on Thursday and Sunday afternoons the Châtelet is filled by row on row of pigtailed
little girls.

England is a muddling-through, a middle-way, a
Laodicean country, its politics are neither hot nor cold,
its drama is neither romantic nor classical, but a mixture
of both: everywhere it shows the mark of compromise.
The annual exhibitions of the Royal Academy modify
their traditionalism with small flirtations with modernist
tendencies, and the most admired forms of speech are
graced with trifling imperfections. It is the same with the
London theatres. The characteristic London theatre is no
more a vast palace than it is a rabbit-hutch or a pocket
handkerchief. What one remembers from the French
landscape is the château and the peeling cottage: from the
English, the moderate-sized country house; and the
normal London theatre conforms to the same national
pattern. It is an average-sized place, seating about a
thousand people or a couple of hundred more. There
are sixteen such theatres in the West End, but in Paris
only five: the Marigny, the Sarah-Bernhardt, the Variétés,
the Comédie-Française, and the Théâtre de Paris. There
are about a dozen of the same size as the Haymarket and
the New, and it is in these that, since the War, the most
active theatrical life of Paris has been concentrated. The
work of Sartre is associated with the Antoine; Anouilh
has been played chiefly at the Atelier; Louis Jouvet
annexed the Athénée, which, since his death, has been
taken over by Jean Mercure; and the comedies of
Bernstein and Roussin have glittered at the Bouffes-
Parisiens, the Ambassadeurs, the Michodière, and the
Nouveautés. All these are playhouses varying between the
size of the Haymarket and Wyndham's. The Marigny,
where the Madeleine Renaud–Jean-Louis Barrault company has given many dazzling performances, holds
almost exactly the same number of people as the Picca-
dilly, being just a little larger than the New.

But where Paris differs most strikingly, in the sphere of theatre architecture, from London is in its wealth of tiny playhouses. The Parisian public seems to have an insatiable affection for theatres holding fewer than five hundred people. The smallest public theatre in London is the Fortune, which has 473 seats. The Fortune has had one or two successes in recent years, with plays like Agatha Christie's thriller *The Hollow*, but its record has been far from triumphant. Certainly no London manager would be encouraged by its experience to build another theatre of the same limited capacity. Yet in Paris there is the astonishing number of sixteen theatres as small as or smaller than the Fortune. The Saint-Georges seats the same number of people—473—but the others, the Capucines, the Studio des Champs-Élysées, the Charles-de-Rochfort, the Comédie-Wagram, the Gramont, the Grand-Guignol, the Huchette, the Bruyère, the Michel, the Monceau, the Noctambules, the Œuvre, the Potinière, the Théâtre de Poche, and the Vieux-Colombier, are all smaller than the Fortune.

These miniature theatres do not always sail the turbulent theatrical seas confidently. On occasion since the War, the Œuvre has taken as little as £18 at a performance, while, with a farce called *Ce cher trésor*, the Potinière once fell to £13. But the Œuvre and the Vieux-Colombier are among the most famous of Parisian theatres; they have both been associated with work of the highest quality; and several of the other smaller theatres have attained notable success, at any rate in the financial field. A farce about a comic psychic maid—*Le Don d'Adèle*—ran for over six hundred consecutive performances at the Comédie-Wagram between 1950 and 1952, and *Monsieur de Falinder*, by G. Manoir and A. Verhylle, was played two thousand times at the Monceau between 1943 and 1948.

Generally speaking, then, apart from a few playhouses of truly monster size, the Parisian theatres are smaller

than those of London. This has had a considerable effect
upon French styles of acting and production. The comparatively restricted French stages do not encourage
elaborate and expensive scenery. There are artists of
great ability, like Georges Wakhevitch, among the Paris
scene-designers, but they work under difficulties; little
money is spent upon their efforts, the result of which
often seem gimcrack and sketchy to English eyes. The
principal reason for this goes down to the roots of the
French conception of the true nature of drama; for the
moment it is sufficient to note that a contributing factor
is the limited area of most Paris theatres.

The tiny confines of these theatres encourage the
writing of light and frothy little farces and comedies
without enough substance to fill a big playhouse. One
does not ask for elaborate plays in a theatre hardly larger
than a drawing-room. When one of these trivia is
brought to England or the United States, and is blown
up to twice its proper size, and acted three times as
emphatically as it ought to be, in order not to be lost
from both sight and hearing in one of our bigger theatres,
all its life, colour, gaiety, and wit depart from it. This
presumably is what happened to Jean-Bernard Luc's
light-hearted satire on psychiatry, *Le Complexe de Philémon*, when it failed disastrously in New York. Jean
Anouilh's *Ardèle* was not a frothy comedy, but it was a
little play, and it was a grave error to stretch it out painfully in an effort to make it fill the Vaudeville in London
for a whole evening.

The smallness of most Parisian theatres lifts a great
strain from the actors' voices. However quietly or
casually they speak, the players can be heard in every part
of the house. They can also be seen, not merely in bulk
but in detail. French actors like Henry Guisol, the husband in *Le Complexe de Philémon* who so disturbs the
psychiatrist by being obstinately faithful to his wife, or
Robert Vattier, the husband in André Roussin's *Nina*,

who is overwhelmed with naïve admiration for the multiple conquests of his wife's lover, indulge in a richness of facial play that would go for nothing in most London theatres, for the excellent reason that it would be invisible at the back of the stalls and dress circle, and in the upper circle and gallery. At the Monceau, the Michel, or the Wagram a wink is as easily seen as an epileptic fit at the Prince's or Winter Garden. Stendhal, writing of Julien Sorel's embarrassed silence in the presence of women, says in compensation that his eyes flashed "like a good actor's." This is not an English novelist's metaphor. One could go to theatres every week for half a century in either London or the British provinces, and still not be able to tell whether actors' eyes flash or not.

The Paris theatres are widely scattered. The Atelier is in the north, on the slopes of Montmartre, while there is a small cluster of playhouses—the Gaîté-Montparnasse, the Bobino, the Casino Montparnasse, and the Montparnasse-Gaston Baty—far to the south even of the Luxembourg Gardens. Yet the great majority of Paris theatres are on the right bank of the river; and no fewer than thirty are concentrated in the eighth, ninth, and tenth arrondissements, along the Champs-Élysées and in the neighbourhood of the Grands Boulevards.

The Grands Boulevards still carry a suggestion of wealth and luxurious idleness. They are close to the fashionable shops between the Ritz and the Louvre. The Café de la Paix still has its gilded decorations and its shining mirrors, and its tables on the pavement, at which one can sit and watch the long lines of motor-cars passing the great stairs and the Second Empire entrance of the Opéra. Here, amid the white-aproned waiters, and under the lights, it is still easy to recall the days of carelessly ostentatious riches, days when La Belle Otero (who is still alive) used to dance wearing three necklaces, the first of which had belonged to the Empress Eugénie, the second to the Empress of Austria, the third

bought for her by an admirer at the auctioneer's for
£25,000; eight bracelets of rubies, emeralds, and sap-
phires; in her hair a tiara of diamonds; diamonds in her
ears; and on her shoulders a bolero made entirely of
diamonds. For this Spanish gipsy it is said that six men
in the early days of the century committed suicide. But
though these legends, and others like them, linger in
Paris more vividly than in London, they are not receiving
many contemporary additions. There are to-day more
sacrifices made to the whirling traffic of the Place de
l'Étoile than to *femmes fatales*.

Because many theatres are close to the Grands Boulevards, and the Grands Boulevards used to be synonymous
with expensive pleasures, it would be a mistake to assume
that even Paris's most fashionable theatres blaze with
dazzling dresses. A gala première at one of the famous
theatres still remains more splendid than anything we
know in London, and enormous efforts are made to give
the house a magnificent appearance. When André
Gide's *Les Caves du Vatican* was presented at the Comédie-
Française a few months before the author's death, the
Comédie's secretary, Frank Bauer, excelled himself. He
secured the presence of the President of the Republic, half
the members of the Academy, nine Ambassadors, three
generals, a maharajah, and in the front row of the dress
circle he placed sixty of the prettiest women in Paris,
filling the orchestra stalls with the runners-up. Admiring
references to M. Bauer's achievement that night continued to crop up in the newspapers for weeks afterwards.

But a gala première is very different from ordinary performances. At these there is an almost complete absence
of evening-dress. When there is a ballet at the Opéra,
one is told that evening-dress is essential; and across the
vouchers are printed the unequivocal words, *Tenue de
soirée est de rigueur*. This rubric appeared on the ticket that
admitted me to the stalls one evening when Lycette
Darsonval and Serge Lifar were dancing in *Giselle*. The

Opéra, which holds between two and three thousand people, was crowded. But I could see only four couples who wore anything resembling evening-dress.

Nevertheless, French audiences are better dressed than English, but not in the line of ostentation. Their clothes, in general, are neater, cleaner, they fit better, are better pressed, and are worn with greater care and style. They do not smell of tobacco smoke. The seats are too small for their wearers to crease and spoil their clothes by lounging and lolling. These seats are not, however, too small to talk in. A French audience is inclined to chatter. It applauds loudly at the end of each act, bringing the players before the curtain at every intermission, but it rushes away without ceremony at the end, in order to catch the last train, for French performances begin late. Most plays are due to start at nine, actually the curtain goes up between ten minutes and a quarter-past nine, and the whole audience is generally seated by 9.30. The play begins with the famous and traditional "Trois coups." The audience shushes and hisses late-comers, who reply by banging their seats down defiantly. In the intervals there is a screen-newspaper to read, and the attendants walk about shouting in shrill voices, "Esquimaux, Esquimaux," the name of a chocolate-ice that is apparently popular in France. There is a general impression of eagerness and excitement, nothing like that feeling one sometimes gets on entering an English theatre, that one has wandered by mistake into a museum.

Before he has seen many plays in Paris—I mean serious plays—even while the conditions and atmosphere I have described still remain strange to him, the English theatre-goer will be struck by an apparent paradox. He will observe a violent contrast between the coarseness and daring of the things that French actors say, and the restraint and Puritanism of the things they do. And he will find that, in explaining this paradox, he has come upon the primary characteristic of the French theatre, a characteristic that differentiates it entirely from our own.

The coarseness which is so obvious in the script of French plays—not only in deliberately bawdy farces, but in the considered work of Paris's acknowledged masters —is at times so unbounded that it arouses protest from the Parisian critics. Jean-Jacques Gautier, for example, was moved to indignation by the verbal freedom of *La Valse des toréadors*, one of the latest plays of Jean Anouilh. He found in it some fine scenes, especially that in which the old general, the lecherous and pathetic and comic hero of *Ardèle*, explained to the doctor how, all his life, he had had to struggle with his soul. But he rebelled against the play's gross language: particularly against a lengthy episode in which a woman shouted, and screamed that she would never give up her husband. "For me you are this, . . . you are that," she cried. "*Tu es ma boîte à ordures.*" And I admit that I myself, accustomed to the greater restraint of English dialogue, was surprised to find, in Marcel Aymé's bitter satire on the French magistracy, *La Tête des autres*, an attractive woman saying, "Un officier me confiait l'autre jour que dans le bled tunisien ou ils sont privés de toute présence féminine les soldats se rattrapent sur les mules," and adding, "C'est d'ailleurs une chose que j'aimerais bien voir."

To a degree even greater than is the case with us and the Americans, the French theatre is preoccupied with questions of sex. But it cannot be said that it is because of this that it exploits to so notable an extent its singularly vivid verbal licence. No modern French writer has taken for his theme a subject more inviting to the abandonment of discretion than Terence Rattigan did in *The Deep Blue Sea*, in which he probed and exposed a woman's pitiful obsession with the pleasure of physical intercourse. But it is hardly an exaggeration to say that in this play Mr Rattigan did not introduce a single phrase or image that violated the most admirable propriety. It is a measure of the skill with which he used the English method of restraint, and also of the potentiality of that method, that, in spite of this, he never for a moment left his audiences in any doubt as to what he was writing about.

But the most striking example one can give of the contrast between the English and the French styles of writing is the opening speeches of a play that is well known in both London and Paris. Anouilh's *Colombe* ran for nearly a year at the Atelier, with Danièle Delorme and Yves Robert in the principal parts; and Denis Cannan's admirable adaptation, under the same title, with Joyce Redman and Michael Gough, occupied the New Theatre in London for three months.

This is how *Colombe* began in London:

ACT ONE

MADAME ALEXANDRA'S *dressing-room, and a corner of the passage outside. Enter* JULIEN *and* COLOMBE.

JULIEN. If we wait for her here we can't miss her. . . . That's the door to her dressing-room.

COLOMBE. Shall we see some of the actors, do you think?

JULIEN. We might. They're not much to look at when they're not on the stage.

COLOMBE. Where is the stage?

JULIEN. Along the passage and down the stairs.

COLOMBE. Could we go and look at it?

JULIEN. Why?

COLOMBE. It was where we first met. . . .

JULIEN. Two years ago. . . . You were a flower-girl, and I was a first-year student. We hadn't ten francs between us—remember?

COLOMBE. Your brother lent us twenty to go and have supper at Poccardi's.

JULIEN. We must have been mad.

COLOMBE. Why?

JULIEN. Getting married, with less than the price of a supper to keep us. . . . I never thought I'd have to bring you back. I never thought that after two years we'd have no more money than we had on the day we got married. Colombe, my darling. . . .

COLOMBE. Yes?

JULIEN. I do love you.

COLOMBE. I love you too.

JULIEN. And I'm sorry.

COLOMBE. What for, my darling?

JULIEN. Because I haven't any money. Because I can't support you as a husband should, and I have to come begging to my mother. . . . Kiss me, to show you don't blame me. . . .   [*They kiss.*

[*Enter* GEORGES. *She looks at them for a moment in surprise before they notice her and break apart.*

JULIEN. Georges!

GEORGES. Master Julien! Well, this is a surprise.

JULIEN. This is Madame Georges, my mother's dresser. Georges, this is my wife.

GEORGES. Your wife? You've gone and got married?

JULIEN. Yes. Don't you remember her?

GEORGES. I can't say I do. She wasn't in the company, was she?

JULIEN. No. She worked in the flower-shop around the corner. Two years ago she brought a bouquet for my mother——

GEORGES. Of course I remember! They offered her the part of the flower-girl in *The Princess and the Beggar*—and she turned it down—and you had a row with the author because he wanted to look at her legs. It was poor Monsieur Robinet, that's who it was—and you gave him such a kick that you tore half the seat off his trousers! The best playwright in France, Member of the Academy, Legion of Honour, and he couldn't sit down for a fortnight! Well, to think it's the same girl, and you've married her! She's so grown up I'd never have known!

JULIEN. We've a child now, too. . . .

GEORGES. You have? A boy or a girl?

COLOMBE. A boy.

GEORGES. How old is he?

COLOMBE. He's just a year.

That is how *Colombe* began at the New Theatre in London. This is how it began at the Atelier in Paris:

ACT ONE

A backstage passage and MADAME ALEXANDRA'S *dressing-room, one side of which is open to the view. The passage is dimly lit, and the dressing-room is still dark.*

On stage; COLOMBE, *sitting on a chair, and* JULIEN *impatiently walking up and down. They seem to be waiting for something. The dresser,* MADAME GEORGES, *enters, carrying a chair.*

GEORGES. Sit down, Mr Julien. It's a long time to wait.

JULIEN. Thank you, Georges. I've already told you I'm better standing.

GEORGES. People say that, and then their legs ache. My eldest son, he was like you—standing all the time. What's happened to him now? Varicose veins. I'm always sitting, and with me it's just the opposite. With me it's the behind that aches.

JULIEN. I'm sick of your behind, Georges. I wish the old woman would come. Quickly.

GEORGES [*to* COLOMBE]. It begins with pins and needles; after that the bone in the backside goes numb, and then it gets into the kidneys. The flesh rubs away, in little lumps.

JULIEN [*to* COLOMBE]. Tell her she bores you, and you don't want to hear any more about her bottom. If you let her go on for five minutes, she'll show it to you.

GEORGES. Sitting down for thirty years, Madame Julien, waiting for the end of the performance! And there are plays that never seem to finish. It's hard on dressers.

COLOMBE. But you aren't forced to sit down all the time?

GEORGES. No, but then my legs get tired. My sixth gave me phlebitis. I can still feel it.

JULIEN [*impatiently*]. Georges, we're fed up with your phlebitis. Go and see if the old woman is on the stage.

GEORGES. No. She always comes up to her dressing-room before the rehearsal. The old woman! That isn't half bad, to call your mother old woman, here.

JULIEN. And, please, no moralizing.

GEORGES. Listen. Listen. He's exactly like my first. When

they brought my husband home with his two legs cut off
—he had slipped under the machinery at Panhard's while
he was cleaning it—I said to myself, Now, I can be quiet,
he won't go fighting any more. But, Madame Julien, it
doesn't do to prophesy: my eldest started fighting like his
father, just as drunk, on Saturdays. Children bring a lot
of bother. My third child, the one who died of con-
sumption, he was different. Always quietly spitting in his
corner, or playing by himself with bits of wood. . . . Your
child, Madame Julien, I hope he's all right?

COLOMBE. He's a year old.

Except for the setting, and the names of the characters,
there is hardly any resemblance between the two open-
ings. Julien in one is a romantic young fellow who dotes
on his wife; in the other, an ill-tempered boor who takes
scarcely any notice of her. In London Colombe was a
lively girl who chattered to Julien on equal terms; in
Paris she shrank frightened and silent into a corner. All
these changes were made, I gathered from conversation
with Peter Brook, the director of the London production,
because it was thought that the English public would
misunderstand the frank and physical language of the
French original. The talk about backsides and varicose
veins and the rest had to be suppressed because it did not
fit in with the linguistic conventions of reputable English
playwriting.

The English playgoer whose researches into the French
theatre are confined to establishments where chorus-girls
do various things that would not be permitted in London
may be inclined to explain the linguistic freedom of the
Paris theatre by the theory that the French stage is in all
ways less inhibited and Puritanical than our own. But
here he encounters the paradox I have already mentioned.
Aurally, the Paris theatre is enterprising and daring;
visually, the serious Paris theatre is primmer than the
English. This can be illustrated by reference to the production of one of the plays quoted from earlier. The hero

of *La Tête des autres*, Valorin, has escaped from the law
courts on the day he was sentenced to death, and taken
refuge in a house which proves to be the home of the
prosecuting counsel, Maillard. His defence has been that
he passed the night of the murder in a hotel with a
woman he had casually met on the streets, the weakness
of this defence being that he was unable to produce the
woman in court. But when he opened the curtains of
Maillard's drawing-room, there she was, standing before
him, none other than the lawyer's own mistress, and the
wife of his closest friend. (The French serious theatre
does not blench either at coincidences or melodrama.)
Naturally, this woman, Roberte, denies Valorin's accu-
sations; naturally, Valorin insists on them, and naturally
the lawyer demands proof. Then follows this short
scene:

MAILLARD [*to* ROBERTE]. Don't bother to answer him. [*To*
   VALORIN] To me, who know the tricks of the trade, your
   lies are almost laughable.
VALORIN. Really? I congratulate you, sir. But if I am lying,
   how do I know that this woman has a scar on her right
   hip, and another on her back? How do I know she has a
   mole on her left breast?
MAILLARD [*waiting for a reply that does not come, turns towards*
   ROBERTE]. Roberte! Say something!
ROBERTE. I don't know this man, and I don't have to answer
   so ridiculous an accusation. And I don't understand how
   you can let me be insulted by a murderer.
MAILLARD. You know quite well, Roberte, that I only want
   to believe you. But, all the same, here is something
   definite. How can Valorin know these things if he hasn't
   seen them?
ROBERTE. Ah! What do you want me to say?... I don't
   know.... Perhaps he's heard some one talk of them....
VALORIN [*smiling*]. Your friends, perhaps? And the Chinese
   hat decorated with a feather, and the black dress with
   the big red flower, I've heard tell of them as well? And
   under the dress, the girdle and the black suspenders

striped with yellow that make you look like a wasp? But
perhaps you are wearing them now?

[*He lifts* ROBERTE'S *skirt and shows the suspenders.*

At least, that is what would happen if the play were
presented in London. There is nothing here to alarm any
English actress or producer. But if Monique Melinand,
who played Roberte at the Atelier, was wearing these
suspenders when Yves Robert as Valorin made his per-
functory grab at her skirt, the audience got no chance of
seeing them.

Here, in this trifling detail of production, we come
upon a vital distinction between the English and the
French ideas of the theatre. It is not a distinction that
every one will admit; indeed, I have seen it implicitly
denied. When I was discussing a performance of Alec
Guinness's, I once remarked in *The Sunday Times* something to the effect that the greatest actor is not the man
who can successfully mimic the largest number of others,
but the one with something of his own to say. Now I do
not know whether other dramatic critics' experience is the
same as mine, but I have noticed for some time that the
plays in which Mr Guinness appears are more productive
of correspondence, both intelligent and foolish, than
those of any other player whatever. Letters, therefore,
came from all parts of the country, telling me that my
premise was wrong, most of them good letters, firmly and
closely argued. I was assured from Arbroath and Gal-
way, from Bognor Regis, Welwyn Garden City, and
Gloucestershire, from Norwich and Bournemouth, from
Highgate and Denmark Hill, that the true actor is really
the man who confines himself faithfully to interpreting
his author, not to revealing his own vision of life by
being, in the deepest sense, himself more and more
abundantly.

In spite of these asseverations of theory, in practice the
English public has reserved its greatest praise and wor-
ship for rich and colourful personalities who often have

treated their authors with cavalier disregard. Who are reputed the most eminent English actors of all time? Garrick and Irving, both of them men who would chop Shakespeare about, invent spurious endings, add their own lines of dialogue, and generally behave as though the playwright's work were merely the raw material out of which they set themselves to fashion what they would.

The view which my Guinness correspondents maintain, but which the English theatre, rightly or wrongly, has steadily denied, is really and in practice a guiding rule of the French stage. In England, not only the actor, but the producer, has an enormous influence upon the drama. I do not doubt for a moment that the final form in which *Colombe* reached the English stage owed a great deal to that fanciful, elvish, and witty genius, Peter Brook. But in France the producer occupies only a subordinate position. Men like Copeau, Dullin, and Jouvet won considerable renown as producers, but they did not enjoy the freedom of action of their English counterparts. In England and America enormous attention is paid to the presentation and staging of a play. Parisian scenery is often charming at a hasty glance, but closer inspection reveals that it is apt to be sketchily made of pasteboard. What Paris considers closely is the speaking of the author's lines. The word is master. English audiences, some one once said, remember what they see, French audiences what they hear. The French theatre is one in which the presiding genius is the author. That is why he is given such complete freedom of expression. It is also the reason that stage directions, even when it is the author himself who provides them, are treated so casually. They come within the sphere of production, of which the French theatre thinks comparatively little. This is the resolution of the paradox I have noted.

The fundamental attitude of the French towards the true method of theatrical production has been most clearly stated by Jean Giraudoux in his introduction to

Claude Cézan's biography of Louis Jouvet. Giraudoux points a sharp contrast between the methods of production of France and those of Germany (which approximate more closely to American and English notions). "The Frenchman," says Giraudoux,

> out of his concern for economy and to show the excellence of his taste, does not wish to exercise all his senses at the same time. While the German conception of the theatre tends towards a general amalgamation of its component parts, the French conception tries to separate them. In art, as in cookery, mixing things up disgusts him. Everything he demands in ballet or opera irritates him in a play. He comes to the play in order to listen, and is wearied if he is expected to look as well. He believes in the word and not in the décor. Or rather he believe that the great battles of the heart are not fought out in bursts of light and shade, in collapses and catastrophes, but in conversation. The real theatrical stroke is not for him the noise made by a stage crowd, but the shade of irony that the hero or heroine gives to a particular phrase. The fight, assassination, or assault that the German attempts to represent on the stage is replaced in France by a counsel's harangue, and the spectators are not passive witnesses, but members of the jury. A Frenchman's soul can be opened, like a safe, by a word; and he disapproves of the German blow-lamp. He insists on regarding dialogue as the supreme form of the duel for a being endowed with speech; it is the power of this dialogue, its efficiency, its form, and then its purely literary merits, which he wishes to test for himself. For him theatrical action consists, not in submitting himself to a wild and almost physical attack of sight and feeling, from which he staggers away exhausted, but in matching the cares and struggles of his life and imagination against a living script that can illuminate them.

This understanding of the theatre as a human and not demoniacal thing does not allow the passionate attention it gives to the text to be distracted by irrelevant strokes of production. The spectator at the Comédie-Française would not understand—an invention common enough elsewhere—

how anyone could put on the stage a procession of real camels during Mithridate's speech to Monime, or, in Becque's *La Parisienne*, twelve different Parisiennes, innumerable symbols of the symbol. He does not believe in décor. For him the décor is the auditorium itself, with its lights, its balconies. It is the spectator who needs dressing up, not the dialogue.

That is Giraudoux's idea of the relative importance of the author and the producer. It is a notion that would stagger Komisarjevsky, Tyrone Guthrie, or Mr Brook, but, though Giraudoux unhappily is dead, his ideas are alive. France is the country of the author's theatre.

2

The Occupation

CULTURE plays a more important part in the life of France than in that of England. The superior number and excellence of Parisian bookshops is evidence enough of that. The dirty, unarranged litter of the book-barrows in the Farringdon Road is a depressing sight compared with the gay attractiveness of the bookstalls on the Seine, offering to the towers of Notre-Dame across the river their prints of brightly plumaged birds and first editions of old poems and novels. The Charing Cross Road is a poor substitute for the dark and wondrous treasure houses of the Rue Bonaparte and the Rue des Saints-Pères, down which during the War the serious-minded Captain Ernst Junger, of the Occupying Forces, used to wander, looking for studies of salamanders and early issues of Baudelaire.

Nor is the theatre in England as important in what cultural life exists here as it is in France. In the worst days of paper shortage most English newspapers reduced their theatre reviews to a couple of inches, whereas in France many publications never ceased to give the better part of a page to the theatre every day. The theatre in France at the present time is enjoying a rich harvest; its golden days have returned to it. And for this there are two principal reasons.

The first is the War of 1939–45, and more specifically the defeat that France suffered in the spring of 1940, when the Germans swept across the country and captured Paris without resistance. No one can understand the position that the theatre occupies in France, and has occupied since the War, without realizing something of what life in Paris was like between the invasion of Poland and the advance in 1944 of Leclerc's troops on the dominated city.

We who lived in London in the winter of 1939–40 can hardly forget the darkness and depression that enveloped the English capital. There was nothing of this in Paris. People danced every night until midnight, and the great factories produced, not tanks, but 30,000 motor-cars. Every Sunday the roads to Rambouillet and Fontaine-bleau were packed with happy tourists, and when the weather was fine it was estimated that a million gold francs flowed abroad each day through tubes of petrol. The enemy aeroplanes that frequently circled in the sky hardly served to remind anyone of war; many of them dropped photographs of Hitler addressing crowds of peaceful workmen. The highest optimism prevailed everywhere, and it continued until the last possible moment. Paris did not know of its danger until it was actually doomed. Three days before the city's surrender an influential journalist declared that the "German High Command was plunged in gloom." The next day, June 12, 1940, the *Petit Parisien* asserted that "the time is not far off when Weygand will . . . turn and attack the Germans. These attacks will certainly be crowned with success." On the 13th Reynaud telegraphed to President Roosevelt, "We shall fight in front of Paris, we shall fight behind Paris"; and immediately afterwards the city was handed over without a shot being fired.

No wonder the citizens of Paris were bewildered and distressed. They had been repeatedly assured that every-thing would be all right, and now, without warning, they discovered that everything was lost. The field-grey uniforms that had been driven back by an army in taxi-cabs a quarter of a century before spread rapidly, silently, over the entire city. The motor-cars that the factories had been turning out in thousands during the winter now became as though they had never been. The Place de la Concorde was a deserted waste: the only sign of existence was a forlorn row of horse-carriages standing outside Maxim's.

After a little while the stunned people returned to life. Papers once again appeared in the street-kiosks. But they were not the old papers, though some of them bore familiar names. There was no more defiance of the enemy, no expression of confidence in victory. Instead, the people were admonished to be polite to the conquerors. "What," demanded one of the papers of June 17, 1940,

> what are your duties towards the guests that War has brought to you? First of all must come a correctness and politeness from which you must never deviate. Stop, even among yourselves, from calling them Boches. This slang word, I know, is not intended by you as an insult. We used to say Alboches before 1914. But many Germans think the word is an insult; don't use it, if only to avoid unpleasantness for yourselves. Call them Fritzes, as our soldiers do. It is a familiar word that shocks nobody, and it reflects your absence of hatred against the Germans, for even when you find them exacting, you do not hate them.

This negative attitude of merely not annoying the Germans soon ceased to be sufficient. Active collaboration was demanded, and one of the newspapers with the largest circulation declared roundly and without equivocation, "We have had the luck to be beaten by a man of genius. . . . Every real Frenchman who cares for the future will to-day put his trust in Hitler."

Sitting in an easy-chair in the comparative security of London, a city that did not know invasion by foreign troops, whose greatest danger was the hazard of bombs, it is easy to look askance at the apparently spiritless way in which the people of Paris at first responded to the challenge of the German occupation. But what was there to nerve the temper of resistance? They seemed to have been deserted on every hand. Their generals had failed them; their newspapers had misled them with an absurd and irrational confidence; their allies had refused them the help of their air force, and were even treating as a great victory what to them appeared to be at Dunkirk a flight before the enemy. Yet even in these terrible circumstances the people of Paris did not long brook without retaliation the presence of the invader. Two days before Christmas 1940 there appeared this brief notice on the walls of Paris:

> Engineer Jacques Bonsergent of Paris has been condemned to death by the German Military Tribunal for an act of violence against a member of the German army.
> He was shot this morning.

This notice was signed by Otto von Stulpnagel. Stulpnagel was regarded by Ernst Junger, who thought himself a merciful man, as too gentle for the task he had to perform as Governor of Paris during the first years of the Occupation, and he was recalled on February 16, 1942, Goebbels considering that he ruled with too light a hand. But he had signed orders for more than four hundred executions.

In their early days in Paris, before their prospects of victory became doubtful, the Germans set before themselves three principal aims. They were firm in their treatment of the Paris population from the very start. A young woman, for example, ignored the pedestrian crossing in the Rue Druot. An *agent* called out to her, but she persisted in leaving the pavement at an unauthorized spot. A German officer walked up, took her by the arm, and marched her up and down the crossing six times. There were many irritating incidents like this, but overriding them was the German desire, in the interests of ultimate triumph, to keep more or less on good terms with the people of Paris. The invaders circulated tactful cartoons and posters. One of the most famous of these, playing on the traditional amorousness of the French, showed a French girl and a German soldier embracing under a street-lamp. The collaborationist Press strove to represent the occupying army, not as victors in battle, but as an army of tourists, every member of which, by a notable coincidence, spoke the same language.

The second aim of the invaders was to destroy whatever affection Paris might have for the British. Under their inspiration the walls of Paris sprouted placards, often posted up by collaborationist Frenchmen, representing the British, not only as cowardly, but as the betrayers of France: and not only as the betrayers of France in 1940, but during the whole of modern history. A cartoon of the first type symbolized Dunkirk in the figure of an English soldier leaping hell-for-leather into the sea beneath a signpost pointing across the Channel to London. He is being chased by German shells, but has no leisure to glance at them. He is in too great a hurry to get back to his island.

A typical example of the second kind of poster showed Saint Joan at the stake, with the flames licking round her, and a silhouette of Napoleon brooding at St Helena, his cocked hat and substantial stomach black against the setting sun. Underneath are the words, "Our two great national martyrs, Joan of Arc and Napoleon, are England's victims."

The third object of the Germans was to suppress all resistance. Their behaviour during the Occupation of Paris was in many ways correct. But at the least sign of opposition their vengeance was terrible. The first German soldier to be attacked and killed in the streets of Paris met his death on August 21, 1941, at the Barbès station. Within twenty-four hours eleven thousand Jews, Communists, and others were rounded up, and sent to concentration camps.

Ernst Junger, who had come to Paris a few months

earlier, and who stayed there until he was sent to the Eastern front at the end of 1942, doubted whether the effect of this severity would be salutary from the German point of view. He himself settled happily, if rather sombrely, into Parisian life. His Journals reveal him as a man of taste, but without humour. The grace of Paris hardly touched his heavy spirit, and he was much troubled by bad dreams. But the bookshops in the sixth arrondissement, between the church of Saint-Sulpice and the quays, solaced him, and he spent many hours turning over their dusty treasures. The booksellers seem to have been polite and even helpful, and he had many friends in Parisian Society. He dined often in French houses, and at the Tour d'Argent, where he talked about entomology and the theatre. But sometimes, walking through the streets at night, he had an uneasy feeling that he was surrounded by enemies; and once when he bought a notebook in the Avenue de Wagram he was profoundly disturbed by the girl who served him. "I was in uniform," he says.

A young girl serving customers struck me by the expression on her face. It was clear that she considered me with enormous hate. Her clear blue eyes, with the pupil contracted almost to a point, looked straight into mine, with a sort of pleasure—perhaps the same as the snake feels when he darts his fangs into his prey. I had the feeling that things have been like this for a long time. Such looks can bring us nothing but destruction and death. And I suspect that they can pass into oneself like a germ, which can be cured only with difficulty and violence.

The hatred that the German Occupation, with its terrible and, in the later years, incessant execution of hostages, inspired in the people of Paris grew to tremendous proportions. How vast it became in the end is shown in a note in Marcel Aymé's *Le Chemin des écoliers*. Michaud, the hero of this novel, one morning watches four German soldiers climbing up the slopes of

Montmartre towards the Church of the Sacré-Cœur, and
envies them their freedom from domestic worries, his
own wife being in hospital, and his children difficult to
manage. These soldiers, he thinks, have nothing to do
but mount guard, obey orders, and wander round Paris.
Michaud did not know it, but the turn of these men was
coming later. Their names were Arnold, Eisenhart,
Heinecken, and Schulz, and M. Aymé tells us what happened to them. Arnold was killed in Russia; Eisenhart,
wounded in the Crimea, came home with both his legs
amputated, and was poisoned by his wife; Heinecken,
whom every one thought a quiet and serious man, became
guard at a Displaced Persons camp, and killed an old
refugee (when M. Aymé wrote *Le Chemin des écoliers* he
was a prisoner in Belgium). The fate of Schulz was the
most terrible. He died in Paris in the American sector in
August 1944. He got separated from his unit, went into
a little café, got drunk, and emerged without helmet or
uniform, wearing only his shirt, trousers, and boots. He
staggered along, shouting and singing, and a crowd
gathered round him. Under the windows of a shoe-
maker's he was attacked and cut to pieces. The dammed-
up hatred of four unhappy, tormented years broke
through its restraints. Women and children, says M.
Aymé, were especially savage. One of these cut off a
finger, another an ear. When the crowd dispersed, all
that remained of Schulz was a few splashes of blood on
the pavement.

That is what Paris felt like in 1944, the year of the
creation of Anouilh's *Antigone* and Sartre's *Huis Clos*.
Then, however, the direction of events was clear;
emotions were simple if frightening. But in the early
days of the Occupation the atmosphere was one, not of
hatred, but of bewilderment. The people of Paris did
not know what or whom to believe. Their newspapers
were, of course, steadily pro-German: otherwise they
would not have been allowed to appear. But they were

full of inconsistencies, and contradicted themselves in an astonishing manner.

In 1940, then, the people of Paris were cut off from help and hope. Their allies had left them, their Government, after bold words, had surrendered, their newspapers were urging collaboration with the invaders, but were plainly untrustworthy; and threats of death and violence were latent in the very presence of the Occupying Power. It was in these circumstances that Paris, looking in vain for sustenance elsewhere, found it in the theatre.

The Germans themselves, by one of those grave miscalculations which they never ceased to make throughout the War, helped them to find it there by encouraging the theatres to open. They declared that if the Théâtre-Française did not resume its activities, they would bring over a company from Germany to occupy its boards. They themselves patronized the theatre. The première of Claudel's *Le Soulier de satin* in 1943 was attended by nearly all the notabilities of the German army then in Paris. But already, before 1943, before Stalingrad, as early as El Alamein, the Parisian theatres had become, from the German viewpoint, centres of disaffection.

The movement began, paradoxically, with Bernard Shaw. Shaw's attitude during the early days of the 1939–1945 War was characteristically exasperating. He was not exactly defeatist, but he took a perverse pleasure in annoying those who most firmly believed in Britain's capacity to resist the Nazis. He used his dialectic skill in defence of the Russian invasion of Poland, proving that this invasion was a great benefit to all freedom-loving peoples, and especially to the Poles, just as, no doubt, the hypochondriac should be grateful to the man-eating tiger who gobbles him up. Shaw in 1940 was far from being a stay and comfort to the British nation, but more than any other British writer he stimulated the hopes of those French men and women who had the spirit of resistance nascent in them.

Mme Béatrix Dussane shows in her invaluable *Notes de théâtre* how this came about. Plays about Joan of Arc, says Mme Dussane,

> deserve a prominent place in the long story of the struggle of the theatre with the censorship [during the Occupation]. In times when there was a scarcity of everything in Paris, it was almost enough to announce a production of a *Joan of Arc* to obtain heat, raw materials, and costumes. Towards the end of 1940 Bernard Shaw's *Joan of Arc* [*Saint Joan*] was produced in this way. The German authorities thought they were being particularly clever, because it was a case of a French heroine fighting the English, and the author was the most troublesome of Irishmen. It was, in fact, a success that encouraged another company, in July 1941, to mount the *Jeanne d'Arc* of Péguy: that same *Jeanne* in which, a little later, writers in the clandestine Press were without difficulty to find admirable appeals to individual resistance. It was, however, permitted, presented, and played . . . and passionately applauded. The censorship, reading the text literally, was delighted with those speeches which talked of driving the English out of France—but never guessed that the public, by a natural transposition, understood "Germans" every time that Jeanne said "English"—and therefore allowed the production to take place. It was the *Jeanne avec nous* of Vermorel, in January 1942, which finally opened their eyes. Its success was too striking not to rouse suspicion. The censorship had learned by then, if not to devine all the concealed meanings, at least to suspect anything that gave the public too much pleasure, and the piece had to be taken off at the height of its popularity.

This, eventually, is what happened to *Le Soulier de satin*, whose production at the Comédie-Française was the most important dramatic event of the whole four years' Occupation. Claudel's play had long been held impossible to stage, his rhythms unsuitable for theatrical speech. *Le Soulier de satin* was produced by Jean-Louis Barrault, and it was his chief triumph at the National Theatre. The first performance, in spite of the hunger

that long before this had made itself evident in Paris, was
a magnificent occasion; and the German forces themselves contributed to it, by occupying a large proportion
of the auditorium. But soon the success of the play rendered the censorship uneasy; after the fiftieth performance it was intimated to the Comédie that it would be
discreet not to play it too frequently; and after the six-
tieth it was removed from the repertoire.

Meanwhile the condition of Paris was becoming
harsher. On the avenues leading to the Bois de Boulogne,
the Place de la République, or the Lion of Belfort
appeared plaques pointing to Lisieux, Reims, and Com-
piègne, as though Paris were no longer the centre of the
civilized world, a place to stay in, but a city for motorized
columns to pass through. This was only one of the many
trifling signs of humiliation that daily met the eyes of
Parisians. The most elegant of Frenchwomen were now
riding bicycles and wearing woollen stockings, and
people were getting hungrier, thinner, and more tired.
They had to conserve their energies, they walked more
slowly than formerly, and gesticulated less. The very
carriage-horses had to zigzag in order to climb the modest
slope of the Champs-Élysées to the Arc de Triomphe.
Yet even as late as the high summer of 1941 Paris still
on occasion tried to assume an air of gaiety. At the Long-
champs races were many German soldiers, but they
mingled with the crowd without attracting much attention, inconspicuous in their quiet grey uniforms. At the
end of the afternoon there was a picturesque procession
through the woods back to the centre of the city, and
people sat on the grass in the Bois to watch it go by: a
few cars, and then brakes, and victorias, and landaus:
completed by a man in a carriage smoking a cigar, and
drawn by a Negro, and a pretty girl in shorts.

But it was in the theatre that the rising spirit of national
pride and hope reasserted itself. In the noble Alexandrines at the Comédie Paris found a heroism and a dignity

she had lost in life; and at the Atelier and the Théâtre de
la Cité she discovered the possibility of living them
again. "In 1942," says Mme Dussane,

> a decisive date was marked by Sartre's *Les Mouches*. Sartre
> had been called up, taken prisoner, and had been returned
> to France. He was already known to the intellectuals
> through his first stories, and was completing his great
> philosophic system. He had taken an important part in the
> resistance movements of the world of letters and of the
> Latin Quarter. His name, like Camus's, became a rallying
> cry for many people, who arranged to meet at his pieces, as
> others before them had made rendezvous at the funerals of
> Armand Carrel or General Lamarque. Applauding his plays
> was like joining a secret society.
>
> With *Les Mouches*, put on by Dullin at the Théâtre Sarah-
> Bernhardt [renamed the Théâtre de la Cité during the Occu-
> pation], Sartre established himself in the theatre, and used
> methods reminiscent of Giraudoux, whom in general he
> little resembled. Once again an ancient story was used to
> give undying reality to the contemporary adventure, and
> prudently to disguise the characters and their thoughts from
> the eyes of the censorship. Sartre retained from the old
> Oresteiad its essential theme: Clytemnestra giving herself
> to the murderous tyrant of her people; Electra, the true
> heiress, reduced to a hateful and hungry misery at the gates
> of the palace; Orestes brought back from exile by the un-
> dying determination of his sister, and by destiny itself; and
> in the end the final massacre. Beyond that Sartre had sent a
> mysterious plague upon the town (later this plague was to
> be the origin of Albert Camus's *La Peste*), an ironic and
> derisory Jupiter, and giant flies, the evil personification of
> the Erinnyes. His Orestes had led afar off a rich and agree-
> able existence, under the supervision of a fanciful tutor. He
> came back from happy Corinth into his sad city, he aban-
> doned peace for murder, because he could not resist the
> impulse to be in the bosom of his own people. He flung
> himself into alliance with them, exclaiming, "What do I
> care for happiness? I want my memories, my native soil,
> my place among the men of Argos. . . ."

I do not know if the censorship put down to the credit of Æschylus this under-estimation of happiness as a source of comfort, this deliberate preference of a more ardent life stretched between risk and action, or even whether it considered it merely as rhetoric. . . . But what is certain is that a whole generation of youth recognized there its own excitement, and clearly heard the appeal that was made to it.

The next drama of a high order to play an important part in the spiritual resurgence of the French people was Jean Anouilh's *Antigone*. It did so largely by accident. "The appeal launched by Sartre," says Mme Dussane,

was deliberate and calculated, and closely connected with the circumstances of the time.

The same scorn for happiness ("a poor word, eh," says Creon) was to break out the following year in Anouilh's *Antigone*. There was nothing deliberate about this; Anouilh remained during the whole Occupation immersed in his work, declaring that he cared nothing for politics. But Anouilh had not waited for the War and the Occupation to put on the stage characters who refused, if I may so call them. *L'Hermine* with its Frantz in revolt dated from 1931; *Le Voyageur sans bagage* from 1937, and *La Sauvage*, still more striking, from 1938. The refusal of happiness, of comfort, of compromise, and concessions, offered, not in honour of such or such a system of thought, but simply arising out of natures too exigent, indomitable, or savage for ordinary life, is the major theme of his *pièces noires*, and sometimes it is latent in certain plays that are relatively *roses*. Of all our leading contemporary authors, Anouilh is the most wholly romantic, the most instinctively at odds with the rules of the social contract.

On emerging from adolescence he had undergone two great influences which had marked him profoundly: Claudel (which hardly appears in his work) and Giraudoux, who on the other hand is clearly apparent there. It is no surprise, then, that in the most bitter period of his career Anouilh had in his turn flirted with mythology, and had written a *Médée*, for the pleasure of giving life to a little witch, thin and dark (his eternal savage), planted at the gates of a city . . . which in the last act will burst into flames. Such were the paths that led him, when he was surrounded by persuasive rationalizations that stumbled on systematic refusals, to the very heroine of refusal: Antigone. It is pointless at this time of day to tell the story of the play or to make quotations. It had a record number of performances, before and after the Liberation, and in various revivals. It has been played in every country [including Britain, by the Old Vic at the New Theatre shortly after the end of the War, with Sir Laurence Olivier and Vivien Leigh] . . . .

The piece was given at the Atelier during the season 1943–44. Somewhat earlier Anouilh had given the public a *pièce rose*, one of his best, *Léocadia* . . . and a *pièce noire*, *Eurydice*, morbidly haunted by death, and—the victim perhaps of some mischances of production—this last [seen in London as *Point of Departure*] had not been very well understood. Both in the Press and among the public its supporters and its opponents had shown themselves equally excited, dividing themselves according to whether they preferred the author's *rose* or *noir*. No party, resistant or otherwise, formed a group round him beforehand. Better still, or worse: as soon as *Antigone* was produced, a quarrel broke out. Since Creon expressed with considerable eloquence the Governmental thesis of expediency, short-sighted critics were deceived, and the word ran round, "Don't go to *Antigone*— it is a Nazi play!"

It was, however, enough to have seen or read *La Sauvage* or *Le Voyageur* to know that, whatever the dramatic situation might be, Anouilh would be on the side of revolt and non-acceptance. . . . The public realized this, and its instinct was not deceived. Little by little the groups of excited young people in the Place Dancourt [the site of the Atelier] increased. The electricity supply failed; the theatres in the spring of 1944 played by daylight, which, for the Atelier, meant gathering the players round the prompter's box, in a narrow space on which fell a shaft of light through the roof. . . . No obstacle, no discomfort kept people away: and this public, which always ran the risk of having to return home on foot during the incessant alerts of the period, stayed when the piece was finished to recall the players five or six times. Nothing is rarer in the [French] theatre than this enthusiasm which prolonged itself to the point of inspiring what we call with melancholy irony the *"rappels de vestiaire."*

What took place during these performances? Something similar to the deliberate misunderstandings of *Jeanne d'Arc,* but which, instead of depending on a few particular speeches, lasted from the beginning to the end: Antigone's refusal became the symbol and the sublimation of the personal refusals of all and every one. Her stubbornness, her "I am not here to understand, I am here to say no," may seem inexplicable to audiences in happier times, but they struck to the heart people watched by the Gestapo, and familiar with every misery. And each time she declared or let it be understood that no argument or force should prevent her from returning to bury her brother, the public exulted in its heart, You shall not prevent us from helping the men hidden in the wood behind the farm. This is by no means imagination: I felt like that myself when I saw the play, and others have confessed to the same experience. It was confirmed also in another way. The triumphal career of the piece was interrupted for a few days by the Liberation, but was resumed soon after the departure of the Germans. When I took friends to see it who had recently come back to Paris, I was astonished to feel no longer the same tension between stage and audience. . . . Certain parts of the public continued to follow the play with enthusiasm, but others visibly fell away. The explanation is that with the Liberation the tension between constraint and clandestinity suddenly vanished. It was now necessary to sympathize with *Antigone* by an intellectual effort, whereas formerly one had been in a conspiracy with it.

An admirable phrase. We have seen that during the Occupation the French public was indeed engaged in a conspiracy with the theatre. The theatre was the permitted spokesman for its aspirations and its anguishes and its searchings of the soul. It was in the four years between 1940 and 1944 that conditions became ripe for the Paris theatre to assume its position of ascendancy in

French life. That, however, is only one of the reasons
why the French theatre to-day has such great importance.
The War gave to it its opportunity. But it was the men
and women in it who enabled it to seize that opportunity.
The second reason for its ascendancy is that it has many
workers whose talent approaches genius.

3

The Dramatis Personæ

THE dominating figure in the French theatre, as I said in my first chapter, is, all things considered, the author. Yet the man who has had the greatest single effect on the French theatre since the end of the between-the-wars period is Jean-Louis Barrault, who is an author only in the sense that he has written *Réflexions sur le théâtre*. This makes him a writer in a considerable sense enough, for this mixture of aphorism, analysis, and autobiography is stimulating, pungent, and witty. But it does not make him a dramatist. Yet his work at the Marigny Theatre has had such an influence that I cannot but place him at the top of the roll-call of those men of outstanding talent who have been the second factor in the Paris theatre's pre-eminence in recent years.

The Marigny is one of the loveliest theatres in Paris. It is situated near the gardens of the Champs-Élysées, not far from the spot where the hero of *Remembrance of Things Past* wrestled happily in his not wholly innocent childhood with Gilberte Swann. On Sunday afternoons, underneath the trees at its side, there is an open-air stamp-market. The entrance hall is smaller than those of most Parisian theatres, and it opens into a circular corridor like that of Covent Garden, and, again like that of the English Opera House, decorated in a rich red fabric. Red is the keynote too of the oval interior, which, after the manner of French theatres, has its walls lined with boxes. Everywhere the eye travels it meets this rich, deep red, which if it makes the theatre slightly oppressive also makes it magnificent.

Barrault and his wife, Madeleine Renaud, who for twenty years had been one of the great figures at the Comédie-Française, took over the Marigny in 1946. There they began one of the great theatrical occupations of all time, comparable with Irving's at the Lyceum. The Renaud–Barrault company's quality of achievement at the Marigny is apparent to anyone who has seen a performance there; but in defining the nature of that quality some care is necessary.

M. Barrault is known in London better than most French actors, both the screen and the stage having introduced him to us. For three weeks in the autumn of 1951 his and his wife's company filled the St James's Theatre, in the West End, in a series of performances of Molière's *Amphitryon* and *Les Fourberies de Scapin*, Marivaux's *Les Fausses confidences*, Gide's *Oedipe*, Armand Salacrou's *Les Nuits de la colère*, and Paul Claudel's *Partage de midi*. But before this he had become familiar to London in the film *Les Enfants du paradis*.

That film of the turbulent, romantic life of the actors on Paris's 'Boulevard de Crime' during the eighteen-thirties made a tremendous impression; especially Barrault's performance in it as the melancholy, white, bony-faced clown who, in his loose, too large Pierrot's costume, played the tragic pantomime of Baptiste. This film did Barrault enormous service, and at the same time sowed certain misconceptions about him. It gave the impression that his sole title to notice was as an actor; and that as an actor his chief qualification was his skill in mime.

To identify Barrault's capacity as an actor with his mastery of mime is an error; yet it is an error that has more justification than is given for it even by his performance as Baptiste. Barrault was born at Vésinet on September 8, 1910, the son of a chemist, and at the age of twenty he offered himself as a student to the celebrated director Charles Dullin, who at that time was the manager of the Atelier. Barrault as a young man haunted the Atelier: he rehearsed there, played there, and slept there, once in a cloakroom, and once in Volpone's bed, which is left on the stage after the performance to be ready for the first act next evening. His passionate devotion to the theatre was almost frightening: it knew no bounds nor reason. His sharp, pale, tormented face, with the black depths of his eyes glinting above his too prominent cheek-bones, his outbursts of rage, his nervousness, the ambition that pushed him on towards the future, and the fears that gnawed at his hopes were rapidly gathered in among the legends of that playhouse in the Place Dancourt, opposite the general provision merchant's little shop where you can buy everything you cannot get at the second-hand bookshop next door, and towered over by the steep-rising tenements of Montmartre.

While there he met Étienne Decroux, of the cruel tongue and eccentric character; the expert practitioner of what he called "expression through the body." The first time he spoke to Barrault it was to wound him to the quick, and a few days later, in a tone without hope, he asked him if this expression through the body interested him. Doubtless, says Barrault, he expected him to steal away . . . as so many others had done, for Decroux had frightened many young men and women in his time. But Barrault replied that he was interested, and the next day received his first lesson in mime.

From the first moment, says Barrault, mime enthralled him, and it enthralled him all the more that for the first time he felt within himself what he calls "the gift." He had for many months, even years, passionately desired to be an actor; but it was in this first elementary and tentative exploration of mime that he felt within himself not only the desire to be an actor, but also the power. It is evident, then, that mime corresponds to something fundamental in Barrault's nature and ability.

The correspondence is so close and true that it was through mime he achieved his first success upon the stage. He had been considerably affected by reading William Faulkner's *As I Lay Dying.* The book, he says, absorbed him, and he put all his powers to the task of absorbing it in its turn. In *As I Lay Dying* a certain wild young man tamed a horse wilder than himself. From the point of view of mime, says Barrault, the horse interested him. It was with the image of the horse in his mind that he worked at his translation of the book into mime during the days of his studentship. He rehearsed his own part at all hours, but more particularly in the mornings, when he took advantage of the electric light needed by the women who cleaned the theatre auditorium. Normally, he would have been embarrassed by their presence, but in his enthusiasm he hardly noticed them. And they were the source, he says, of one of the greatest encouragements he has ever received in his life.

"I wore," continues Barrault,

> nothing but a slip. I had absolutely nothing to indicate the presence of the imaginary horse I was trying to tame. In my excitement I easily forgot the women who were sweeping up the litter left by the public the night before. The slight noise made by their brooms did not disturb me. However, one morning my attention was distracted by something. I stopped and saw that one of the women had planted herself in front of me, leaning on her broom, and I quickly realized that she had been looking at me thus for several minutes. I looked at her in a rather embarrassed way, as if I had been caught doing something ridiculous. She did not move, but continued to stare at me abstractedly, as if both of us were stupefied.
>
> Then I smiled at her, and she said: "I'd like to know what you have been doing, all the time I've been looking at you, on that horse. . . ."
>
> What a victory, what joy, what an encouragement, what a spectator this woman was, what a reward!

It is evident that Barrault's interest in mime, and his reliance on it, are considerable. I have said that in general the French theatre is interested in hearing rather than in sight. This is true of all the great figures of the Parisian stage except M. Barrault. But Barrault realizes that men have eyes as well as ears, and he appeals to the eye, not in mime only, with a thoroughness that often disturbs his critics. He has put on productions, such as *Le Procès* and *L'État de siège*, in which he has experimented with crowd scenes and lighting as daringly as Tyrone Guthrie or Peter Brook; and for this he has been severely reprimanded by many of the most influential critics in Paris, on the ground that he was tending to exalt the producer above the author.

But it is unjust to Barrault to exaggerate this aspect of his work. There is no man in France more sensitive than he to the beauties and delicacies of speech. Before him the plays of Paul Claudel, with their long poetic lines, and apparently monotonous rhythms, were thought to be impossible to present on the stage. It is entirely due to Barrault that a method has been discovered of speaking the lines of Claudel so that they delight the ear, and yet never weary it. He is himself a very fine speaker, and some of the greatest things in his own performances are a tribute, not only to his powers as an actor, but to his strength of character.

Barrault is by nature taut and restless. His dark eyes burn with uneasy fire, and French critics are fond of calling his face tormented. At rehearsals he bounds from the stage to the auditorium, and from the auditorium back on to the stage. His rages, he says himself, are Olympian, and he enjoys them greatly. Life to him, though he lives in the solid bourgeois surroundings of the Avenue President Wilson in the sixteenth arrondissement, is a continuous tempest, which he loves to ride and to direct. This, of course, is not always to every

one's taste. There are times when even his friends think
that he takes too much upon himself. Through all the
rehearsals, for example, of Henry de Montherlant's
Malatesta at the Marigny the author had little opportunity of opening his mouth in the face of Barrault's
exuberance. He spoke for the first time just before the
dress rehearsal. "M. de Montherlant," said Barrault,
addressing the company, "is kindly going to rewrite a
few speeches." "Don't you believe it," said Montherlant, with a smile. "Dear Jean-Louis, rewrite them
yourself."

To a man like Barrault, repose is perhaps the hardest
quality in the world to come by. But he is constant in
self-criticism. Naturally hasty and impulsive, of quick
tongue and impatient movements, he all the time tries
to acquire the qualities he lacks. To such a man, for
example, the answering of letters is a bore and an irrita-
tion, and he by no means answers every letter he receives
even now. But he claims that the proportion of the
letters he replies to grows year by year. He remembers
the kindness and indulgence with which Dullin treated
him when, as a young and unknown and unrecommended
man, he first approached the Atelier; and this memory
makes him more sympathetic to the young and probably
gauche of to-day than the impatience of his nature would
suggest. In this development of his character it is more
than likely that his marriage has played a considerable
part. Madeleine Renaud and Jean-Louis Barrault have
contrasting and complementary characters: she is gentle,
patient, prudent, and pleasantly malicious, he fierce,
impulsive, and turbulent. Her influence upon him has
been an inspiration, a salutary restraint, an enrichment.

Thus Barrault has become one of the few actors who
can triumph against the run of his own nature. That in
moments of torment and stress, as in the temptations of
Partage de midi, when he is inexplicably rejected by God;
or in the ecstasy of Mesa's passion in the Hong Kong

cemetery in the second act of the same play; or in the boisterous high spirits and horse-play of *Les Fourberies de Scapin*—that Barrault should be excellent at such moments is not to be wondered at; they answer to something fundamental in his eager, excited, restless, and troubled nature. But that this player should also, on occasion, be able to spread a peace over the theatre, that he should be able, not to heighten tension, but to relax it, is genuinely surprising, as surprising as if the sly malice of Jane Austen were to compose a saga, or the solemnity of Milton to shed itself into a limerick. Yet this unexpected miracle Barrault can and does perform, though no doubt the cost to him is great. We have in London, at the St James's, seen how he can do it, in the very last words of Salacrou's *Les Nuits de la colère*, in which he plays the part of the betrayed and blinded Resistance leader. After the tortures and agonies of that tremendous and understanding drama, with its treachery, cowardice, courage, and despair, Barrault steps forward out of the framework of the play, and speaks for a moment of the hope that mankind may gain from the fact that in a time of difficulty and distress some men have shown themselves capable of living worthily. He spoke with solemnity, but a serene solemnity, and with a quiet sadness in whose pride was no shadow of argument or assertion; and the syllables of the last word of the speech—*honorablement*—rolled out like the completion of a piece of noble music, like the calming of a world's sorrow.

As an actor, then, Barrault is not to be thought of only in terms of vision and of mime. But he is not to be thought of, either, only as an actor. If Barrault were no more than an actor, his reputation in France, and his influence on the French theatre, would by no means be what they are. He would still be a notable figure on the Parisian stage, but he would not have a pre-eminent position. If one asks ordinary French theatregoers, or indeed expert workers in the French theatre, who are the greatest French players they will reply, for the women, Edwige Feuillère, Madeleine Renaud, and for the men, Pierre Fresnay, Pierre Brasseur. Barrault's name will come third or fourth on the list, and it may even not be mentioned at all. It is not as an actor that Barrault's chief work is done. I discussed this matter with a leading French dramatist. "Barrault," he said to me, "Barrault is not an actor, he is a bomb."

In the end we came back to that explosiveness in Barrault's nature which he tries to control, but not to suppress entirely. This explosiveness is a source of great creative energy. It has made the Marigny, when Barrault is in it, the world's leading theatre. There was a time, a few years ago, when the Old Vic company offered us one tremendous experience after another, following Olivier's Richard III with Richardson's Falstaff, and both with Guinness's Richard II. In those days, about the end of the War, the New Theatre in St Martin's Lane, where the Old Vic then gave its performances, could legitimately reckon itself a leader in the world's theatres. It was not content only with interpreting Shakespeare. It had ambitions to be an enricher of the contemporary drama. Its fostering of James Forsyth, however, though well intentioned, and right enough in principle, did not bear immediately rewarding fruit. Mr Forsyth's grandiose historical plays had no life in them. The great actors left the Old Vic before it discovered substitutes either for themselves or for Shakespeare; and the glory over the New Theatre faded.

Some beams of it reappeared above the horizon in the neighbourhood of the St James's when Sir Laurence Olivier assumed the management of that celebrated playhouse. His opening production of Christopher Fry's *Venus Observed*, and his employment, in regal disregard of economy, of the best and most magnificent scene designers, suggested that Sir Laurence intended to make of the St James's a creative home of the modern theatre. But Sir Laurence is a busy man. He has to think of the cinema as well as of the theatre; America beckons to him, and cannot be wholly ignored. During Sir Laurence's tenancy of the St James's some fine things have been seen there. But they have been separate and unrelated successes rather than products of settled policy.

But the Marigny, under Barrault, is an entire theatrical world in itself. Sometimes Barrault emerges from that world, and comes to London, or tours South America, or visits the nearer Continental cities, or makes a film. (Like Sir Laurence, he finances his theatre from his pictures.) But his absences from the Marigny are strictly limited in time. For six or seven years he has spent at the Marigny eight or nine months out of every twelve. The Marigny is his special creation, and he devotes to it all his care. There is no aspect of theatrical life in which Barrault is not actively, and indeed passionately, interested. He loves the high moments of theatrical drama, when Mesa makes love to Ysé, or Hamlet soliloquizes. That is clear enough. But he is fascinated too by the conditions underlying the sale of programmes; they are, he says, enthralling. He theorizes about the mental approach to her job of the girl who shows you to your seat with the same gusto as he considers an actor's attitude to the crisis of his part.

He desires, therefore, that the Marigny should be a home of great plays, and so produces Molière and Shakespeare. But the presentation of past masterpieces, though important, is only a part of his work. He wishes the Marigny to be a complete theatre, the source not only of great performances of plays already known, but the inspiration of new work. He wishes this work, both new and old, to be presented with every advantage that the French theatre can offer. In consequence he has brought to the Marigny not merely Madeleine Renaud and himself, but players like Edwige Feuillère, Brasseur, Blanchar,

Jean Desailly, and Jacques Dacqmine; and, in the designs of the late Christian Bérard, he has made the Marigny a centre of stage decoration.

The Marigny, under Barrault, has recovered for the theatre treasure that otherwise would have been lost. I have already said that, but for Barrault, the world would probably never have seen either *Partage de midi* or *Le Soulier de satin*. Barrault did not discover Georges Feydeau, but he rediscovered him. It is unlikely that the Comédie-Française, for example, would have revived Feydeau (with an excellent influence on its finances) had not Barrault made so huge and unexpected a success of his production of *Occupe-toi d'Amélie*. The coupling of the work of Feydeau and Claudel, of the writer of farces and of the grave, religious ambassador, shows the range of Barrault's tastes and sympathies.

Barrault is catholic-minded. I recognized this the first time I met him. The French theatre began to impinge forcibly on the minds of English theatre-goers about the time of the production of *Ring Round the Moon* in the early days of 1950. But before this Viscount Kemsley had perceived the great force of the post-War movement in the French theatre, and it was as early as 1948 that he sent me on the first of many visits to Paris to investigate this movement for *The Sunday Times*. Had it not been for Lord Kemsley's recognition of the relevance of the French theatre to the English, which no one else had at that time realized, and his action upon this recognition, my opportunity of meeting Barrault, and of appreciating his especial qualities, would have been long delayed, and might never have occurred at all.

I came upon Barrault at one of the most depressing moments of his career at the Marigny. His successes at that theatre have been accompanied by three considerable failures. The first of these was Bruckner's *Elisabeth*; another was André Obey's *Lazare*; and the third was Albert Camus's *L'État de siège*. Two nights before I met him, Barrault had produced *L'État de siège*, and the Parisian critics had already made clear their unfavourable opinions. On these occasions there is a great deal of plain speaking. No feelings are spared. The rasping notices carry no suggestion of English understatement. Parisian critics are quite capable of heading a review of a play they have disliked with a heavily printed title such as "Barrault Surprises: Even Worse than Usual." This was the heading that the now defunct *Opéra*, under the editorship of Roger Nimier, placed over its notice of André Obey's *Lazare*.

Something of the same sort had occurred over the production of *L'État de siège*. Nevertheless, Barrault did not seem unduly discouraged. He recognized plainly enough the play's failure; and we discussed whether Camus was, or was not, an Existentialist, Existentialism then being much in the public eye. Barrault preferred to call Camus revolutionary, thinking of the dramatic innovations of his play rather than of his political opinions. "Are you, too, revolutionary?" I asked. " Je suis homme libre," he replied.

A free man, with complete freedom of choice; a freedom of choice not bounded by any political shackles, or æsthetic limitations. That is why Barrault has found theatrical vigour in authors as widely differing in their outlook upon life, and in their conception of theatrical propriety, as Claudel and Feydeau. It is why, in his production of new work, he has gone, with fervour and success, to authors as divergent as Salacrou, Montherlant, and Anouilh.

These three writers have little in common except that they are among the principal figures in the contemporary French drama, and that each of them has contributed work to Barrault's theatre. I have already mentioned Salacrou's *Les Nuits de la colère*, which was one of Barrault's most notable productions; Anouilh gave to the Marigny *La Répétition*, and Montherlant *Malatesta*.

Montherlant lives on the Left Bank, Salacrou in the
Avenue Foch, and Anouilh has a villa at Neuilly, on the
other side of the Bois de Boulogne from Salacrou. Thus
the three men are not neighbours, and in view of the
divisions that exist in France between writers so much
more sharply than they do in England, it is possible they
are not even friends.

I have no wish, and I certainly lack knowledge, to go
into the complications of French politics, but Barrault's
association with these authors shows that the sole values
in his theatre are dramatic. Anouilh has always asserted
his complete independence of politics, Montherlant is
romantically conservative in temperament, while Salacrou would probably find himself in agreement with many
of the views of a British Labour Government. It is significant that Barrault is in artistic sympathy with all three.
With Jean-Paul Sartre and Marcel Aymé, they are the leading dramatists of contemporary France, and must be considered in any roll-call of the Parisian theatre.

Armand Salacrou, a member of the Academy Goncourt and of the Legion of Honour, was born in Rouen
in August 1899, and is, like Barrault, the son of a
chemist. He spent his early life in Le Havre, and then
studied law, medicine, and philosophy in Paris. He became Secretary at the Atelier under Dullin some years
before Barrault joined the theatre, and in 1930 founded a
publicity organization which has met with great success.
He is a married man, has two daughters, and his collection of paintings by Picasso, Modigliani, Bracque, and
Dufy immediately impresses any visitor to his elegant
and spacious apartment.

His plays have been produced in many of the most
celebrated theatres of Paris. In 1944 one of his pieces,
Les Fiancés du Havre, was presented at the Comédie-
Française. Charles Dullin's last part on the stage was in
Salacrou's *L'Archipel Lenoir* at the Montparnasse in 1948.
The Atelier took his *Patchouli* and *Atlas-Hôtel*, as well as

his later play, *La Terre est ronde*. *Une Femme libre* and
Un Homme comme les autres were put on at the Œuvre in
1934 and 1936 respectively, and his *Histoire de rire* had a
great success at the fashionable Madeleine in 1939.

M. Salacrou's apartment is bright and light, dustless,
and modern. Anouilh, who was born at Bordeaux in
1910, has a liking for an older, richer, darker, more
romantic luxury. I last saw M. Anouilh in the morning-
room of the Athenæum, whose walls are hung with heavy
embossed gold paper. It was decorated by Alma-
Tadema, and its atmosphere is discreetly *fin-de-siècle*. A
heavily shadowed portrait of Matthew Arnold lowers
across the room at a fading picture of Frederick the
Great. In one corner there are coffee-cups, but the
favourite drink is a tawny yellow sherry. Nowhere is
there a suggestion of anything more modern than a cigar
divan or a hansom cab. As he looked round him
Anouilh's dark eyes shone in his shy and sombre face.
He would have preferred to live in almost any century
rather than the present. "Here," he said, "is the best
of England."

In his youth he was very poor, and wrote advertisements for a living; now he must be one of the richest
dramatists in the world. He was married early, to the
actress Monelle Valentin, who has played many of his
curiously helpless and determined, pure and fràil heroines.
His first success was *Le Bal des voleurs*, which André
Barsacq, the present manager of the Atelier, directed in
1932. M. Barsacq has since been associated with the
majority of Anouilh's pieces, though it was Claude Sain-
val, at the Comédie des Champs-Élysées, who presented
one of the most famous of them, *Ardèle*, and Barrault both
directed and played in *La Répétition; ou, L'Amour puni*, at
the Marigny.

The third of these Barrault dramatists is Henry de
Montherlant, who was born in Paris on April 21, 1896.
Montherlant also is a romantic, but his romanticism is not

the doomed and defeatist sort that fascinates Anouilh.
It is a romanticism based on battle—the battle of sport,
the battle of medieval war, the battle of the sexes. There
is something of the swashbuckler about Montherlant,
though his swashbuckling is done with impressive style.
He admires power and ruthlessness and the magnificent
taste and cruelty of the Italian Renaissance. He is thrilled
by the massive evidences of the wide-flung Roman Empire
that lie scattered over France and North Africa; he
glories in the thought that at one period of his life he went
down into the bull-ring as an amateur matador, and was
wounded more than once. He despises the feminine
virtues of pity and compassion, and has never admitted
women to equality with men. He takes a loud and
sometimes strident pride in his ability to live independently. When a young woman urged him to marry,
he replied with characteristic vigour and too demon-
strative brutality that he would rather have tuberculosis,
proving unintentionally that emotion is more the foundation of his thinking than is logic, since weddings and con-
sumption are not, after all, inevitable alternatives. The
splendid, highly coloured, and dramatic dominate his
imagination. His style is dyed in the purple. His *La
Reine morte* was presented at the Comédie-Française in
1943, his *Maître de Santiago* at the Hébertot in 1947, and
his *Malatesta* at the Marigny in 1949.

Distinguished as is the record of the Marigny, there are
some Parisian dramatists, and those among the most
famous, who have not been represented in the Barrault
seasons there. One of these is Marcel Aymé, who, after
building up a great reputation as a satirical novelist and
short-story writer, is now devoting himself to the theatre
with outstanding success. M. Aymé was born at Joigny
on March 29, 1902, and is the son of a blacksmith. His
mother died when he was two years old, and he was
brought up by an aunt at Dôle. His military service was
in the Rhineland during the Occupation after the First

World War. He came to Paris in 1923, intending to take
up medical studies, but had to earn his living. So in
turn he became a bank employee, an insurance salesman,
and a reporter.

The Parisian dramatists do not as a rule make things
easy for journalists. They dislike interviews. Anouilh,
for all his shy, deceptive charm, can be quite savage where
the Press is concerned, just as he can be entirely delightful, friendly, and co-operative. Aymé, whom I have
never met, can, I believe, be as difficult as Anouilh. He
lives in Montmartre, in the Rue Feval, in an Alpine area
of houses, amid the staircases and chimney-pots of the
Butte, narrow cobbled streets, and village shops. Beneath him all Paris is stretched out in a golden view, a
spread counterpane of domes and towers crossed by the
recurrent river, while, above, the great bell of the Sacré-
Cœur reverberates down the shaken hillside. Every
night the tourists' motors painfully climb the steep and
twisting slopes, making for the jammed tables and the
violins of the Place du Tertre, passing M. Aymé's home
without knowing it. If their occupants saw M. Aymé's
long and silent form they would be able to make little of
it. When interviewed it is Aymé's disconcerting practice
to sit motionless and quiet, saying nothing. He writes
every evening between 8.30 and midnight, slowly, two
pages a day, with a pen held between the index and the
middle fingers. When the French journalist Paul Guth
interviewed him the only time he showed animation was
when he noticed Guth writing in the same peculiar fashion.

The secret of great output, of course, is not speed, but
regularity. It has been calculated that a man who wrote
a couple of pages every day would, if he lived a fairly
long life, produce as much as Voltaire. Aymé, though
still comparatively young, is well on the way to proving
the truth of this. He has written sixteen or seventeen
novels, of which the most famous, *La Jument verte*, has
exceeded its three-hundredth printing. He has also

published half a dozen volumes of short stories and several plays.

I have already spoken of Aymé's *La Tête des autres*. The first of his plays to achieve outstanding success was *Clérambard*, which was produced at the Comédie des Champs-Élysées in 1949, and ran for more than three hundred performances. In Anouilh's opinion *Clérambard* was the best play to be seen in Paris at the time, but he thought it too extreme for English tastes. Extreme it is. The Count de Clérambard at the beginning of the play, when he compels his whole family to work incessantly at indoor looms in order to earn a few shillings, is, according to English tastes, unbelievably mean; after he has seen a vision of St Francis of Assisi he is unbelievably kind-hearted. Yet in his kind-heartedness there is a domineering ruthlessness, a determination that since he has become holy every one else must be holy too, which is not easy to accommodate to the compromising nature of the English.

Though Aymé's plays, particularly *Clérambard* and *La Tête des autres*, are very popular, though they afford striking acting parts, they do not seem to me to display his genius as well as his other work does. His stories are famous for his apparently inexhaustible facility in hitting upon some preposterous hypothesis whose consequences he works out with impeccable workaday logic to their impossible but quite convincing conclusions. It is the ingenuity which Aymé shows in stories like *La Grâce* or *Les Sabines* that most immediately impresses his readers; but a finer quality than this is the feeling of poetic compassion in which he sometimes envelops his characters. This feeling, despite Clérambard's conversion, does not penetrate either of his most celebrated plays. From *La Tête des autres*, especially, one would never guess that Aymé is a merciful man.

Despite Aymé's great productivity, and Anouilh's theatrical reputation, the most famous of contemporary

French authors, both in his own country and abroad,
is Jean-Paul Sartre. Sartre is three years younger than
Aymé, and his connexion with Existentialism has carried his fame round the world. It has given him the kind
of reputation that the theory of relativity brought to
Einstein in the nineteen-twenties. Few people understand either relativity or Existentialism, but the two
philosophies have brought their authors the highest form
of fame in the modern world, the attention of gossip
writers and of the popular Press. Sartre has always lived
in fairly easy circumstances, though his father, a naval
officer, died when he was a child. He was taken prisoner
in 1940, but released after some mistake had been made
in his papers. During the War he played a great part in
the clandestine Press, and was one of the founders of
the magazine *Les Temps modernes*. Along with André
Roussin, the author of *La Petite Hutte* and *Bobosse* (played
in London as *Figure of Fun*), he is said to earn an income
of more than £50,000 a year.

There are many other figures that occupy a prominent
position in the French theatre. Henry Bernstein, though
he is nearly eighty, continues to enjoy great popularity.
Just as some people always go to the Royal Academy
exhibitions, so there are those who never miss a new
Bernstein. Bernstein is the manager of the Ambassadeurs, in the Champs-Élysées, one of the most fashionable of French theatres. He keeps it open mainly with
revivals of his own works, but he is very perceptive of
talent in others, as he showed by the speed with which
he transferred to the Ambassadeurs a little comedy called
La Cuisine des anges, when it was a great success at
the Vieux-Colombier. Marcel Achard, a considerably
younger man than Bernstein, has been for twenty-five
years a leader of the French lighter stage, though his
work is little known in England. His *Marlborough s'en
va-t-en guerre* was produced at the Oxford Playhouse in its
Woodstock Road days in the middle nineteen-twenties.

So far as I know, that is the only play of his that has been
seen in England, though the Lunts have acted him in
America. Such pieces of his as *Voulez-vous jouer avec
moâ?*, *Auprès de ma blonde*, *Nous irons à Valparaiso*, and
Le Moulin de la galette are light, gay, and attractive.
Achard's admirers say that he knows his job; his detrac-
tors that he knows little else.

Jean Cocteau is still the most versatile of French
dramatists; Paul Claudel is finding that the plays he wrote
in his spare time when he was serving as Ambassador
in distant parts of the world, plays designed as closet
drama, without a thought of public representation, are
winning him in France the same sort of reputation that
T. S. Eliot enjoys in Britain, that of a master of a more
rarefied world than the theatre who nevertheless finds it
possible to employ successfully the theatre's conventions.
Most popular of all is Roussin. Roussin is about the same
age as Anouilh, and came into public notice first during
the Occupation, both as an author and as an actor in the
Marseilles area. The comparison between Roussin and
Rattigan is an obvious one. They are almost exact contemporaries. They write the wittiest plays of their
respective countries. They write about the same social
classes, the well-to-do and the Bohemian. They are both
fashionable. By their own exertions they are both rich.
But there is an important difference between the two.
Rattigan has greater emotional power than Roussin;
Roussin has more poetry than Rattigan. Roussin has
not written anything that touches the emotions so
poignantly as Rattigan's *The Browning Version* or *The
Deep Blue Sea*. On the other hand, is there anything in
Rattigan that so surely rises out of the particular into
the universal, that so suddenly illuminates the entire
landscape of life, as Nina's speech on the unpromising
topic of married people lying in bed together, physically
so close, yet in thoughts and dreams and longings
separated by impassable oceans?

Another author who has been enjoying a good deal of success recently is Gabriel Arout. M. Arout's *La Dame de trèfle* at the Saint-Georges was one of the few satisfactory productions of the early 1952–53 season. It is a melodrama about a respectable woman who, in order to carry on an affair with a passionate lover and at the same time preserve her good name, offers herself to him, under an alias, at a brothel he frequents. He, poor fellow, is driven nearly out of his mind by his inability to decide whether or not the Ada of the brothel is really the Isabelle of the drawing-room. The author himself is said not to have decided the point, and most of the Parisian critics represent themselves baffled by this recondite problem, which is as about as difficult to see through as a clear-glass window. M. Arout prints in his programme sundry quotations from the play, on such topics as happiness, desire, and what is an honest woman? He is obviously not averse to being treated as a bit of a philosopher, and his admirers play up to him by discussing *La Dame de trèfle* in terms of Pirandellian exploration of the duality of the soul. The play did not strike me as this kind of thing at all: Isabelle and Ada, with the same emotions and in the end the same clothes, seemed to me plainly to be the same person. I saw no philosophy in the piece at all, but I found the wretched Roland's efforts to trap Isabelle, first with rhetoric, then with a bottle of scent, and finally with a horse-whip, vigorous, ingenious, and exciting.

In the opening scene Madeleine Robinson's strongly defined features and powerful figure seemed a rather inadequate excuse for Roland's transports, but thereafter, especially as Ada, Mlle Robinson gave an impressive Robsonish performance.

La Dame de trèfle, excellent entertainment as it was, could easily be used to confirm the general English impression that the only problems the French theatre is interested in are those of fornication and adultery.

Fornication and adultery do in fact reappear on Parisian stages with formidable frequency, but it is inaccurate to suppose that they are never banished therefrom. Not only are there French plays completely devoid of sexual pre-occupations, but some of such plays are among the most popular. I have not often been in a theatre in which, even before the curtain rose, there was such a spirit of expect-ancy and excitement as pervaded the Hébertot during the run of *Dialogues des Carmélites* in 1952. This play was adapted by the late Georges Bernanos from a novel by Gertrud von Le Fort, and it suggests that in Bernanos the theatre lost an original force of passion and skill. There is no sex in *Dialogues des Carmélites*; the relations between men and women are scarcely glanced at. The relations between human beings, and between human beings and God, are what mattered to Bernanos; and in this play their consideration leads to high spiritual drama and to magnificent theatre. *Dialogues des Carmélites* sounds like one of the dialogues of Plato, which, however their style may delight, are not, and are not intended to be, dramatic. But Bernanos's play satis-fies as much on the vulgar but essential ground of theatrical thrills, as upon that of thought and feeling. In fact, its ending is a *coup de théâtre* to be remembered along with the slamming of the door in *A Doll's House* and the last words of Sydney Carton.

The play is about the conquest of fear. To escape from the demands of life, and the terrors from which the world, with all its pleasures, is never immune, a young French aristocrat, Blanche de la Force, enters the Carmelite order. There she hopes to find security and protection; but, as one might foresee, she is deceived. The time is the late eighteenth century. The Revolution breaks out, the order is persecuted, and Blanche in panic-terror flees in disguise to Paris. The other nuns are taken, and condemned to the guillotine. Then comes the scene of which I have spoken. It shows the last few steps

of the sisters, through a crowd of townspeople, before
execution. In the crowd a priest, hidden in a cloak, makes
a furtive sign of the cross and disappears. Off-stage, the
doomed sisters intone the *Salve Regina*, and then the *Veni
Creator*. One by one they cross the front of the stage,
mount the scaffold, and the knife falls. Each time it falls,
the singing diminishes in volume, until there are only two
voices left, and then only one. But at this moment a new
voice is uplifted, stronger, clearer than the others, unwavering, but with something childlike about it, and
Blanche, her face now serene and untroubled, walks
through the crowd, and, still singing, follows the last of
her companions up the steps. Once again the knife falls
and the curtain comes down on the deep, hushed silence.
Until this scene Hélène Bourdan's Blanche had seemed to
me vague and indeterminate, but the actress played this
final brief and moving episode as if she had been waiting
for it all the evening, and had reserved for it all her
power. In the full, true notes of her voice sounded the
triumphant joy of a spirit released from long terror, and
the effect upon the audience was, as well it might be,
overwhelming.

I have called the ending of *Dialogues des Carmélites* a
coup de théâtre, and I almost regret having done so, for
there is something derogatory about the phrase. It suggests the subordination of truth to theatrical effect, and
in this superb climax there is nothing like that. There is
only and happily and overwhelmingly a coming together,
a perfect matching, of the inner life of the play with
its most intense dramatic expression. But in another
author who has done much more work for the stage
than Bernanos, and by it has provoked that constant
and animated and acrimonious discussion which is one
of the marks of fame, there is, I fear, incontestably a
falsification of values such as the words *coup de théâtre*
imply.

Jean Cocteau is a man of multiple talents. He writes

films and directs them, and even, as in *Les Enfants terribles*, accompanies them with a commentary in his own sombre and impressive voice. He is a poet, a critic, a writer for the ballet, even a novelist and artist, as well as a most prolific dramatist. There is no form of æsthetic expression that does not stimulate his imagination, and yet that imagination, which superficially is the most fecund of its time, always seems forced and strained.

Cocteau's work is well known in Britain. His films, especially *Orphée* and *Les Enfants terribles* (shown here as *The Strange Ones*), have had comparatively wide publicity in London. His play *L'Aigle à deux têtes* (*The Eagle has Two Heads*, translated by Ronald Duncan) caused a minor sensation when it was produced, soon after the end of the War, in London, when it brought an extraordinary celebrity to its principal actress, Miss Eileen Herlie; and the Arts Theatre has given at least two Cocteau plays, *Les Parents terribles* (*Intimate Relations*) and *Les Monstres sacrés* (*The Holy Terrors*).

The impression that Cocteau makes upon his audience is one of bewildering cleverness. In everything he does there is something to astonish and astound. At the first night of *The Eagle has Two Heads* at the Lyric Theatre, Hammersmith, the audience listened in amazement to a speech of Miss Herlie's that lasted for nineteen minutes without a break, and contained more than 2000 words. In *The Strange Ones*, that terrible picture of an incestuous brother and sister living in a dream-world of bric-a-brac and the morbidly preserved treasures of their unclean childhood, there was a remarkable nightmare sequence. The incestuous and eventually murderous sister, distracted by the thought that her brother has fallen in love, dreams that she is being led through a woodland glade, along a slight declivity on which lies a rich blue carpet. On the top of the hill she comes upon a billiard-table bearing the dead body of her brother, whose outstretched arm hangs listlessly, while a bell rings. It may, says the dark and solemn voice of Cocteau himself, be the automatic billiard-marker. It is, however, some one at the door, and Elizabeth is wakened from her uneasy sleep, and springs out of her untidy bed.

It is a mark of most authentic literature that everything in it should be at once unexpected and inevitable. Interest is often killed if the audience or the reader can see what is coming, and the manner of its coming; but it is killed equally if, the moment the thing has come, it is not recognized that nothing else was possible. Now, when Elizabeth sets out on her alarming journey no one can foresee what she will arrive at, nor pass on her way. The wood, the carpet, the billiard-table, and the dead body are all unexpected. But they are also arbitrary. There is no artistic logic by which they seem inevitable. Their sole quality is the quality of surprise. One feels that Cocteau has racked his brains in order to devise a series of astonishing images.

He is always racking his brain in order to astonish. His interest is not in the thing said, but in the manner of its saying. His principal characters in *The Holy Terrors* are a famous actress and her husband, whose happiness is threatened by a strident and selfish young girl-student of the Comédie-Française. A quarrel between husband and wife is inevitable. Now, instead of giving us a straight quarrel depending for its interest on the depth of emotional disturbance the two players feel, Cocteau's translator, Edward O. Marsh, cleverly interpreting the spirit of the original, mixes the episode with a rehearsal of *Romeo and Juliet*, and makes the climax a visual parody upon the balcony scene in that play. It is clever and amusing, but it does not in any way touch the heart, because Cocteau is not concerned with his characters as people, but only as marionettes whom he can exhibit in the most surprising aspects possible. A quarrel between a devoted husband and wife is a moving and terrifying thing: it shakes the universe. But to Cocteau it is nothing, except as providing the opportunity for a theatrical scene unexpectedly embellished.

Later in *The Holy Terrors* Cocteau launches his hero into a full-blooded attack upon the cinema in contrast with the theatre. In the Arts Theatre production in November 1952 Ballard Berkeley delivered this speech with rasping fire, but it consumed nothing. It had no warmth. I do not believe for a moment that Cocteau despises the cinema. If he did he would not give to it as much time as he does. He is capable of writing just as cleverly against the theatre. Cocteau does not give the feeling of inner sincerity that is essential to a work of art.

This question of sincerity is not as simple as it looks. To ask of a writer that he should be sincere in everything he writes is not the same thing as asking him actually to believe all that he puts down on paper. I remember a lunch at the Ivy one autumn day with Christopher Fry and Robert Cowen a young, American scientist interested in the connexions between science and art. The conversation happened to turn upon the processes of scientific discovery and artistic creation. Fry, who was then writing a play about the Hungarian revolution of 1848, said that artistic composition was really like a process of discovery. It was like seeing the words dimly, through a glass darkly, and writing them down. "Come," I said, "you don't really believe that the play is already composed in its perfect Platonic form somewhere in heaven, and that you have merely to copy it out? You don't really *believe* that, do you?"

"Well," said Fry, "whether I believe it or not, that's exactly what it feels like."

It is perfectly possible for a poet to feel sincerely many things he does not philosophically believe. Thomas Hardy represented himself towards the end of his life as a conforming member of the Church of England. As such he could not believe that the President of the Immortals really sported with Tess. He was, on the other hand, bound to accept the doctrine of an all-bountiful Father. But that does not involve any insincerity in the writing of *Tess of the D'Urbervilles*. The imagination frequently tells us things that the reason rejects. Insincerity comes in only when the imagination is forced and misrepresented, and the feelings exaggerated, for the sake of making an effect.

This forcing of the note seems to me to be perpetual in Cocteau. I do not ask that when he denounces the cinema he should be expressing firmly held convictions. It is enough if at the moment of writing the speech against the cinema in *Les Monstres 'sacrés* he merely felt as if they were his convictions. But somehow I cannot believe that he did. The speech, like all his speeches, is rhetoric, coinage of the brain. It does not ring true to anything around the heart. I cannot think that Cocteau even has a heart. He is purely a subtle brain seeking, and not vainly, to take one's breath away.

Friends of mine both in England and in France with whom I have discussed this book tell me that my judgment upon Cocteau is harsh and unjust. There are many people who regard his work as reaching the summit of contemporary French achievement. I do not agree with this valuation of Cocteau, but I feel that in equity I ought to record it.

Far, far deeper in feeling than Cocteau is Paul Claudel, the author of *Partage de midi* and *Le Soulier de satin*. M. Claudel is intensely religious, and a living proof that, though religion is compatible with genius, it is not always allied to charity. Paul Guth, whose interviews are almost as lively as Cyril Ray's, once asked him if the growing influence of religion on literature would lead to more charity and gentleness of manners. "Charity?" he exclaimed indignantly. "What do you mean by charity? Charity towards evildoers or to_ wards their victims? There isn't a psalm that doesn't

talk about God's enemies. David's hand wasn't nerve-
less, and the Fathers of the Church were not easy-going."

Claudel's probing into the recesses of the heart, and his
abiding consciousness of the dogmas of religion, his inexhaustible outpourings of often abstract words and
images, and the loose rhythm of his verse at one time
brought him abundant and savage criticism. The acid
Paul Léautaud said of his work, "This sort of literature,
with its hodge-podge of images, its verbal delirium, and
its foundation of bigotry, does not give the idea of great
intelligence." Another critic remarked that "what is
called the genius of Claudel is only aphasia. He power-
fully emits noises some of which are true and the others
unintelligible." He is a man who has no control over his
eloquence. The lightning flashes, and then the night
comes down in thick blackness again. One has the feeling that he is not much liked personally. André Gide
said of him, "He is a man who thinks he can travel to
heaven in a Pullman." Claudel retorted, "Gide is going
to hell in the Métro."

Whatever may be the ultimate standing of Claudel in
the history of the French theatre, I cannot do less than say
that the performances of his *Partage de midi* which the
Renaud–Barrault company gave at the St James's in the
autumn of 1951 were among the most tremendous and
moving theatrical experiences I have ever had. The hot
glare of the tropic sun on the white deck of the becalmed
ship; the heat, and the languor, and the *malaise* of the
three passengers; the sharp torment of Mesa, the man
whose soul, offered to the service of God, had been
summarily rejected, the warm, languid fascination of Ysé,
the uneasy exultation of Amalric, rejoicing in the splendour of physical strength and desire; the keen, pointed
face of Barrault; the soft, caressing voice, the eyes
glimmering through tears, the slow movements of Mme
Edwige Feuillère, who gave to the tight corset and
sweeping dresses of the late Victorian era an incom-

parable grace; the sudden clang of the ship's bell breaking the mid-day silence—all these are things that return
to me night after night as I sit watching dull comedies
and vulgar farces, gilding otherwise miserable evenings
with reflections of Paradise.

There are, of course, also the players. Pierre Fresnay
has, I think, the highest reputation among French actors.
It is claimed for him that he can act anybody or anything.
Versatility is a considerable quality, but it is not in my
opinion necessarily the mark of a great actor. François
Périer is also said to be able to range over the entire gamut
of human types and nature. He has played with equal
success the excessively scrupulous hero of Sartre's *Les
Mains sales* and the actor in *Bobosse*. Périer is no conventional matinée idol, and he cannot always keep his
unruly hair out of his eyes; but he has great spirit and
tenderness, comic verve and pathos, and is undoubtedly
one of the best players in the world. Pierre Brasseur's
celebrity too is great. Rotund, restless, and dynamic,
he would accept with delight the charge of overacting.

Danièle Delorme is sweet and small and timid and
simple; Jean Marais has a fine presence, and the prestige
of his film reputation, but his season at the Comédie-
Française brought much criticism of the weakness of his
voice; Yves Robert can give stiff, ramrod performances
when these are called for, or be easy, suave, and supple;
Jacques Dacqmine has repose and considerable elegance;
Elvire Popesco has comic fire and gusto, with energy
that suggests that she is trying to get through a thousand performances in nine hundred nights, and will
probably succeed; Suzanne Flon and Jacqueline Porel are
leading ladies of more conventional charm. This list
could be extended almost indefinitely, but the French
performances that I personally have most enjoyed have
been those of Périer in *Bobosse*, Madeleine Renaud in *Les
Fausses confidences*, Robert Vattier in *Nina*, Fernand
Gravey in a light-hearted little crime play, *Je l'aimais*

trop, which is set in a flower-shop, Henry Guisol as the worried husband in *Le Complexe de Philémon*, and Edwige Feuillère as Ysé in *Partage de midi*, and as the heroine in Pol Quentin's *La Liberté est un dimanche* who seeks to beguile the Governor of a prison island in order to arrange the release of one of his captives.

Of these the impression that most vividly and movingly remains is that of Mme Feuillère, tall, languorous, incomparably magical. Mme Feuillère is the only actress I have seen who unites extreme physical allure with the highest mastery of her art. Her movements have a slow, incantatory grace, her voice is grave and enchanting, she can give the feeling that she has bewitched the entire universe so that it is caught in a net from which there is no escape. She breathes an atmosphere of the warm, spell-binding, perhaps demoralizing South, bringing into her theatre that lotus-eating world of sensuous delight from which one would not depart even if one could.

4

Jean-Paul Sartre

THE time has come to examine more closely the work of some of the leaders of the French stage. The obvious subjects for detailed study are Sartre, Salacrou, Montherlant, Anouilh. The long runs and frequent revivals which the works of these men have enjoyed in Paris during the last twenty years is proof of their feeling for the stage, and the genuineness of their dramatic instincts. But they are more than writers who have the trick of engaging and keeping the attention of the playgoing public. They are men whose work has a corporate significance in relation to the problems and difficulties of the age.

They differ from each other in almost every way— in political conviction, in faith, in technique, and in personality. But they are alike in this, that in their work the great questions that humanity has asked itself, often with anguish, are always present, overtly or implicitly. What is right? What is justice? What is happiness? How can mankind have life, and have it more abundantly? They are Paris's most consistent entertainers, and at the same time they stand to it in the relation of philosophers. When the achievement of the contemporary French theatre is finally assessed it is the plays of these four dramatists that will be the decisive factor; and it is unlikely that they will be neglected in any account of the thought-pattern of Western Europe at this particular historical juncture.

There are several reasons for beginning with Jean-Paul Sartre. I do not think that Sartre's reputation in

Paris, purely as a dramatist, is as high as that of Anouilh;
and there are many good judges of the theatre who think
that he is inferior to Aymé, despite the fact that the career
of Aymé as a dramatist, however well established he
may be as a novelist and writer of short stories, has only
just begun. On my first visit to Paris after the War
Sartre's *Les Mains sales* was playing to crowded houses at
the Théâtre Antoine; yet I could not help noticing that
the playgoers to whom I spoke, if left to direct the conversation themselves, enthused, not over this production,
but over Anouilh's *L'Invitation au château*.

Nevertheless, Sartre is the most significant contemporary post-War dramatist. He is the symbol of that
théâtre engagé of which in London we have heard only
weak echoes in the productions of organizations like
Theatre Workshop, and in such plays of J. B. Priestley
as *Home is To-morrow*. Sartre has accepted the theory
that the political life of man to-day is increasing in giant
progression at the expense of his private existence. There
was a time when individual people could, if they wished,
very largely ignore the political situation in which they
lived. In the Middle Ages farmers and yeomen sowed
and reaped placidly while the nobility a couple of
fields away fought to its extinction. As late as the
beginning of the nineteenth century wars had only a
local and partial significance. The heroes of Jane Austen
rarely or never speak of Napoleon; Mr Darcy and Mr
Bingley were undisturbed by thoughts of Ulm or
Trafalgar, the retreat from Moscow or Amiens.

Such a divorce between the public and the private no
longer exists. At any moment the rhythm of our lives
may be shattered by decisions arbitrarily taken thousands of miles away from us by people over whom
we have no possible means of control. Broadly speaking,
the English theatre does not reflect this new condition in
which private affairs are governed by public events.
Sartre's *Les Mains sales* and Rattigan's *The Deep Blue Sea*

both deal movingly with young people sorely perplexed. But whereas Sartre's Hugo is distressed only by the shifting perspectives of Communist policy, Mr Rattigan's heroine is caught up exclusively in the dilemma of her own personality.

Many plays, of course, continue to be produced in Paris on the development of which public policy and affairs impinge no more directly than they do on the story of *The Deep Blue Sea*. In this sense the plays of Anouilh and Roussin, for example, are private studies. These authors exclude from their view of life most things that take place outside the homes of their characters. Like their predecessors, they find sufficient drama in the hearts of men and women without making excursions into their politics.

But there is another, and a powerful, school of French drama whose creators are engulfed in the turmoil of national and international discussion and controversy. Out of this school come plays so savagely anti-American that they are stopped by the police; plays so fiercely critical of the processes of French democracy that they provoke riots; and the plays of Sartre. Some are Communist and in favour of Russia; some are Communist and against Russia; some are simply against Communism. But they are all political. They all belong to the *théâtre engagé*.

It is plays of this kind that lead Mme Béatrix Dussane to say that the principal modern French dramatists are not merely playwrights, but philosophers and leaders of thought. People go to a production of Sartre's not merely for an evening's entertainment, but for a statement of political and philosophical belief; and they continue to do this, although they do not always agree what the statement of belief is. For example, most audiences at *Le Diable et le Bon Dieu* thought they were seeing an attempt to prove that God does not exist, while Sartre himself said that the play suggested the unhappy position of Europe poised between the U.S.A. and the U.S.S.R. No matter: the best philosophers have always practised the uses of ambiguity.

Sartre's position in France, then, is a high one. His *obiter dicta* are listened to with as much eagerness as they would be in England if they were spoken by a film star or a Wimbledon champion. Young men and women seeking an evening's diversion walk up and down the Rue Mignard, looking reverently at the windows of the ground floor where it is supposed that Sartre was born. His books sell in scores of thousands. In England too he made a sharp impact after the War. With his *Men without Shadows* and *The Respectable Prostitute*, he was the first contemporary French writer to be chosen for presentation on the London stage of to-day.

These plays were hardly popular successes. Even *Les Mains sales* (*Crime Passionnel* at the Lyric Theatre, Hammersmith, and later at the Garrick) did not pass beyond being a *succès d'estime*, and Sartre's later play, *Le Diable et le Bon Dieu*, has not yet had a London production, though it has been admirably translated by Kitty Black. But to offset the comparative failure of his plays in London, he has had the advantage of becoming entangled with a catchword. There are millions of people who know that Einstein is a famous man simply because they connect him with a word of vaguely magic meaning, Relativity. Sartre too has a magic word that is none the less impressive for being largely incomprehensible, or at least uncomprehended. Existentialism has won for Sartre a place in the public's mind that his plays, at any rate in England, would not have gained for him.

It has also given rise to several misconceptions, among which the most serious is that the other Existentialists in France are all Sartre's disciples. M. Sartre is not the headmaster of a school that happens to contain promising pupils like Albert Camus and Simone de Beauvoir. Mlle de Beauvoir, for example, propounded the problem of

Existentialist liberty in *L'Invitée*, before she became acquainted with any of Sartre's work. Sartre and she are great friends, and in his playful moods the author of *Les Chemins de la liberté* is said to enjoy romping round the furniture with her. This horse-play, which would be unbecoming in the austere relationship of lecturer and student, is appropriate enough between comrades in their moments of relaxation; and it is as comrades, not as master and disciple, that she and Sartre pursue their explorations into the new philosophy.

New the philosophy may be, especially in the criteria it provides for the judging of human behaviour; criteria so unusual that the reader of the series of novels that Sartre calls *Les Chemins de la liberté* has great difficulty in knowing whether any of the characters at any given moment is acting well or ill. "Let justice be done, though the heavens fall," is a saying that sounds admirable; but do you, asks Sartre, know what justice is? He and his friends may, is but he certain that no one else does.

Yet, though the philosophy is new, the question it is designed to answer has been with us through many centuries. It is implicit in the title of Sartre's main series of novels. The problem the Existentialists face, that led them first into orthodox Communism, and afterwards away from it, is the problem of freedom.

"In Thy service is perfect freedom" is a Christian conception that Existentialism repudiates. It involves the acceptance of a code of rules external to the individual; and though the individual may change in his increasing or decreasing approximation to the practice of that code, the code itself remains immutable; and to the Existentialist immutability is the prime, the cardinal sin.

The Existentialist attitude towards it may most easily be understood by an examination of Mlle de Beauvoir's *Le Deuxième Sexe*. This enormous work, which has nearly half a million words, is widely read in France; my own copy was published in 1949, and it shows that it had then run through eighty impressions. What is the reason for the inferior position of women, asks Mlle de Beauvoir: and, in eight hundred pages, she proceeds to tell us.

Immutability is at the bottom of it. She has, of course, no patience with the explanations that once were thought sufficient: with St Thomas's decree that woman is "a failed man," or with the implications of Bossuet's scornful remark that Eve was created from one of Adam's "superfluous bones." Nor is she impressed with the traditional retorts, that woman was created after man, and second thoughts are best, that woman's brain, though smaller than man's absolutely, is greater relatively to her weight; and that since Christ took the form of a man, it must have been through humility.

Mlle de Beauvoir then makes an excursion through the insect world, as a result of which she denies that her biological functions are what differentiates the female from the male. Both male and female insects, she maintains, are destined to serve merely for the creation or the nourishment of their offspring. Neither the male mosquito, who dies after the act of fecundation, nor the female, who survives only till the fate of the succeeding generation is assured, is an end in itself. They are both instruments in the service of the continuation of the species. Spiders, frogs, and bees are called in to reinforce Mlle de Beauvoir's claim that among insects the female cannot philosophically be distinguished from the male by her sexual functions. Even the male praying mantis, gobbled up by his wife after coition, is somehow shown to have an existence that is really not very much different from that of the female. The cannibalism of the latter sinks into a position of comparatively trifling importance.

But with mammals there is another story. The female receives, the male gives. The female is passive, the male active. Moreover, the male's task in creation is entirely completed by the act of coition. After that he is altogether free of physical responsibility or service, while the female continues to nourish the creation within her own body. In other words, the male has won that independence from the species the struggle for which among insects causes his death: but the female animal continues in subjection.

It is woman's creative capacity that Mlle de Beauvoir hates and fears. Women reproduce and repeat life, but men change it. It is due to men that the pattern of life varies, that one civilization gives way to another, that the Greeks cede place to the Romans, and the Romans to the peoples of the North. Women, on the other hand, alter and develop nothing; they only give to life a perpetual encore: their outlook upon existence is immutable.

Men invent tools, and fire, and dwelling-places, and by means of these things they take life into their hands, and transform it into something other than it was. In doing so they often risk their lives, proving that there are values greater in importance than mere life itself. The inferiority of women is due to the circumstance that they have never in the past been allowed to share in this existence of change and development that is exclusively known to men. "What they claim to-day is to be recognized as existing by the same title as men, and not to subordinate existence to life, man to animality."

It is thus in relation to the Existentialist philosophy that Mlle de Beauvoir explains the inferior position of women. Existentialism is a philosophy of becoming; every moment man is faced with some situation which he must resolve by an act of volition, by a choice. On the nature of that choice depends his freedom. If he makes it by any of the traditional doctrines he is in bondage. Only if he makes it in accordance with his own character, without external interference from creeds or society, is he free: only then does he behave existentially.

Of the three strands in Sartre's life (of the novelist,

the philosopher, and the dramatist), the novelist made
his appearance first. Sartre began to write at the age of
six, when he turned into Alexandrines the fables of La
Fontaine. Later he became an admirer of Jules Verne.
The War 1914–18 had a great effect upon his imagination, and he contemplated the production of a group
of historical romances. But at sixteen the second
strand appeared, and began to interweave itself with
the first. Nevertheless, his earliest adult writing was
a novel, which was refused by several publishers. And so
it was as a philosopher that he first saw print, with an
essay on "The Imagination," in *La Nouvelle Encyclo-
pédie philosophique.*[1]

In 1938 Sartre impinged for the first time on the French
public consciousness as a novelist. In that year his present
publishers, Gallimard, accepted *La Nausée*. Marc Beigbeder in his study of Sartre, *L'Homme Sartre*, describes
this as an essay, but says that it was called a novel in
order to attract wider attention. That is precisely what it
did. To the general surprise it caused a sensation, and
became a best-seller. It did not, however, receive any of
the literary prizes which in France are almost as numerous as Governments. Beigbeder says the reason for this
is that the book contains several scandalous passages, and
that on this account no literary jury dare honour it. But
it made a considerable impression on young intellectuals;
and henceforward Sartre was a leader of the *avant-garde* in
both literature and politics.

In 1939 M. Sartre, like his hero Mathieu in *La Mort
dans l'âme* (published in England as *Iron in the Soul*), was
drafted into the French army, and he served, short-
sighted though he is, in the demoralized retreat of the
spring of 1940. After a year in Germany as a prisoner, he
came back to Paris in 1941. By profession Sartre is a
teacher; and when he returned to the occupied city he
sought for some activity in which his pedagogic gifts

[1] This happened in 1936.

could find expression. Nevertheless, he was unwilling to sink the creative capacity he had discovered in himself just before the War in the resumption of an ordinary teaching career. Schools, even universities, did not attract him any more. He became a friend of Charles Dullin, whom we have already met at the Atelier in the company of Jean-Louis Barrault. About this time Dullin moved from the tiny Atelier in Montmartre to the huge Théâtre Sarah-Bernhardt, which faces the Châtelet, that great home of spectacular musical comedy near the Louvre. Dullin had a theatrical school, and Sartre became one of its professors, taking as his subject classical Greek drama.

These influences determined Sartre's next creative work, which was *Les Mouches*, a play. This reflected his recent absorption in classical literature, since it was a new version of the *Oresteia*. It was affected by Sartre's association with Charles Dullin, in that Dullin played in it the important part of Jupiter; and it was presented, under Dullin's direction, at the Théâtre Sarah-Bernhardt.

Les Mouches did not introduce Sartre to the theatre as successfully as *La Nausée* had brought him to the novel. There were political as well as dramatic reasons for this. *Les Mouches* begins with an orgy of repentance and emotional self-flagellation. Orestes, with his tutor, comes to Argos on the fifteenth anniversary of the murder of his father, Agamemnon, by his mother, Clytemnestra, and her lover, Ægisthus. He finds the streets deserted, the walls daubed with blood, millions of flies blackening the air, and everywhere the smell of a shambles. He has been joined by Jupiter, disguised as an old traveller. Jupiter is talking to a bent and ancient woman, who asks him who he is. "Don't bother your head about who I am," he replies.

> You would employ your time better in trying to win
> heaven's pardon by your repentance.

THE OLD WOMAN. Ah! But I do repent, my lord. If only you

knew how I repent, and how my daughter repents, and my son-in-law sacrifices a cow every year, and my grandson, who is only seven, we have brought him up in the spirit of repentance: he is as wise as an image, fair, and already he is saturated with the feeling of original sin.

"And does Ægisthus repent?" asks Orestes.

JUPITER. Ægisthus? I should be surprised if he did. But what does it matter? The whole city is repenting for him. [*Terrible screams in the palace.*] Listen! So that they should never forget the agonized screams of their king, a cowherd chosen for the strength of his lungs shrieks like this, every anniversary of the murder, in the great hall of the palace. . . .

Ægisthus himself has no remorse, he is incapable of feeling it, but he has instead a bitter regret for his emptiness, and it is out of great unhappiness that he cries to his wife, Clytemnestra:

I am weary of having for fifteen years upheld in the air, with my own arms, the remorse of a whole people. For fifteen years I have dressed myself like a scarecrow. These black garments have ended by draining the colour out of my soul. I know, wife, I know: you are going to speak to me of your remorse. Well, I envy you; it gives meaning to your life. I have none; but there is no one in Athens more miserable than I.

As for Clytemnestra herself, she carries her remorse like a banner; it is her solemn joy, her pride, and her distinction. She clings to it more than to her palace or her life, certainly more than to her reputation. She cries to her daughter Electra, "Anyone may spit in my face, and call me criminal and whore. But no one has the right to sit in judgment on my remorse."

Some critics of Sartre, notably Robert Campbell, author of *Jean-Paul Sartre; ou, Une Littérature philosophique*, argue that the repentance of the people of Argos is purely hysterical. They are hypnotized to such an extent that they take the sins of others for their own, blaming themselves for a murder that was committed only by Ægisthus and Clytemnestra. But this view is inconsistent with Sartre's text. The people of Argos, if they did not actually join in the murder of Agamemnon, were passive accessories before the fact. They had seen in the face of Ægisthus, as he leaned over the battlements of the city watching the return of Agamemnon from battle, that he meditated some terrible deed. Yet they did nothing to stop it.

The people here said nothing because they were bored, and they wanted the excitement of a violent death. They said nothing when they saw their king appear at the gates of the city. And when they saw Clytemnestra stretch out her beautiful and perfumed arms, they said nothing. At that moment one word would have been enough, a single word, but they were silent, and each one of them saw, in his imagination, the picture of a great corpse with the face split open.

They even found in this crime, as the characters of Sartre are prone to do in other things beside murder, an obscene sexual thrill. The old woman we have already met talking to Jupiter was no doubt typical.

JUPITER. Why are you wearing mourning?
THE OLD WOMAN. It is the costume of Argos.
JUPITER. The costume of Argos? Ah! I understand. You are wearing mourning for your assassinated king.
THE OLD WOMAN. Be silent! For the love of God, be silent!
JUPITER. You are old enough to have heard those tremendous cries that rang round the streets of the city for a whole morning. What were you doing?
THE OLD WOMAN. My husband was in the fields. What could I do? I bolted the door.
JUPITER. Yes, and you half opened the windows to hear better, and you pricked up your ears behind the curtains, and you held your breath, with a little tickle between your thighs.
THE OLD WOMAN. Be quiet!

JUPITER. And you had a vigorous time in bed that night, you and your husband. It was quite a celebration, wasn't it?

The people of Argos, then, were not as free from guilt as Robert Campbell supposes. But, guilty or not, their insistence on repentance, their constant harping on the theme of their sin, had uncomfortable repercussions in the France of the early nineteen-forties. This talk of repentance was far from being a pale echo from the egendary past: something very similar to it had been heard recently from the lips of Marshal Pétain. It was as if, in England at that time, a play had turned into ridicule defiant phrases about fighting on the beaches and the landing-grounds. The Vichy Government had adopted a policy of national repentance, of acknowledgment of past sins, and of pleading for forgiveness; and the words that Sartre put into the mouths of the people of Argos, and of their rulers, had an uneasy ring. The play had a luke-warm reception from the collaborationist Press. It encouraged, of course, the nascent spirit of resistance in Paris, but many of those who approved it were not unreserved in their admiration. Marc Beigbeder, for example, found the elaborate stage settings distracting and at odds with the simplicity of the text. He thought it more impressive when he saw it in rehearsal, without either scenery or costumes, than on the big stage of the Théâtre Sarah-Bernhardt.

These political considerations were not the only reasons for the comparative lack of success of Sartre's first play. *Les Mouches*, with its story of murder and expiation, and, in the new development that Sartre gives it, its breaking of expiation, is not more melodramatic than the other tales that its author puts into his plays. But his dialogue, which in certain scenes of *Huis Clos* and *Les Mains sales* gives the thrill of dancing lightly over a sinister trap-door, is here ponderous and heavy-footed. Orestes, Electra, Clytemnestra, Ægisthus, and Jupiter do not converse: they hurl blocks of rhetoric at each other:

and the strain on their muscles is very visible. Moreover, Sartre when he wrote *Les Mouches* was still exceedingly conscious that he was a philosopher, the author of, among other things, *L'Imagination*, and he desired actively to behave as a leader of thought. This would have been all right, except that he had not yet discovered how to make his philosophy implicit in his play, or contribute to the development of his drama. Here is one of the most important statements of Sartre's philosophy, put into the mouths of Jupiter and Ægisthus, in the fifth scene of the second tableau of the second act of *Les Mouches*:

JUPITER. All crimes do not equally displease me. Ægisthus, we are among kings, and I will speak to you frankly: the first crime was mine, in making mortal men. After that, what could you others, you murderers, do? Give death to your victims? Very well; but they already carried it in themselves; the most you could do was to hurry it on a bit. Do you know what would have happened to Agamemnon, if you hadn't killed him? Three months later he would have died of an apoplexy in the arms of a beautiful slave. But your crime was useful to me.

ÆGISTHUS. It was useful to you? I have paid for it for fifteen years, and it was useful to you?

JUPITER. And what of that? It is because you are paying for it that I find it useful. I love crimes that pay. I like yours because it was a blind and underhand murder . . . more like a cataclysm of nature than a human act. Not for a moment did you defy me: you struck in the fury of rage and fear: and then, when the excitement passed, you thought of what you had done with horror, and tried not to admit it. What a profit I've got from it! For the death of one man, twenty thousand others plunged into repentance. That's the balance sheet. I haven't made a bad bargain.

ÆGISTHUS. I see what all this talking conceals. Orestes will feel no remorse.

JUPITER. Not the least shadow. At this moment he is making his plans carefully, with a cool head, modestly. What am I to do with a murder that isn't followed by remorse, with an impudent murder, a murder untroubled, as light as a breath in the murderer's soul? I will see that it doesn't happen. I hate the crimes of the new generation: they are as sterile as weeds. This gentle young man will kill you like a chicken, and then he will go away with red hands and a clear conscience; in your place, I should feel humiliated. Do something. Call your guards.

ÆGISTHUS. I have told you no. The crime that is being got ready upsets you too much not to please me.

JUPITER [*changing his tone*]. Ægisthus, you are a king, and it is to your royal conscience that I am speaking. You love to reign.

ÆGISTHUS. Well?

JUPITER. You may hate me, but we are relations; I have made you in my image; a king is a god upon earth, as noble and as sinister.

ÆGISTHUS. Sinister? You?

JUPITER. Look at me. [*A long silence.*] I have told you that you are made in my image. We both make order reign, you in Argos, and I in the world; and we both have the same heavy secret in our hearts.

ÆGISTHUS. I have no secret.

JUPITER. Yes. The same as I have. The sad secret that belongs to gods and kings is that men are free. They are free, Ægisthus. You know it, and they don't.

This dialogue contains some of the most important ideas in the play. Sartre believes that it is men's own self-condemnation that lets them be tormented and dismayed; they are damned because they believe they are damned; and they can save themselves simply by not believing it any longer. That is what Orestes does at the end of *Les Mouches*, when, after slaying both his mother and Ægisthus, as in the old story, he walks out of Argos untouchable and unpunished only because he resolutely declines to regret what he has done. But the fact that Sartre felt it necessary to expound these ideas through the mouth of Jupiter is a confession that he had failed to make them spring spontaneously out of the action.

Furthermore, he put them at a point in the story where
they considerably hamper the action. All the time that
Jupiter is lecturing Ægisthus, Orestes and Electra are
hiding behind the god's statue, waiting patiently for his
interminable expository powers to weaken so that
Orestes can get on with his job.

The last scene in the play, when, in an atmosphere of
allegory, Orestes marches triumphantly out of Argos
with the Furies impotently following him, and leaving
Argos free, is greatly praised by Robert Campbell, who
says that theatrically it is the best thing in the piece. It
did not seem so in the English production which the
Group Theatre presented for a single Sunday-night performance at the New Theatre in 1951. David King-
Wood was Orestes; perhaps he delivered Orestes's last
long and important speech too monotonously. But part
of the fault at any rate was Sartre's. There was something altogether incongruous in ending this heavy philosophical melodrama with a recollection of the Pied Piper
of Hamelin and his rats. It was certainly necessary if the
play was to end in fitting dignity and impressiveness to
do more than change the name of Hamelin to Scyres.

The Group Theatre production was an elaborate one;
and the crowd, wailing, terrified, and ecstatic, at the
ceremony of the opening of the graves and the emer-
gence of the dead, was finely directed. Here, the performance of Yvonne Mitchell, in Electra's shameless,
white, transparent dress, dancing in the midst of everybody else's lamentation, was at its best. But the thing I
remember most vividly from the production was the
entrance of Mary Hinton as Clytemnestra. She glided
from behind a pillar in a flaming scarlet robe; and above
the robe was a face once beautiful, but now in ruins: the
lines of its still visible nobility overthrown, marked by
the evil years.

Men are free, says Jupiter, and they do not know it.
Freedom is the theme of *Les Mouches*. To Sartre the

man who, in any crisis of his life, chooses between alternative courses of action according to the rules of his
party, the dictates of his religion, or the laws of his
morality, is denying the freedom which, by the mere
exercise of his will, he could assert: for he is then behaving, not in the fulfilment and development of his own
personality, but in obedience to the resolution of others.
He is handing over his right to decision, in the Sartrian
view, to Lenin, to Moses, or to Christ. To the Existentialist, the triumph of Orestes is that he refused to abdicate
his freedom. By refusing to feel remorse, by flinging
aside that family morality of ancient Greece which has
become the morality of the entire Western world, the
Orestes of Sartre differentiates himself from the Orestes
of all other dramatists from Æschylus to Eugene O'Neill.

Sartre's hero murders his mother, and experiences no
regret. This lack of feeling, this absence of any revulsion
of affection, this disregard of the Western recoil from acts
of blood, instinctively affronts the conceptions of what is
just and even natural that have been built up during two
and a half thousand years in European civilization. Yet it
is precisely this that Sartre finds admirable. The whole
play is conceived and written so that, at the end, Orestes
may issue this flagrant and triumphant denial of traditional values.

One difficulty in appreciating Sartre is that he is an
imperfect artist who does not always succeed in external-
izing effectively upon the stage the drama that is taking
place in his imagination. This is a difficulty that is met
with in all playwrights, even the greatest. One imagines
that there were things in Shakespeare's mind which did
not altogether come out when he wrote *Pericles*. But
with Sartre there is a bigger stumbling-block still. For
Sartre writes out of a moral system entirely different from
that of his audiences. The yardstick which his audiences
instinctively use in judging the incidents and characters
of his plays is not the yardstick that Sartre has employed

in constructing them. The result is apt to be extreme confusion and bewilderment as to which are, and which are not, the people in his dramas and novels that one is supposed to admire. Most people's notions of what constitutes good behaviour are a synthesis of what they more or less vaguely remember of the teachings of the Christian religion combined with such disciplines of conduct as they carry over from school, home, and business life. The resulting morality is the standard of judgment they apply, without even thinking, to what they see upon the stage or read in their novels. This leads, with Sartre, to chaos.

Sartre must be understood before he is judged. The moral pattern he has in his mind has to be extracted from *Les Mouches* before the spectator can tell even what the play is about. A play, however, is a comparatively simple entity. It can deal with only a few important characters, and it is limited by length and scenic conditions. A novel, on the other hand, especially a novel in three or four sections, each containing a hundred and fifty thousand words, is a far more complicated matter. The difficulty of understanding *Les Chemins de la liberté*, the first volume of which, *L'Age de raison*, was published soon after the War, is, therefore, much greater than that of grasping the point of *Les Mouches*. The novel covers so much more ground, it brings in so many more people, and it presents them in so much greater detail.

L'Age de raison begins by focusing its attention upon a sharply concentrated problem. Mathieu, a teacher of philosophy, gentle in temperament, Left Wing in political conviction, hovering uncertainly on the edge of the Communist party, learns that his mistress, Marcelle, is about to have a baby. Something has to be done, and Mathieu is influenced by Marcelle to seek an abortionist. That, however, is not the solution of Marcelle's difficulty that is ultimately chosen. The action of the novel covers only two days, and in that time Marcelle is provided with a husband. The husband is not Mathieu, but Daniel, a middle-aged, wealthy pederast who confuses the reader's reaction to the story by being almost the only character in it who now and again behaves in accordance with Christian morality and what one would ordinarily consider to be kindly human feeling. Since, in *Les Mouches*, Sartre takes for his hero a matricide, there would be nothing surprising if he gave his admiration to Daniel. But Daniel feels compunction. His conscience is uneasy over his sexual behaviour, and at times he even tries to control himself. These are things, of course, which exclude him from the possibility of being, at any rate in the early stages of the novel, a Sartrian hero.

Marcelle, Daniel, and Mathieu are not the only principal characters in *L'Age de raison*. There is Mathieu's Fascist-sympathetic brother Jacques (the period of the book is 1938); there are Lola, the cabaret dancer who is putting on flesh with the years, and her young lover, Boris. By bourgeois standards Boris is a liar and a thief, though he has some tenderness for Lola, and he has a brooding sense that war will see to it he does not live more than three or four years. His sister Ivich is a Lesbian. Brunet, the Communist leader, tries to persuade Mathieu to join the Party, but Mathieu is unable to make up his mind, just as he is apparently incapable of decided action in respect of Marcelle's threatened baby.

If one's assessment of the characters in *L'Age de raison* is hedged with complications, reservations, and uncertainties, not many readers will fail to recognize Sartre's brilliance in the devising and management of incident. In sordid excitement and in psychological penetration it would be hard to match the scenes of Daniel's abortive attempts to drown his cats in the Seine, or Boris's theft of the bulky etymological dictionary of cant from the bookshop at the corner of the Rue de Vaugirard and the

Boulevard Saint-Michel, or Mathieu's visit to the old woman with the dirty needle.

The second volume of *Les Chemins de la liberté* is *Le Sursis*, and it deals with the week of the Munich crisis. From the starting-point of Mathieu's personal problem *L'Age de raison* widens its scope to include all Paris from Montmartre to Montparnasse. The area that M. Sartre surveys in *Le Sursis* is still wider. The city becomes a continent. Hitler, Sir Horace Wilson, and Chamberlain meet at Godesberg. Mathieu is on holiday at the seaside. Daniel and Marcelle are staying at a farm in the country. A drunken Negro blunders about Marseilles. A group of paralytics is evacuated from Paris; two of them on adjacent stretchers fall in love, and become acutely miserable, because they are immediately afflicted with uncontrollable diarrhœa and are ashamed to call for the bed-pan. On the coast of North Africa a man jellies himself with fear by looking at a book full of pictures of men mutilated in war, from which he cannot withdraw his fascinated and terrified eyes. On the Mediterranean one of the members of a woman's band, in order to get better quarters for herself and her companions, goes to the captain's cabin at night, but turns out to be too thin to give satisfaction.

To the difficulty of keeping in mind Sartre's peculiar moral outlook, *Le Sursis* adds a further difficulty: that of technique. *L'Age de raison* moves in the ordinary way of a realistic novel. The development both of incident and character, so far as technique is concerned, is conventional. But the method that Sartre adopts in *Le Sursis* is the method of cinema montage. Scenes widely separated from each other in space are jerkily juxtaposed, and often it is almost impossible to discern the boundary line between them. In *Le Sursis* there are something like 2000 separate scenes, and some of them are only half a line long. Characters who have no connexion with each other are wrenched out of their background and lined shoulder to shoulder in M. Sartre's undifferentiated prose, brandished before our bewildered eyes, and then pushed back into their several surroundings.

Here, excellently translated by Eric Sutton, is a typical passage from the novel:

Lunch-time! They had entered the blinding tunnel of midday: outside—the sky, white with heat; outside—the dead, white roads, no man's land, and war: behind the closed shutters, they sat stifling in the heat. Daniel put his napkin on his knees, Hannequin tied his napkin round his neck, Brunet took the paper napkin from the table, crumpled it, and wiped his lips, Jeannine wheeled Charles into the large and almost empty dining-room with its smudgy windows, and spread a napkin on his chest; this was a truce; the war—well, yes, the war, but what about the heat! butter in a bowl of water, a blurred and oily wedge of it at the bottom of the bowl, and over it thick, grey water and scraps of dead butter floating belly-upwards, Daniel watched the curls of butter melt in the radish-dish, Brunet wiped his forehead, the cheese sweated on its plate like an honest man at work. Maurice's beer was tepid, he pushed his glass away: "Pah! It might be piss!" A bit of ice was floating in Mathieu's red wine, he drank—first he felt a cold liquid in his mouth, and then a little pool of musty wine, still slightly warm, which promptly melted into water: Charles turned his head, and said: "Soup again! It's crazy to serve soup in mid-summer." His plate was laid on his chest, it warmed his skin through the napkin and his shirt, he could see the edge of the plate quite clearly and dipped his spoon into it, then raised it vertically: but a man on his back can't be sure what is vertical, so part of the liquid splashed back into the plate, Charles moved the spoon to a point above his lips, lowered it, and—hell! it always happened, the burning liquid trickled on to his cheek, and soaked his shirt-collar. The war—ah yes! the war. No, said Zézette, not the radio, I don't want it, I won't think of the war. Well, let's have a bit of music, said Maurice. Cherseau, good—b—b-r-r-r—my star—here is the news—sombreros and mantillas—*I will wait*, at the request of Huguette Arnal, Pierre Du-Croc, his wife and two daughters, Roche Danillac, Mlle Eliane of Calvi and Jean-François Roquette, for his little Marie-Madeleine, and a group of typists at Toul for their soldier sweethearts, *I will wait*, day and night, have some more bouillabaisse, no thanks, said Mathieu, something can surely be arranged, the radio crackled, sped over the white, dead squares, smashed the windows, and penetrated into the dim, vaporous interiors of the houses, and Odette thought: Something can surely be arranged, it's so hot.

Something surely *has* been arranged. All the separate pieces in this elaborate mosaic of which the theme is heat and war and food have been put in place with the utmost deliberation. They have been brought from far and near, from many quarters of France, even from England and from Spain, and set side by side in one enormous paragraph which even yet is not half finished, and which would require, for the identification of its characters, and their location in space and in the story a commentary as lengthy as itself. *Le Sursis* is, in fact, one of the most difficult novels to follow since *Ulysses*, of whose freedom of speech, it will be noticed, it preserves some traces.

The change of style from *L'Age de raison* to *Le Sursis* was much criticized in France, and for the third volume of his series, *La Mort dans l'âme*, M. Sartre returned to the methods of realism and consecutive narrative. It has two main threads: the experiences of Mathieu in the great debacle of the French army in the spring of 1940, and the peculiar sensations of Daniel as he watches the German army enter and take possession of Paris. The picture of the demoralization of the army, of which Sartre no doubt himself had first-hand knowledge, is a particularly fine achievement. The story of Mathieu is to be completed in a fourth volume, which, at the time I am writing this, has not been published.

Les Chemins de la liberté, as its name clearly implies, is concerned, like *Les Mouches*, with freedom. Its theme is the pilgrim's progress of Mathieu towards the discovery in himself of the power of decision and action. Having written of freedom directly, Sartre in his next play, *Huis Clos*, approached the same problem negatively, and set his scene in a prison. But not an ordinary prison, for in an ordinary prison there is room, however little, for development. Sometimes the development is even considerable: it was in a prison that Bunyan wrote *The Pilgrim's Progress*, and Wilde gained the experience for *De Profundis*. But Sartre's prison is carefully designed so that when the proper people are in it no development is possible. It thus becomes, to the Existentialist, the most evil place imaginable. It is, in fact, hell.

Huis Clos was produced, with great success, at the Vieux-Colombier in 1944, and some time later it was presented, under the title of *Vicious Circle*, at the Arts Theatre in London, with Alec Guinness in the part of Garcin. It is Sartre's best play—and undoubtedly a great advance on *Les Mouches*. Sartre is not a tidy constructor of plays; pieces like *Les Mouches*, *Les Mains sales*, and *Le Diable et le Bon Dieu* sprawl considerably, and they require a large number of characters. But *Huis Clos* has only four characters (one of whose parts is very small), and a single scene, and it preserves the unity of time. Once up, the curtain does not come down till the end of the play, which lasts about an hour and a half.

The opening words of the play show how completely Sartre has escaped from the ponderousness of *Les Mouches*. The scene is a room furnished in the style of Napoleon III. Garcin enters and glances round him.

GARCIN. So here we are.

THE ATTENDANT. Here we are.

GARCIN. It is in order.

THE ATTENDANT. It is in order.

GARCIN. I . . . I think that in time one will get used to the furniture.

THE ATTENDANT. That depends on who you are.

GARCIN. Look. Are all the rooms like this?

THE ATTENDANT. What do you think? We get Chinese and Hindus. What would they make of a Second Empire chair?

Here and there in *Les Mouches* there are passages of an agreeable lightness of touch. Orestes's tutor is almost always treated with a pleasantly gay irony. But the tutor is a minor character, hovering on the boundary of the plot. When Sartre comes to deal with the serious business of the play solemnity descends upon him. In *Huis Clos*, for the first time, he hit upon a way of being serious and amusing simultaneously, and the off-hand gaiety of the manner adds another touch of the sinister to the matter.

We have seen, in connexion with Simone de Beauvoir's *Le Deuxième Sexe*, with what horror the Existentialist regards the phenomenon of repetition, which to him is the negation of that reaching out towards something new and different that is the essence of his particular conception of freedom. Repetition, therefore, becomes a leading theme of *Huis Clos*; and it is one of the marks of Sartre's progress as a dramatist that he is able to introduce it, not in one of the thick tirades of Jupiter, but in a swift exchange of question and answer that ends in something like a joke. "What is there outside these walls?" asks Garcin.

THE ATTENDANT [*astonished*]. Outside?

GARCIN. Yes, outside! Beyond these walls?

THE ATTENDANT. There is a corridor.

GARCIN. And at the end of the corridor?

THE ATTENDANT. There are other rooms and other corridors and staircases.

GARCIN. And then?

THE ATTENDANT. That's all.

GARCIN. Still, you must have a day out some time. Where do you go then?

THE ATTENDANT. To my uncle's, who is the head warder, on the third floor.

Nevertheless, "stone walls do not a prison make, nor iron bars a cage." Sartre is as aware of this as any British moralizing poet. These things are not in themselves a prison; they are only considerable contributions to it. Having set the theme of physical repetition, Sartre, with two additional characters, elaborates its spiritual and mental aspects.

The first of the new arrivals in hell is a Lesbian, Inès, and the second Estelle, a fair-haired nymphomaniac who has murdered her baby. Estelle has eyes only for Garcin, whom her fastidious sense of physical attraction cannot bear to see without his coat, which he has wished to remove because of the heat. Of these three people the quickest-witted is Inès, and it is she who first guesses that their meeting after death is not an affair of chance.

GARCIN. I liked living among men in their shirt-sleeves.

ESTELLE [*drily*]. Evidently we haven't the same tastes. This proves it. [*To* INÈS] What about you? Do you like men in their shirt-sleeves?

INÈS. In shirt-sleeves or not, I don't much like men.

ESTELLE [*looking at them in amazement*]. But why are we all here together?

GARCIN. It is just luck. They put the men where they can, in the order of arrival. [*To* INÈS] Why are you laughing?

INÈS. Because your talk of luck amuses me. Do you need reassurance so desperately? They leave nothing to luck.

ESTELLE [*timidly*]. But surely we've met somewhere before?

INÈS. Never. I should not have forgotten you.

ESTELLE. Well, then, perhaps we have common friends? Don't you know the Dubois-Seymours?

INÈS. I should be astonished if I did.

ESTELLE. They know everybody.

INÈS. What do they do?

ESTELLE [*surprised*]. They don't *do* anything. They have a country house and——

INÈS. I had a job in the Post Office.

ESTELLE [*recoiling a little*]. Oh, really? [*A pause.*] And you, Monsieur Garcin?

GARCIN. I never left Rio.

ESTELLE. In that case, you are quite right. It is luck that has brought us together.

INÈS. Luck. That accounts for the furniture, too. . . . And the heat? And the heat? [*A pause.*] I tell you that every detail has been arranged. This room was waiting for us.

ESTELLE. It isn't possible. Everything is so ugly, so hard, so full of angles. I used to detest angles.

INÈS. Do you suppose I used to live in a Second Empire drawing-room?

Inès here almost has her hand upon the solution of the mystery. During her lifetime she has been what she calls *"une femme damnée."* She has taken away her cousin Florence from her husband, and driven her to suicide. To these moral delinquencies, however, there is no evidence that she had added the sin of accepting Existentialism, against which the dramatist Gabriel Marcel has warned all Christians. But she shows a remarkable intuitive understanding of Existentialist doctrine, and within a few moments of the conversation I have just quoted she is able to answer Estelle's question.

INÈS. Wait! I understand. I know why they have put us together!

GARCIN. Take care what you are saying.

INÈS. You'll see how ridiculous it is. . . . There's no physical torture, is there? And yet we are in hell. And nobody can visit us. Nobody. We shall remain here until the end, alone. It's like that, isn't it? And yet there's some one missing: the tormentor.

GARCIN [*in a low voice*]. I know that.

INÈS. Very well, they've economised in personnel. That's all. The customers do the work themselves, as in the self-service restaurants.

ESTELLE. What do you mean?

INÈS. The tormentor is each one of us for the two others.

In that sentence Inès puts the key into the lock. Torment each other is precisely what these people do, Estelle the infanticide and nymphomaniac, Inès the dark and insatiable Lesbian, and Garcin the sadist and coward who has been shot for desertion. Inès desires Estelle, Estelle Garcin, and Garcin cannot satisfy either her or himself because he passionately longs for Inès, the strongest in will of the three, to assure him that he is not really a coward, but a man: and this the tortured but resolute Inès will never do. Sartre has here discovered perpetual motion among the passions. Estelle and Inès will for ever desire, Garcin will for ever plead for reassurance: none of them will ever be satisfied: and they cannot put an end to their misery by killing themselves, for they are already dead. This is the terrible fact upon which Sartre closes his play: his characters have already entered an eternity.

ESTELLE. Dead . . .
    [INÈS *picks up a knife, and plunges it into herself.*
INÈS. Dead! Dead! Dead! Neither the knife, nor the poison, nor the rope. That is *already over*, don't you see? And we are together for always.   [*She laughs.*
ESTELLE [*bursting with laughter*]. For always. My God, how funny it is! For always.
GARCIN [*laughs and looks at both of them*]. For always!
    [*They sit down, each on his own couch. There is a long silence.*
    They stop laughing, and look at each other. GARCIN *rises.*
GARCIN. Very well, let us continue.

"Let us continue." Let it go on and on. Let it never alter.

Garcin's last words are the most terrible in the Existentialist vocabulary. One cannot imagine Mlle de Beauvoir reading them without a shudder.

They bring the play to an impressive conclusion. Æsthetically, *Huis Clos* seems to me to have only one defect. At some point in the action the three characters are able to see beyond the walls of their room, beyond the limitations of their life after death, into what is happening to their friends and acquaintances on earth. This is used as a further tightening of the screw of their unhappiness, for what they see is excruciatingly painful to them. Nevertheless, this extension of their perception is a weakening of the play's central and most impressive conception, which is simply that Estelle, Inès, and Garcin can never escape from each other, but are confined for ever within the narrow circle of their mutual torments. Apart from this flaw, the construction of *Huis Clos* is masterly.

Better than any other of his plays, *Huis Clos* enables M. Sartre to assert his conviction that the most dreadful thing that can happen to any human being is for him to find his liberty of decision limited by other human beings, either in person or in codes of behaviour formulated without any reference to himself. This doctrine is summed up by Garcin in a single sentence—in fact, in half a single sentence. "L'enfer, c'est les autres" (Hell is other people).

These are perhaps the most famous words M. Sartre has written, and they have been often attacked, especially by Mme Dussane. Mme Dussane admits, of course, in the special case offered by Sartre in *Huis Clos*, that each of the three characters finds his or her particular hell in the other two. That is incontestable; it is the point of the play. What she questions is whether what is true for a sadist, a suicide, and an infanticide is necessarily, or even probably, true for other and less unusual people. Is it not as absurd to extract a generalization from characters as exceptional as Garcin, Estelle, and Inès as it would be to base an estimate of the mathematical powers of mankind on an example as rare as Newton?

But Sartre has his defenders, among them M. Campbell. Garcin's sadism, Inès's suicide, and Estelle's murder of her child, he points out, have nothing to do with their mutual torture. They would be misery to each other if Garcin were as kind as St Francis, if Inès had died naturally, and if Estelle's child had wept bucketsful at her funeral.

This is a dangerous argument. It brings M. Campbell, in acquitting Sartre of the charge of weighting the dice, close to accusing him of irrelevance. It is difficult to believe that in so tightly constructed a play as *Huis Clos* Sartre has emphasized in his characters qualities which have no bearing on the main issue.

As a matter of fact, these qualities are of the greatest importance. Before Estelle, Garcin, and Inès can torture each other, they have to meet; and in order to meet, they have all to descend to hell; and in order to descend to hell, they have to have done something deserving such a punishment. It is because one is a sadist, another a suicide, and the third an infanticide that they make each other's disastrous acquaintance. Now, if Garcin's "L'enfer, c'est les autres" is considered, like Macbeth's "To-morrow, and to-morrow, and to-morrow," purely as a dramatic speech, as the expression of a certain character's feeling at such and such a point of his experience, then it is not only invulnerable, but admirable. A light has just dawned upon Garcin: hell has no need of pitchforking devils and the lake of fire; human beings are themselves enough to make it. It is in the illumination of this sudden recognition that he exclaims, "No need for the grid-iron—hell is other people." What words, in the circumstances, could be more appropriate?

But if the speech is not merely dramatic, if it is intended to have a wider philosophical relevance, to be not only a suitable remark of the moment but an eternal truth, then it would seem that Mme Dussane's objection is well founded. What weight, then, did Sartre intend Garcin's observation to bear?

One cannot help feeling that he intended it to bear a good deal. Shakespeare was not a systematic philosopher; M. Sartre is. Shakespeare flung off, with a giant and apparently careless ease, a multitude of emotions and reflections which are often contradictory; M. Sartre is both a more constipated artist and a more thorough thinker. *Macbeth* has not the air of having been written to illustrate any particular point made by any particular character, while at the end of all his plays Sartre has the pleased look of a man who has proved something. The ingenious, interlocking cogs and wheels of *Huis Clos* whir and revolve, and the neat little philosophical package is cleverly delivered; but one feels that with some other machinery the package would have been different. *Huis Clos* is a philosophical proposition in which the demonstration is more valuable than the result.

After *Huis Clos* Sartre wrote two less important pieces, *Morts sans sépulture* and *La Putain respectueuse*, and then resumed his full stature in *Les Mains sales*, which was presented at the Théâtre Antoine on April 2, 1948, where it had a long and prosperous run. We have seen that in Garcin Sartre imagined a man whose spiritual self is ruined by his dependence on other people's belief in him. Shortly after the War the French Communist Party collaborated with others in forming a Government. Out of these two conceptions, the individual and the political, Sartre evolved the problem and the plot of *Les Mains sales*.

The play, like *Le Diable et le Bon Dieu*, which followed it, is not as good a piece of workmanship as *Huis Clos*. In order to tell the story of Hugo Barine, Sartre finds that he requires a prologue, an epilogue, and five acts, and there are two or three changes of scene. The prologue opens with Hugo, after serving some time as a prisoner, coming to the room of his former mistress, Olga. They are in Illyria, a country occupied by the Germans, the frontiers of which the Russian armies are now approaching. Both Hugo and Olga are Communists, yet another Communist, Louis, is hard on Hugo's heels, and intends to kill him. Louis feels that Hugo talks too much. But Olga persuades Louis to wait until midnight, by which time she hopes to have found out that Hugo is still useful to the Party, or at any rate recoverable for it. Two years before, Hugo had been sent, with his wife, as secretary to Hoederer, the leader of the Communist Party in Illyria. Hoederer had then been in process of compromise with the bourgeois and Fascist parties in Illyria. His policy had shocked the more orthodox Communists, of whom Louis was one, and Hugo's orders had been to kill Hoederer. He had done so, but the question no one could answer with certainty was whether he had done this through loyalty to his superiors or through jealousy, for Hoederer had been attractive to his wife. This is what Olga sets herself to find out. The main part of the play, at least in length, consists in the presentation of Hugo's relations with Hoederer.

Sartre has shown much skill in leaving the answer doubtful. We see Hugo shoot Hoederer when his wife, Jessica, is in his arms. Hugo has delayed and pro-crastinated beyond measure, but even so we cannot be sure of the motive that finally impelled him to pull the trigger. It is not at all certain for what reason he did not carry out his orders immediately. It may be that he admired and sympathized with Hoederer personally; it may be that, since neither his wife nor his friends really believed him capable of decisive action, he was not able to fulfil his mission until his will was stimulated by some unexpected shock. Hugo himself, on the night when he came to Olga's flat at the opening of the play, did not know why he had killed Hoederer.

There is, I think, some relapse in *Les Mains sales* into the heaviness of manner of *Les Mouches*. The interview between Hoederer on the one hand and the Prince and the bourgeois leader on the other is interesting philoso-phically in its probing of the true seat of political power in a country lying within the orbit of the Soviet Union, but dramatically I do not think it justifies its considerable length. When Olga, weary of waiting for Hugo to do his job, decides to do it for him, and throws her bomb over the garden wall, the incident allows the Prince to behave with the effective theatrical coolness of aristocrats going to the guillotine with a pinch of snuff in plays about the French Revolution; but also it seems somewhat turgid; and the ensuing scene of Hugo's drunkenness is dull.

The main weakness of the play lies in the exceedingly sketchy treatment that Sartre gives to the character of Louis. Hoederer is a politician who does his best with the means that come to his hands, and sometimes the means are not pretty. "How," he exclaims to Hugo,

> how you cling to your purity. . . . Purity is an idea that belongs to a fakir or a monk. You intellectuals, you bourgeois anarchists, you make it an excuse for doing nothing. For doing nothing, for resting still, with your elbows glued to your sides, wearing gloves. My hands are dirty. Right to the shoulders. I have plunged them in mud and blood. . . . Do you imagine you can govern innocently?

Hoederer's hands are dirty, but they are the hands of a man. He is a character of stature, and there is no surprise in the fact that Hugo cannot but admire him. Hugo himself, the arrogant, young, and eager intellectual, is also potentially a character of stature. His self-distrust, his pleadings with Jessica and Olga to strengthen him with their belief in his determination, are merely painful stages in the development of something that Sartre thinks has value. But Hugo acts only on orders from Louis: Louis is Hoederer's real opponent. He is, according to the requirements of the plot, an opponent capable of dividing the Party with Hoederer. To this need the Louis of *Les Mains sales* is absurdly inadequate. Compared with Hoederer, he is only a gangster—indeed, for most of the time, the shadow of a gangster. When Hugo, defeated in argument, says that Hoederer would not have got out of it so easily with Louis, we not only do not believe it, but we do not believe that Hugo could have believed it.

All the same, the play has some very fine things in it. The early scene of the searching of Hugo's room could

hardly be more tautly done; the political argument
between Hoederer and Hugo from which I have already
quoted is, unlike the conversation of Jupiter with
Ægisthus, really an argument: and it has dramatic point,
because it bears importantly on whether Hugo will, or
will not, kill Hoederer. But the best part of the play, a
fact unaccountably concealed from a critic as excellent
as Francis Ambrière, is the epilogue.

The construction of *Les Mains sales* (prologue and
epilogue, with the play sandwiched in between) reminds
M. Ambrière derisively of *Romance*, a drama that England
has forgotten, but of which echoes can still apparently be
forlornly heard in the *coulisses* of French theatres. Since
the prologue tells us that Hugo did in fact kill Hoederer,
why, asks M. Ambrière, wait until the end of the play to
see him do it? Precisely because the killing of Hoederer
is not the play's real climax, which comes only in the
epilogue, with Hugo's discovery of the true reason for
his act.

While Hugo has been in prison there has been a change
in the Party line. Collaboration between parties has
become the accepted Communist policy for the time
being, and the memory of Hoederer is now revered as
that of a hero. Hugo's "recoverability" depends on his
having committed his murder for private reasons, and his
willingness to forget that Party leaders had been mixed
up in it. It is at this moment that Hugo, in the Sartrian
sense, grows up, and becomes a free man, another
Orestes. These are the last moments of the play, and they
are those for which all the rest has been written.

> HUGO. Listen: I don't know why I killed Hoederer, but I
> know why I ought to have killed him: because his policy
> was bad, because he lied to his comrades, and because he
> risked contaminating the Party. If I had been brave
> enough to shoot when I was alone with him in the office,
> he would have died because of that, and I could think of
> myself without shame. I am ashamed of myself because I

killed him—afterwards. And you, you put greater shame on me still by deciding I killed him for nothing. Olga, what I thought about Hoederer's policy I continue to think. While I was in prison, I believed that you agreed with me, and that helped; I know now that I am alone in my opinion, but I shall not change it.

[*Noise of a motor outside.*

OLGA. They have come back. Listen. . . . I cannot . . . take this revolver, go out by the door of my room, and take your chance.

HUGO [*without taking the revolver*]. You have made Hoederer into a great man. Yet I loved him more than you ever did. But if I denied my act he would become an anonymous corpse. . . . [*The motor-car stops.*] Killed by chance. Killed for a woman.

OLGA. Go away.

HUGO. A man like Hoederer doesn't die by chance. He dies for his ideas, for his policy; he is responsible for his death. If I claim my crime before everybody . . . if I am ready to pay the price for it, then he will have died a death worthy of him.   [*Some one knocks at the door.*

OLGA. Hugo, I——

HUGO [*going towards the door*]. I have not killed Hoederer yet, Olga. Not yet. It is now that I am going to kill him, and myself as well.   [*Renewed knocking.*

OLGA [*crying out*]. Go away! Go away! [HUGO *kicks the door.*

HUGO [*exclaims*]. Not recoverable.

Those words, which are the last in the play, decide Hugo's fate; and Jean-Jacques Gautier tells us that François Périer, who played Hugo in Paris, uttered them with a little ironic bow. M. Sartre undoubtedly intended *Les Mains sales* to end with a flourish, and on a note of triumph. The pseudonym that Hugo took in clandestinity was Raskolnikov, and I daresay M. Sartre chose it for him carefully. Raskolnikov also, it will be remembered, ended with an avowal and acknowledgment of murder. The acknowledgment, in his case, was a spiritual victory. It cannot be questioned that Sartre considers that Hugo won a spiritual victory, too.

It is, of course, a spiritual victory only within the framework of Sartre's peculiar philosophy, a philosophy that runs counter to many of our deepest convictions and feelings. Sartre arouses much instinctive opposition among English readers and audiences. Professor Allardyce Nicoll, for example, is affronted by his squalidness. "Unquestionably gifted with high talent and with a flair for the devising of effective dramatic scenes," says Professor Nicoll in his *World Drama*, "Sartre chooses to employ these in the interests of ugliness." This seems to me to be a rather harsh judgment. Sartre's constant preoccupation is the liberation of the human spirit. His heroes are men engaged in the constant struggle to have life, and to have it more abundantly. Within the Sartrian philosophy, his plays are notable, and even inspiring, studies of the fight of character to establish its own integrity.

He is not a pessimist. The experiences of France during the Occupation have not deprived him of confidence in man. Both Orestes and Hugo in the end assert their redemption through their courage in accepting and asserting their actions without either excuse or regret.

It would, of course, be easier to appreciate Sartre if these actions were not the slaughter, in the first case, of a mother, and in the second, of a friend. Yet it is essential that the actions to be avowed should be such as to arouse instinctive repugnance, or there would be no difficulty, and consequently no courage required, in avowing them. Sartre, therefore, deals in actions which, though justifiable in his own philosophy, are evil in nearly everybody else's. He has not the immense advantage, enjoyed by almost every great dramatist in the world, of writing according to philosophic and religious convictions common both to himself and to his audiences. His good is other people's wickedness, his courage other people's perversity. This is why one's response to the whole impact of a Sartrian drama is intellectual only. These plays do not touch the deep springs of feeling, they do not correspond to what one instinctively is convinced is the truth. A play like *Les Mains sales* resembles a geometrical proposition restated in terms in which straight lines have been redefined as rhomboids, and circles as straight lines. It is still possible, by an intellectual effort, to judge whether the proposition has been set forth correctly; but the effort required is considerable.

Continuing his criticism, Professor Nicoll remarks that Sartre "loves all that is damp, oily, and viscous: in his imagery he displays a strange devotion to metaphors and similes taken from the processes of digestion." This is true, but it is not a peculiar characteristic of Sartre. The sort of passage that Professor Nicoll is thinking of here can be paralleled in any modern advanced novelist. "We get the impression," says Nicoll, "that while Hamlet primarily thought of Alexander, Sartre thinks primarily of the bung-hole." I have already shown that I think this is unjust. Sartre not only thinks primarily of Alexander, but he also thinks primarily of Alexander's finest qualities. He thinks of them, too, in terms of admiration; but—and this is the difficulty—he thinks of them according to standards of moral judgment which ninety-nine per cent. of his audiences repudiate.

Sartre may one day convince them, and then their response to him will be whole-hearted instead of hedged with reservations. He may some time make us look at his plays through his own eyes, as the Impressionists have made us look at their paintings. Speaking for the moment outside my province as a dramatic critic, I may be allowed to remark that if that day comes it will be one to be regretted. It will mean the overthrow of Christian values in civilization, and the substitution for them of standards I view with misgiving.

Sartre himself is aware of the difference between his own moral and philosophical convictions and those of the vast majority of the people who flock to his plays, read his books, and admire his genius. Both *Les Mouches* and *Les Mains sales* are about men who reject the orthodox, conventional standards of their surroundings, and in so doing, in Sartre's opinion, they find their souls. Orestes denies a proposition, that sin should bring repentance, common to every version of the Christian religion, and of most others: Hugo repudiates the standards of the political party to which he belongs. But in his defence of both of them Sartre's intention is to proclaim an individualistic revolt of the widest and least qualified kind: to assert that the righteous man is he who, at every crisis of choice in his life, acts in accordance with his own nature, and not after the teachings of any religious, moral, or political or social code in the world.

Most Western people continue to believe in a standard of righteousness external to themselves: they consider that murder, treachery, dishonesty, are wrong absolutely, and are not, in some cases, to become justified in relation to the nature of whoever happens to commit them. These people, therefore, will not accept Sartre's condonation, and even approval, of Hugo and Orestes, who remain to them essentially murderers. The realization of this had, I think, some effect on Sartre's next play, the longest and the most ambitious he has yet written. It is as if he admitted to himself that those of his audiences were behaving reasonably who asked what would have been the result if Hugo or Orestes had acted, not out of their own feelings, but in accordance with the teachings of one of the world's various moralities. In *Le Diable et le Bon Dieu* he takes a man—Goetz, a captain of mercenaries—who does so behave, and he proceeds, in a play whose performance lasts four and a half hours, to inquire into the consequences.

The notion of writing *Le Diable et le Bon Dieu* arose out of a conversation that Sartre had with Jean-Louis Barrault in 1949. Barrault, I believe, has never appeared in a play of Sartre's, but, as I have suggested before, the influence of this dynamic and tautly conditioned figure is not confined to his own theatre. Barrault told Sartre of a Spanish comedy in which a gambler played at dice for Good and Evil. Sartre saw in this anecdote a reflection of his Existentialist theories. He brooded over the story, enriched and developed it, and, much impressed by a recent visit to North Africa, visualized his hero as a black man.

About this time Sartre dined with Simone Berriau, the director of the Théâtre Antoine. During dinner he announced dramatically, "I have discovered a way of arranging a fabulous theatrical failure: I propose to offer you my next play. Your ruin is assured." To which Mme Berriau replied, "I prefer being ruined by one of your plays to being enriched by anyone else's. Tell me its subject." Whereupon Sartre said the projected title of the new piece was *A Negro's Vengeance*.

Presumably in this conversation there was a good deal of banter. Sartre knew, and knew that Mme Berriau knew, that he was one of the most popular dramatists in France. In Mme Berriau's own theatre, the Antoine, *Les Mains sales* was at that moment in its second triumphant year. The talk about ruin was therefore largely playful. Nevertheless, work on the scale of that which Sartre then had in mind represents a considerable risk. In the form in which Sartre first wrote it *Le Diable et le Bon Dieu* would have played for nearly six hours, and its presentation made enormous demands on the mechanical resources of the French theatre, which are not as considerable as those of New York or even of London. The director, Louis Jouvet, to Sartre's anger insisted on cuts that reduced the play's running time by a full hour, but even so the efforts and expense of putting it on the stage were prodigious. The management derived some prestige from the statistics of these efforts by printing them prominently in the Antoine programme, from which every visitor to the theatre was able to learn, among

other things, that 19,800 hours of labour and £500 worth
of nails had been required to stage the play.

However, I am moving too fast. About the time of his
conversation with Mme Berriau Sartre came upon the
Table Talk of Luther, abandoned his notion of a black
hero, and decided to set his story against the background
of the Peasants' Revolt. He spent well over a year building up a collection of notes, speeches, ideas for scenes,
and psychological observations, and changed the name of
the projected play to that which it now bears. In March
1950 he left Paris for Saint-Tropez, where he had discovered that the gardens of the Hôtel Aioli, hidden by
laurels and old palm-trees, not far from the Place de la
Ponche, offered him a wonderful refuge from interrup-
tion. There he worked for three weeks in absolute
secrecy, pondering not only the shape and content of his
play, but who should take the principal part. His first
choice was Gérard Philipe, but the character of Goetz
developed in such a way that Pierre Fresnay seemed more
suitable. Fresnay could not, however, be obtained
because of his film engagements, and the character under-
went a further modification. Goetz became more
exuberant, excitable, and volatile, qualities that fitted him
particularly for Pierre Brasseur, one of the most bound-
ing, bouncing, and irrepressible of serious French actors.
Brasseur accepted with eagerness the offer that Sartre
made to him, and it was he who finally saw the play on
to the stage.

This huge play about a freebooter who first defied and
then courted God had its *répétition générale* on June 11,
1951, before an extremely brilliant audience. Disturb-
ances had been expected because of what Claude Brulé
calls "its incredible blasphemies," the rumour of which
had already gone round Paris. But the evening passed
off without protest. When Nasty, the Peasants' leader, exclaimed to the Bishop of Worms, "Ton Église est une
putain," the audience gave no sign of displeasure; nor

was it overmuch troubled when, in reply to the accusation, "Tu es un bâtard," Goetz answered tranquilly,
"Oui: comme Jésus-Christ." These phrases caused some
offence in the Press, and a good deal was written about
them, but in the theatre, so far as I have been able to discover, they produced no great consternation. The company, perhaps, was more conscious of the nature of the
play they were presenting than the audience. The players
quickly realized that *Le Diable et le Bon Dieu* could
plausibly be viewed as an atheistic reply to Claudel's
orthodox masterpiece, *Le Soulier de satin.* Soon after
rehearsals began the word ran round the *coulisses*, "We
are playing *Le Soulier de Satan.*" Sartre himself was not
present at the *répétition générale*, having a Left Wing
political meeting to attend. But he arrived in time for
the final applause. His mother had watched the entire
performance, and had eagerly noted the public's reactions.
One of Sartre's earlier works had been *L'Etre et le néant.*
When she heard a young opponent of her son say that
the new play ought to be called *Le Reître et le néant*, her
eyes filled with tears.

This young wit's reaction was not typical. *Le Diable
et le Bon Dieu* was generally treated with respect by the
critics, and it drew large audiences. Sartre had expended
on it tremendous pains, for he designed it to show that
those who said that things would have been better, or at
least different, had Orestes and Hugo acted otherwise,
were wrong. No man, says Sartre, can foresee the results
of his actions; therefore, the only sensible thing to do is
to act in accordance with one's own nature. That at least
saves stress and strain, and the consequence is likely to
be no more unsatisfactory than conduct based on ethical
principles.

His Captain Goetz captures Worms by means of a
secret key given to him by a conscience-torn priest, Heinrich. Goetz exults in evil. He thinks of himself as the
wickedest man alive. He puts crowds to the massacre,

and delights in his mistress only because he believes she loathes him. When he finds that she is in love with him, he throws her to every common soldier in the army who will have her, until she is dying of horrible diseases. Brasseur played him with a bouncing, black-bearded gaiety that some spectators found very alarming, but to me Goetz, in his first and evil phase, exulting in wickedness and volubly prostituting his mistress, Catherine, seemed to verge on the exuberantly absurd. But the point Sartre wished to make about him was that he accomplished nothing by his wickedness. He killed hundreds, even thousands, of human beings, but the society he attacked remained as firm as ever.

In one of his more exalted moments the priest Heinrich deflated him by remarking that there were plenty of men as wicked as he who went about killing people on week-days, and modestly confessing on Sundays. But, added Heinrich, there are few good men. This was a challenge that Goetz found irresistible. During a Palladium pantomime one Christmas there was a pigeon act, and one of the pigeons was extremely officious. Every time a new trick was announced, this particular pigeon marched forward, ready to perform it, in or out of its turn. Goetz had the temperament of this pigeon: whatever was being done, he wished to be the protagonist. Immediately Heinrich had spoken of the scarcity of good men, Goetz conceived the notion of setting up as a saint. To be good or not to be good, he made this question turn on the throw of dice: and so that the dice should come down on the side of virtue, he cheated. It is on Catherine's discovery of this cheating that the curtain of the first act descends.

The second act shows Goetz in the full rush of deliberate sanctity. He gives away his lands to the peasants, and kisses a leper on the mouth, much to the leper's disgust. But his sanctity is of no more avail than his wickedness. Neither as a bad man nor as a good do things go the way

he designs. Saul killed his thousands, but David his tens
of thousands, and Goetz the saint proves more lethal
than Goetz the devil. For the surrounding peoples are
jealous of the prosperity of Goetz's countrymen, which
results from his generosity, and they march in and massacre them. In seeking either absolute evil or absolute
good Goetz achieves only misery. This seems to prove
Sartre's contention that it is pointless to govern one's
actions by any convention of behaviour, since no one can
foretell what the consequences of any action will be.

Yet, of course, it does not prove anything of the kind.
A play is not a history, narrating events over which the
author has no control. It is a story which the author
invents, though authors are often shy of admitting this.
They like to maintain that their characters are real people,
having independent lives of their own. They speak of
them as if they were as actual as the man next door. "As
I see it," Yeats wrote to Sean O'Casey, when rejecting
The Silver Tassie for the Abbey Theatre, "Hamlet and
Lear educated Shakespeare, and I have no doubt that in
the process of that education he found out that he was
altogether a different man to what he thought himself,
and had altogether different beliefs." O'Casey will have
none of this academic fancy that Hamlet and Macbeth,
instead of being offshoots of Shakespeare's imagination,
were a couple of college professors. This fine and irascible
dramatist, who is so strange a mixture of generosity and
envy, maintains the contrary view that the characters of
an author's work are his creations, and not God's. "Of
one thing we can be certain," he says, "namely, that what
Shakespeare makes Hamlet say was not what the living
Prince would, or could, have said, but what Shakespeare
wanted him to say; that the play is largely a biography of
Shakespeare's thoughts."[1]

Le Diable et le Bon Dieu too is largely a biography of
Sartre's thoughts. The development of the plot is an

[1] Sean O'Casey, *Rose and Crown*, pp. 37 and 38.

expression of Sartre's outlook on life. If that outlook were different from what it is, so would the plot differ from that in the play. The consequences of Goetz's actions do not prove Sartre's philosophy; they flow from it. They are not its demonstration, but its fruit. For giving us an insight into Sartre's mind they are invaluable; as a dramatic experience, they have their moments; but as a philosophic theorem they are worthless.

Moreover, even if what happens in the third act of the play were what would have happened, and not what Sartre decided should happen, it would still not disprove the Christian ethics. For Christianity demands more than that men should do good things: it demands that they should be good men.

Now, a good man Goetz never became. A man cannot add to his stature by taking thought, nor become good by an effort of the will. Goodness is a matter of inward grace, and this grace Goetz did not have. He knew it himself, when he exclaimed, " Je n'ai pas agi: j'ai fait des gestes." His actions, in his phase of attempted virtue, did not express anything truly inside himself; he did not give away his lands out of compassion, nor kiss the leper from brotherly love; what he did was merely an imitation of what he thought a good man would have done in similar circumstances.

I do not mean that, in a flamboyant, exhibitionistic way, he did not wish to do good things. When he found Catherine dying and haunted by a sense of sin he genuinely desired to take the burden of her sins upon himself, and free her from her terrible obsessions. But he had not in himself that tranquillity and that peace which could spread a balm over others. Theatrically, calling on God to witness, he could stir faith in her only by leaping up to the great white bleeding statue of Christ which adorned the church to which she had been brought, and stab himself to produce in his hands sham stigmata which made the dying woman believe a miracle had occurred. This is the best and most exciting scene in the play, but it hardly shows Goetz as a good man. He remains a mountebank, a poseur, a self-conscious actor. Christian ethics, then, are neither proved nor disproved in this play, if they could be proved or disproved in any play. In *Le Diable et le Bon Dieu* they do not arise.

This immense and sprawling work is impressive, but it shows a regression in Sartre's dramatic talent. It is too melodramatic, too deliberately shocking, too formless. *Huis Clos* remains his best play. Nevertheless, it is a play that causes some discomfort among Sartre's admirers, or at least among those who revere him more as a philosopher and thinker than as an artist. They feel that the play is tinged with religion. Gabriel Marcel, himself a dramatist of reputation, and known to listeners to the Third Programme for his bitter study of a Puritan, *A Man of God*, has from time to time warned Christians against Existentialism, and *Huis Clos* is markedly an Existentialist play: yet priests are found who say that its influence is better than that of a good sermon.

Their opinion, however, seems to be based on the naïve ground that its scene is hell, and that hell is a Christian religious conception. This view hardly carries more weight than the belief of the old lady who thought that the devil must be a respectable character because he is mentioned in the Bible, yet Sartre's supporters find it necessary to meet it with solemn and serious argument. Marc Beigbeder, for example, maintains that an atheist can legitimately believe in an after-life. Atheism, he says, denies only the existence of God, not survival after death. Sartre's presentation of hell, therefore, in *Huis Clos*, still leaves him in good infidel standing.

This seems a remarkably heavy-handed approach to the question. Sartre's use of the dramatic convention of hell in *Huis Clos* no more involves his belief in the place's physical existence than Ustinov's employment of the

legend of the Sleeping Beauty in *The Love of Four
Colonels* means that the English dramatist accepts literally
the story of the love-struck Prince and the magic kiss. In
the one case as in the other, the author helps himself to a
powerful legend, which is clustered with all sorts of
valuable emotional overtones that he finds convenient to
his dramatic purpose. In *Huis Clos* hell is used merely as
a synonym for the ultimate condition of human misery;
and the philosophic interest of the play resides exclusively
in Sartre's identification of this nadir of misery with the
Existentialist recoil from interference with the individual's freedom of action by the influence of other people.
It has nothing whatever to do with credulity about the
lake of fire and the fall from heaven. Even if it had, the
path from this credulity to faith in and knowledge of
God is long, narrow, and dangerous. If the followers of
Sartre, as they undoubtedly do, look upon the term
Christian as an insult, one can assure them with confidence that there is nothing in *Huis Clos* to cause them
embarrassment. They are unduly sensitive. There is
more in Christianity than the word "enfer."

This is a point, however, on which the Existentialists
are uncommonly uneasy. The world of fiction is a
treacherous one. Many a sincere Christian has taken to
the novel or the drama, and in obedience to his creative
impulse produced pages that have scandalized the faithful. One recalls the horror of the devout editor of *Good
Words* when he found certain passages in Trollope's
Rachel Ray that seemed to him to encourage the sin of
dancing. It is consequently pleasing to discover that the
writing of fiction can just as easily raise doubts about the
good faith of the unfaithful. Sartre's very first incursion
into the drama had led to the raising of atheistic eyebrows, and the muttering of agitated and humourless
questions. The mind of a good atheist, it appears, is as
rigid as that of an orthodox bigot.

In *Les Mouches* Sartre had introduced the figure of

Jupiter, and Jupiter is a god. M. Beigbeder hastily interposes that Sartre gives to his Jupiter no more super-natural capacity than the ability to perform a few parlour tricks, such as the dispersal of the plague of flies by half a dozen words of gibberish. Yet in a hot country, this is a gift not to be despised: it is indeed a capacity more use-ful than the ability to move mountains. The desire to free oneself from the buzzing of insects comes more fre-quently, even in the chills of England, than the wish to rearrange the landscape.

But in fact Sartre makes Jupiter more than the mere prestidigitateur that M. Beigbeder allows. He has the gift of omniscience. How otherwise could he have known what the old woman was doing on the day of the murder of Agamemnon, and in what other way could he have recognized the wandering Orestes? Yet to doubt a man's atheism because he introduces a figure of classical mythology into a reconstruction of a classical play sug-gests an unusual degree of nervousness. Nor is it reason-able, simply because a man writes about paganism, to suspect him of being a concealed Christian. One might just as well imagine a politician to be a die-hard Tory on the ground that he shows a tendency to believe in Karl Marx.

Sartre's position in regard to religion, as Beigbeder himself observes, is to be deduced rather from the per-vading tone of his work than from any particular pas-sages. The logical consistency of the philosopher can-not be expected from a creative artist, who is subject to his moods as well as to his reason. Now in the main Sartre's attitude towards religion is perfectly simple. He hates it. He considers it to be the source of a great part of human misery. It is associated with the things which he dislikes. "Walls plastered with blood, millions of flies, the smell of a shambles, deserted streets . . . is this," he asks bitterly, "what pleases Jupiter?" "Fear and a bad conscience have a delicious aroma in the nos-trils of the Gods."

But in his view religion's worst error is its conception of an end, a goal, towards which men must strive. He shrinks from that verse of St Paul's which exhorts us to act so that "we all come in the unity of the faith . . . unto a perfect man, unto the measure of the stature of the fulness of Christ." For this involves behaviour according to certain standards, in other words, the adoption of a system of ethics. And this leads to the idea of authority, of laws, all of which cripple man's freedom. Others may regard them as the compass by which men guide themselves in the storm. But Sartre advises us that we should go out into the storm without a compass, manufacturing one for ourselves as the waves buffet and pound us.

Sartre's creative work, therefore, is concerned more or less exclusively with the examination of characters who are in process of making such a compass. Recently, however, he has discovered in real life a man who has exemplified in deliberate action his own original philosophy, and in his enthusiasm for him he has temporarily broken off his writing of *Les Chemins de la liberté* in order to compose his biography. This biography he has issued under the title of *Saint Genet: comédien et martyr*, a volume of more than a quarter of a million words in which, in prose sometimes penetrating, but oftener obscure and confused, he presents to us, against a psychoanalytic background, the figure of a strange rebel against society who is also a considerable writer, one of whose plays, *Les Bonnes*, was presented, in London, first at the Mercury Theatre, and later at the Royal Court during November 1952.

Jean Genet, the author of two novels, *Notre-Dame-des-Fleurs* and *Miracle de la rose*, spent much of his early life in prison. In one of his gaols he met a criminal, Maurice Pilorge, who was beheaded at Saint-Brieuc on March 17, 1939, for the murder of his friend and paramour Escudero, whose life he took for the sake of less than a thousand francs. This Pilorge both infests and inspires the imagination of Genet. "His body and his radiant face haunt," says Genet, "my nights without sleep." He speaks of the "double and unique splendour of his soul and his body." After Pilorge's condemnation Genet, helped by a warder who also was bewitched by his fascination and his terrible fate, used to go each morning to his cell to take him a packet of cigarettes. Pilorge, already up, would be singing under his breath, and, with a bright smile, would greet Genet with the words, "Hail, Jean of the morning." But for Pilorge, whose "death has not ceased to poison his life," Genet would never have written *Notre-Dame-des-Fleurs*, and it is to his memory that the book is dedicated.

Genet's life and experiences have not been such as to give him a conventional outlook. That he has not such an outlook is the point about him, rather than the sometimes breathtaking musical beauty of his prose, that commends him to Sartre, who is interested in him, not as a writer, but as a practising philosopher. Genet has a less explicit dislike of Christianity than Sartre: indeed, the Christian ritual and its ministers are frequently mentioned in his books with that casual naturalness which suggests a certain familiar affection. But his hatred of the ethics derived from Christianity is far more active and real than Sartre's. In private life Sartre is a model citizen, whatever his theoretic views may be. But Genet boasts of robbing and betraying his friends. He cannot forgive kindness; he hates generosity of spirit if it comes from above. "Madame is good!" scornfully exclaims one of the maids in *Les Bonnes*. "Madame loves us. She loves us like her chairs . . . like her bidet . . . like the pink china seat of her toilet." A lady once said, "My maid ought to be contented. I give her my clothes." Genet replied, not without point, "Very good. Does she give you hers?" Genet exemplifies in his life, or perhaps I should say, he *has* exemplified in his past life, the open, deliberate defiance of Christian principles that Sartre merely

preaches. It is because he has actually lived irreligion
that Sartre calls him a saint, a saint of the new, the
Existentialist, church.

Genet was born in 1909, a foundling, and was sent to
foster-parents in the country. He is illegitimate, a fact
that Sartre finds remarkably significant and apparently,
to judge from the vigour it brings into his prose,
stimulating. Genet, says Sartre, is not his mother's son:
he "is her excrement." We who are born of the species
are justified in continuing the species, but "Genet, born
without parents, is ready to die without children. His
sexuality will be abstract tension and sterility." Thus
from the very beginning Genet is destined to be sexually
perverted. As one reads this sort of thing it becomes
increasingly difficult to avoid the impression that Sartre,
in leaving orthodox Christianity, often wanders down
byways of extreme absurdity. Whatever may be the
handicaps of illegitimate children, there is no reason, outside of Sartre's overheated imagination, to suppose that
they are necessarily cut off from the normal instincts of
humanity.

As a child Genet fell into the way of thieving, and soon
found himself at a reformatory. The experience was in-
expressibly bitter to him. "He suffered cruelly . . . felt
the disgrace of having his hair cropped, of wearing an
infamous uniform, of being put in that vile place."
Genet himself has described his feelings. "I was sixteen," he says. "In my heart there was nowhere to preserve the conviction of my innocence. I recognized in
myself the scoundrel, traitor, thief, and pervert that others
saw in me . . .; I found myself full of uncleanness. I
became abject."

It is the mark of the practising Existentialist that,
surrounded with the snares and pitfalls of life, and its
multitudinous possibilities, he makes unhesitatingly a
deliberate choice. Genet chose. That is why Sartre
thinks him worthy of one of the longest books even he

has written. Regarded by society as a thief, Genet decided
that a thief was what he would be. He deliberately
vowed himself to evil. As the devout Catholic surrounds
himself with the images of saints, Genet surrounded
himself with the mementoes of criminals. On the walls
of his prison cells he pinned up pictures of murderers like
Pilorge and Harcamone which he had cut out of sen-
sational newspapers. To these he said his prayers, and
longed passionately for their spirit to enter into and to
inspire him. He lay on his bed at night, gazing up at
them, and indulging in ecstasies which until recently
could not be publicly described even in French.

Sartre sees a mystical connexion between sanctity and
evil. Like salvation, evil is a matter of grace. The commission of a crime does not make a man evil: it is because
he is evil that he commits a crime. The commission of a
crime may be a moral accident: in that case, the man who
commits it has no title to the Sartrian compliment of
being called evil. On the other hand, a man's crimes may
remain only potential: he may never commit them at all.
Even so, such a man, on whom the grace of wickedness
has been conferred, is truly evil. It is in this sense that,
in *Les Bonnes*, Genet speaks of the "eternal union of the
criminal and the saint." This is why, on the walls of his
cells, he hung, not only the portraits of Harcamone and
Pilorge, but pictures of footballers and boxers of blame-
less reputation, but with faces showing the required
degree of degeneracy. It is to morbid depths like these
that the rejection of the traditional philosophy and
religion of Europe has brought two of the most remarkable of contemporary French authors.

Genet is not a voluminous writer. His two novels,
Notre-Dame-des-Fleurs and *Miracle de la rose*, even with
the poems *Le Condamné à mort* and *Un Chant d'amour*, do
not make up a book as long as Sartre's *Saint Genet*. When
it was announced that a leading French publisher was
going to issue his Collected Works there was even a

certain amount of derision among some Parisian critics, who did not think that Genet was old enough or had written enough to deserve an honour generally accorded only to very prolific authors at the end of their careers.

Whether Genet has written much is one question; the value of what he has written is quite another. A great deal of both the novels is scandalous stuff, and neither of them for some years could be sold openly in Paris. On the other hand, Sartre compares Genet with Villon and Rimbaud; Cocteau calls him "a great poet"; and it is claimed by his admirers that some passages he has written, such as the trial of the sixteen-year-old murderer, Notre-Dame-des-Fleurs, and the ending of *Miracle de la rose*, put him among the very greatest figures of French literature in his capacity to unite poetic imagination with the realism of sordid situations.

I have not enough knowledge of French literature either to endorse or to throw doubt on the high position thus accorded to Genet. The realism of his work is, however, very striking. It is through the medium of a dream or a reverie that he creates in *Notre-Dame-des-Fleurs* the horrible and frightening world of the Parisian tough and his male paramour, with their mean luxuries of soft hat, English Raglan, and yellow pointed shoes. But through the shifting fabric of this dream the terrible figures emerge with astounding clearness, pursuing their obscene activities in rooms crowded with bottles of stolen liqueurs, silk ties, cases of scent, and sham jewels, and, in their perverted delicacy, crossing half Paris in order to get to the W.C. at the Terminus Saint-Lazare, because it is decorated with mauve mosaic. They know every café in Paris that has a W.C. with a seat. "To get a good rear," says Mignon, the tough of *Notre-Dame-des-Fleurs*, "I must sit down."

There is a great deal of this kind of thing in Genet: he dwells with an astonishing freedom of vocabulary on the violence of his characters, their physical needs, and the details of their perverted sexual activities. But he can, and frequently does, write prose of absolute simplicity and perfect music. He writes, in the opening paragraph of *Miracle de la rose*, on the prison of Fontevrault with a solemn and tender eloquence, as some men have written of the towers and spires of Oxford. He evokes the influence of this gaol in words that sound like bells tolling men to church, for one of his strangest and most troubling powers is to be able to subdue the understanding with a high and sombre music, with insidious guile mingling the pure and lovely with foul and evil things. The noble ending of *Miracle de la rose* itself, with its magical litany of criminals echoing in the memory like Lord Chief Justice Crewe's "For where is Bohun? Where's Mowbray? Where's Mortimer?" follows a particularly scabrous passage. And it is to a thief and murderer that he offers the words of classical and horrifying simplicity, of revolting and tender affection, that conclude *Le Condamné à mort*.

The only one of his plays seen in London is *Les Bonnes*. In 1947 Louis Jouvet produced *Les Bonnes* at the Athénée, where it ran for ninety-two performances. There are only three characters, the two maids and their mistress. Sartre, in his lengthy analysis of the play, insists on the numerous aspects of it which suggest that things are not what they seem. The lady of the house, for example, is not really a lady at all: she is a street-walker. When the curtain rises one of the maids is dressing the other: but this other is wearing, not her own clothes, but her employer's, and some time goes by before one realizes that the second maid is not actually the mistress. They poison their mistress's tea, so great is their hatred of her, and one of them, a baleful creature clothed in black, has a murderess's vision in which she sees all the maids of the *quartier* following her to the guillotine. But it is not the mistress who dies, but the first maid. The maid, however, is not murdered; she commits suicide. She commits suicide, not as herself, but as her loathed mistress, dressed in her mistress's garments. And so on, and so forth. In this terrible and haunting *mélange* of guilt and hatred and darkness and evil, everything is deception. Genet wished that even the actresses should not be what they appeared; he wanted to have their parts played by adolescent boys. But Jouvet, who did not protest against the Lesbianism, sadism, flagellation, and blasphemy which have their parts in the play, refused to allow this.

Les Bonnes, played in London by Selma Vaz Dias and Olive Gregg as the maids, and by Oriel Ross as the mistress at the first two performances (subsequently by Betty Stockfield), has many of the qualities that make it impossible openly to import into Britain English translations of Genet's work. (I believe that an English version of *Notre-Dame-des-Fleurs* exists, but I have never seen a copy either of this or of any other translation of Genet.) But in only one passage does *Les Bonnes* seem to me to possess the characteristics for which alone Genet is worth reading—namely, his extraordinary ability to write of sordid and disgusting things in a high, sometimes horrible, always singing, and assured strain. In the terrible nightmare speech of one of the maids concerning the procession of servants to the scaffold, with its disturbing, perhaps blasphemous, certainly impressive echoes of religious ritual, Genet in *Les Bonnes* comes nearest to his Villonesque master's manner. This is the best thing in the play; there is about it a memorable passionate horror, a revolting grandeur.

What is Genet's future as a writer? It cannot be divorced from his future as a man. All his books have been born out of an experience of life unspeakably ignoble. In prison after prison he has lived in the company of men singularly vile, and his books make of these men's degradation a norm of behaviour. He is the first writer for many generations who has made something that can at any rate be colourably called literature out of a defence of mean, cruel, and cowardly crime.

The commercial success that has followed on his literary achievement, however, has lifted Genet out of the world of the sewers that nurtured his genius. He is to-day a figure of fashionable Paris; he spends his leisure on the Côte d'Azur. He discusses with fascinated interest the education of his well-to-do friends' children. The luxurious hotels of the Riviera are far from the prison of Fresnes; and it is prison that has been Genet's "most kindly nurse."

5

Armand Salacrou

TO go out on the high seas with no compass. This is
Sartre's advice. It is gallant, but is it practical?
This is the question that haunts Armand Salacrou. It
causes Sartre himself no distress, for Sartre is convinced
of the possibility of human perfection. But Salacrou cannot believe in human perfection unless it is modelled on
and inspired by the divine; and he is tormented by the
doubt whether this divine perfection exists.

He was born into a Catholic family, but as a child he
lost faith on reading some elementary scientific text-book
which explained the universe in purely mechanistic
terms. Later, as a young man, the mechanistic explanation in its turn seemed to him unsatisfactory. But he did
not return to religion; he felt only a profound and distressing need to return to it, and a disabling inability to
do so. No modern French dramatist, says Serge Radine
in his study, *Anouilh, Lenormand, Salacrou,* is so concerned with the religious problem, with metaphysical
questioning, with longing for a paradise lost.

The distress, the creative ferment in Salacrou spring
from the fact that he can neither believe in God and the
Christian faith, nor free himself from an impelling sense
of their necessity. He has not the gift of faith, yet
passionately desires it. At one point in his life, just after
the conclusion of the War, it seemed for a moment that
he had discovered an alternative to it which would bring
to him the philosophic peace he has long sought. But, as
we shall see, this hope was only an illusion. After the

brief optimism of 1946, when new altars raised themselves, he still, in words that he wrote many years before, feels the need for God without being able to believe in God.

If this makes him distressed and melancholy he does not inflict his melancholy on his friends. Whatever may be Salacrou's interior miseries, questionings, and fears, he overcomes them in society enough to be a remarkably merry and animated companion. He is a man who has lost God, and the loss may have marked his soul. But it has left his gay and eager face untouched. With his sharp, keen eyes, his bright and almost transparently clear complexion, and his agile gesticulations, he looks less depressed than a Scotsman who has mislaid sixpence. I have seen him in his charming apartment in the Avenue Foch, of which the walls are rich with early works by Modigliani, Braque, and Picasso, leaning forward from his easy-chair, nose thrust impetuously out, words pouring from him like a torrent, his arms waving like flags in a tempest. I have lunched with him in London at the Caprice, where he has been filled with exuberant joy to find steak and kidney pie on the menu, recalling the dinners he used to eat in England when he was a schoolboy in Salisbury. And both in England and in France I have found him incessantly lively, entertaining, and cheerful.

His is a nature capable of great happiness; and sometimes this happiness has been fully attained. There is a record of one such period in his life in the postscript he wrote for *Le Pont de l' Europe*. This was one of Salacrou's earliest plays, written before anything of his had been acted, while he was still only twenty-five. Salacrou says that everything he writes turns into a play, and maintains that he could not compose a novel. The descriptions, he says, would come out as speeches. But he does himself an injustice. For when he chooses to exercise it he has a very fine descriptive style, whether of people or of landscapes and feelings. Besides a greater talent than he admits—he is one of the most modest of dramatists—he has also a more considerable love for description than he believes. Much of the interest of his early play *Patchouli* resides in the penetrating analysis and presentation of his romantically-minded hero that he offers between brackets and in italic type. Nor has any writer —novelist or critic—produced a more living evocation of Louis Jouvet and his admirable company than does Salacrou in a single paragraph in the postscript to *Atlas-Hôtel.* "Jouvet had accomplished his masterpiece"—he is speaking of the Jouvet of 1930, just before that great actor and director entered on the film career which was to bring him fame even in London and New York—

> Jouvet had accomplished his masterpiece: a company of five players, made for each other in their voices and their gestures. They were like a magnificently co-ordinated team of sportsmen playing some invisible and tragic football; Renoir, hard, violent, intimidating in appearance, disturbing; Jouvet, one hand in that of Ariel, the other in Caliban's; Michel Simon, who could have been Renoir, who could have been Jouvet, hiding his strength, his tenderness, his intelligence in a sort of comic illumination that our generation will probably never know again—and between these three men, all the women of history and of geography reflected turn by turn in the grace and splendour of Valentine Tessier and Lucienne Bogaert. Five people like five notes perfectly attuned to each other, notes that could be broken up, opposed, alternated, and mingled to play all the varied music of human destinies.

This was written of a time when Salacrou was meditating a play for the outstanding company. "I was," he said, "like a child in front of a piano open and mute." Like a child—have I not already said that Salacrou is the most modest of authors?

A description equally fine, and more to our present

purpose, since we are speaking of the capacity for happiness of this man who is haunted by the ineffective desire for religion, is to be found in the passage in which he recollects the place and temper in which he wrote *Le Pont de l'Europe*. This play was written on the banks of the Seine in the first days of harvest, while the cargo-boats were drifting up the river to Rouen; and Salacrou has retained from that time the memory of many long and silent weeks, spent among simple folk, during which he was writing, writing, always writing. This, he says, was happiness, true happiness; and then one Sunday—and what delight still lives, after a quarter of a century, in the unadorned, straightforward phrase—one Sunday his play was finished.

It was presented by the Jeunes Auteurs at the second of the French National Theatres, the Odéon, now the Salle Luxembourg. Salacrou did not attend the opening performance, but wandered round the neighbouring Luxembourg Gardens, wholly satisfied to feel that at last words which he had written were being spoken on a real stage. His friends kept him fully informed of the impression his piece was making. Three of them, authors themselves, ran out at the end of each act, sought Salacrou under the trees, and gave him the exciting news. "It is a disaster," they exclaimed. "You will have a terrible Press." But Salacrou was not discouraged. The speeches he had written for King Jerome were being declaimed a hundred yards away, and people were listening to them. It was too much to expect them to listen with pleasure. That would come later.

This King Jerome was one of Salacrou's most romantic creations, preoccupied, like so many of the characters of the later and more famous plays, with love, with its evanescence, its unfaithfulness. A penniless wanderer from Paris, a young student who had been hopelessly in love with a Spanish dancer, he had come on foot into the capital of an east European state on the very day when it had been prophesied that just such a man should be chosen as its new king. Installed in power, and surrounded by clownish Ministers, he invited to his palace a company of players, including the Spanish dancer, in an effort to recapture the passion he had felt when poor and young. It is a baffling and confused play, the characters appearing and disappearing with disconcerting swiftness, a sort of charade, influenced no doubt in its technique by the surrealism of some of the artists whom Salacrou most admires. But out of its disarray and helter-skelter darted more than once a flash of poetry, of imagination, which ought to have shown that a new author had arisen, as yet uncertain of himself and his medium, but of splendid promise. I am thinking particularly of Jerome's speech on the artificiality of Paris—"the walls which are of iron, the light that does not come from the sky, and carriages that move without horses and even without smoke"— and of the dancer's sigh over the melancholy of stage doors—"no more illuminations, no more applause! A little door on an empty street, behind the Music Hall, with a few shadows of old people like provincial charwomen, and little pigtailed girls standing on the pavements." But there were others, too.

On the whole, the Parisian critics, faced with the new and unusual talent of *Le Pont de l'Europe*, did not do badly. Some of them at least adopted a more reasonable tone than most of their London colleagues when called on to judge the Frank Sundstrom production of Kafka's *The Trial*, or John Whiting's Arts Theatre prize play, *Saint's Day*. They recognized a high and ambitious intelligence, condemned the play's ramshackle construction, and perceived "sparks of genius, as if from a smoky fire." There were also, of course, judgments passed that might have come from a London notice of *Saint's Day*. "Whatever," wrote the critic of the Havas Agency, "whatever anyone says about me, I cannot admit that this ambitious play will be understood by ordinary folk having a night out." And another critic thought of a joke which might have been invented in Fleet Street itself. "This bridge," he said, "is less gay than that at Avignon."

The best authors write what they must: they express the thoughts and feelings which compel them to utterance. But they also pay some attention to the problem of making this expression attractive to the largest possible audience. This is a question that is as urgent for Mr Rattigan and Mr Priestley as it is for the multitude of youthful authors whose heads are bursting with ideas and pockets with unacted manuscripts. It is one that M. Salacrou has been pondering for many years, and on which he has written entertainingly and instructively.

His next play after *Le Pont de l'Europe* was *Patchouli*. The hero of *Patchouli* was a young man who preferred to live in the past. He liked delving into memoirs of the Second Empire better than going to parties in the Third Republic. In fact, he had fallen in love with one of the ladies of the Franco-Prussian War, simply because she had refused herself to a young nobleman of the time. This insistence on feminine virtue, which becomes on occasion almost morbidly intense, is a theme to which Salacrou often returns, and which he was later to treat with masterly skill in *Histoire de rire*. Between this subject and that of *Saint's Day*, which I take to have been the warning that unless mankind listens to its poets and prophets there is no hope for it, there is no resemblance. But the fate of the two plays bears strikingly on the question of the public reception of plays that are unconventional in inspiration and technique.

There is a general impression among young authors that the reason their plays remain in manuscript is the stupidity and cowardice of managers. This feeling I believe to be unjust. Far from being timid and shrinking, managers, it seems to me, are almost incredibly rash in presenting, at enormous expense, the works of untried authors. Mr Whiting offers an obvious example. The first thing that anyone in London heard of him was that his *A Penny for a Song* was to be presented by the greatest of London managements, in one of the most exquisite of London theatres, in a production by one of the most eminent, inventive, and witty of London directors. The only other play of his of which we have heard, *Saint's Day*, was accepted by the management of the Arts Theatre, and awarded a prize of £700. When they read it in manuscript the judges who awarded the prize, Christopher Fry, Alec Clunes, and Peter Ustinov, were considerably impressed by its poetic merit.

Mr Whiting, then, has little cause to complain of the managers; neither had the young and experimental Salacrou. He sent the manuscript of *Patchouli* to Jouvet, but heard nothing from that great man. He showed a copy to Charles Dullin at the Atelier, the same Dullin who shortly afterwards was to give his theatrical training to Jean-Louis Barrault. Dullin at once accepted it. That evening Salacrou and his wife, to celebrate the occasion, dined at a restaurant in Montparnasse, which was still in the days of its ascendancy. The next table was empty, but reserved. A few minutes later a man came and sat down at it: he was Jouvet. "My dear young fellow," he exclaimed, "your piece will do. I was going to write to you . . . I will play it." Salacrou explained that he was at that moment celebrating its acceptance by Dullin. Jouvet changed colour. "Don't do that," he said. "I will arrange it all with Charles." Dullin, however, hung on to the play. Salacrou, therefore, though *Le Pont de l'Europe* had failed, found two of the most famous Parisian managers competing for his next play.

Dullin did more than produce *Patchouli*. He found regular work for its author. As Mr Clunes supported Christopher Fry and William Templeton for a year till they found their dramatic feet, Charles Dullin gave Salacrou employment at the Atelier which helped to free him

from the drudgery of his connexion with one of the film
companies of the nineteen-twenties. He had passed
dreary months zigzagging across France on behalf of the
screen, trying to find something resembling the shore of
the Côte d'Azur at Honfleur, looking on the Côte d'Azur
for the scenery of Martinique, and, in Austria, rebuilding
Maxim's of the Rue Royale. I have spoken earlier of the
size and informativeness of French programmes, and of
that at the Atelier Dullin made Salacrou a sort of editor.
This did not give the young author quite enough to live
on. To supplement his income Salacrou started an
advertising agency which has since grown to outstanding
proportions. To render his mind still more easy, Dullin
sent Salacrou a letter, on the evening of the *générale*,
undertaking to produce his next five plays. When the
curtain went up on the critical and decisive performance,
all the auguries were fair. Salacrou's feet had been placed
on the road to artistic independence: he had the confidence of both Jouvet and Dullin. He was free of his
unrewarding work for the films. What every one had
forgotten was the audience.

In Salacrou's theory of the theatre the audience, over-
looked until that *générale*, now plays an enormously important part. On this evening the author, not knowing
that he was establishing a habit, dined alone at a restaurant in the Boulevard Rochechouart, reading and re-
reading the small advertisements in the *Temps*, which he
propped against an empty bottle of wine. At ten o'clock
exactly he rose, and went to the theatre.

Patchouli, he says, had already failed, and the failure
was turning into a catastrophe. The public had no artistic
sympathy with the play whatever. It did not in any way
share the æsthetic experience that was happening on the
stage. "It looked at it as one looks at a drunken man
in the street." As the second act finished, Salacrou was
in the wings, and he heard a tremendous burst of
laughter in the auditorium, so loud that it made the

scenery shake. Dullin was behind the backcloth, his head thrust forward, his hands in his hair. Then he lifted his head, and gazed at Salacrou, who saw that beads of sweat were rolling down his face like tears. The last words of the act were, "What a failure!" and as they were being spoken, the descending curtain stuck. The audience applauded madly. But the applause was for the curtain, not the play.

In the third act the actress Tania Balachova had to say, as she sat down in a chair, "I wish something violent would happen." The chair collapsed as she spoke, leaving the unfortunate Mlle Balachova's arms and legs in the air. Everything, says Salacrou, turned to burlesque.

After the first-night failure of *Saint's Day*, Fry, Ustinov, and Clunes formally declared their unshaken confidence in it. This is what Charles Dullin did with *Patchouli*. He put enormous advertisements in the papers, carrying only these words, "I believe in *Patchouli*. Charles Dullin." But he found the nervous strain upon him too great, and after fifteen performances gave up his part. And when Salacrou went to see Jouvet, he said merely, "Well, young man, so it didn't succeed, after all?"

Dullin and Jouvet may have weakened in the end, but it is not on them that Salacrou blames the peculiar failure of *Patchouli*. It is not the managers, but the audience, that he finds unsympathetic to new authors. It should be made clear that M. Salacrou does not complain of the failure, as such, of any of his plays. He is able to perceive (as some English authors, for example, are not) that some of his work may be defective. What makes him wistful about *Patchouli* is the particular nature of its failure. The audience did not listen patiently to the play, and then, as is its right, find it wanting. It was unsympathetic, even hostile, from the beginning. It treated the piece, not as something honourably uninteresting, but as contemptible. Its attitude was a continuous jeer. "Little by little," says Salacrou,

I discovered that a play does not begin its life at the last rehearsal, but on the first evening of its presentation to the public. A poem is born in solitude with a pencil and a sheet of paper. A dramatic poem begins to breathe only before the public, with the public. Tristan Bernard said: "Dramatic art is an exact science whose laws no one knows." These undiscoverable laws are found in the collaboration of the public.

I have on occasion protested against the behaviour of London audiences when the gallery has booed at first nights. But in general the booing has been of plays of no intellectual or artistic pretensions. It has been the rule in London during my experience of the theatre that audiences have shown themselves intolerant and hostile only when the play has been by its own nature contemptible. I can remember only a single exception to this, when, on the night of a General Election, a mildly Tchekovian piece called *All the Year Round* was treated with ribaldry almost from the rise of the curtain. The company presenting the play was young and talented, and the gallery treated it with great cruelty. Even in this instance the author had no claim to the artistic promise of the Salacrou who wrote *Patchouli*, and I do not think it could be maintained in London, as Salacrou maintained, no doubt justly, in Paris, that audiences are ever unwilling to attempt to co-operate with a dramatist of talent, simply because that talent is unusual. I do not say that the attempt invariably succeeds. It was obvious that the audiences both for *The Trial* and *Saint's Day* never understood the language the playwright was speaking. But this was not for want of trying, and no one connected with either production had any need to leave the theatre feeling he had been humiliated. In England the lack of sympathy for new dramatists is perhaps more widespread among critics than among audiences. But that is a subject on which it would be tactless for me to dwell.

Though *Patchouli*, like *Le Pont de l'Europe*, was a failure, it left Salacrou in a strong position in the *avant-garde* theatre, and Jouvet commissioned him to write a play for his company. The invitation both delighted and intimidated Salacrou. I have already shown the admiration Salacrou entertained for Jouvet and the group of fine actors and actresses with which he had surrounded himself. But Salacrou's talent is not one that reveals itself to order: offer him a young lady's autograph-album and ask him to write something in it, and the words freeze inside him, not from reluctance, but terror. At first the thought of writing a play for a particular company dried up inspiration, but then he remembered a fantastic character he had once encountered in the African desert, took himself off to a provincial town with pen, paper, his wife, and his daughter, and wrote *Atlas-Hôtel*.

In the late nineteen-twenties Africa dazzled the imagination of Europeans. The number of young men I knew in Oxford at that time who were resolved to seek their fortunes in Kenya rivalled those who favoured becoming Cabinet Ministers. The Foreign Legion was in the heyday of its reputation, and a popular novelist called Wren wrote a book from which *Beau Geste*, one of the best of silent films, was made. *Beau Geste* opened with a company of soldiers coming in the desert upon a strange fortress manned only by dead men. In *Atlas-Hôtel* a film company visits a scene almost as curious, a half-finished hotel rising suddenly out of the desert sands, without a roof, with no glass in the windows, and a fig-tree growing in the space reserved for the gaming-tables, yet ready to provide luncheon to any passer-by.

On the dividing-line at Pitlochry between the mountains of central Scotland and the desolate moors that run up to Balmoral there is a theatre that reminds me of this peculiar hotel. It is the playhouse in which James Stewart houses the Pitlochry Festival every summer. The foundations of it are laid on an elaborate scale, the seating

is thorough and extensive, the cloak-rooms and bars
excellent. But this solid construction is—or at least was
—enclosed only in circus canvas: the theatre is a building
without walls, as M. Salacrou's hotel was an inn without
roof, and Wren's fortress a citadel without life. The explanation of Pitlochry is found in post-War building
regulations, and Wren accounted for his fortress with
an ingenious plot. It was in character that Salacrou discovered the reason for his extraordinary hotel.

The management of the story in *Atlas-Hôtel* is less
than masterly, and the unexpected reunions that bring
people together in the desert from the ends of the earth
are somewhat improbable, but there are delightful things
in it, especially the dialogue between the novelist Albany
and his lost wife, Augustine. There are charming touches
of poetry, as when Augustine fleetingly recalls the joy of
youth symbolized in "Sur le pont d'Avignon, On y
danse, on y danse." But the success of the play lies in its
central character, Auguste, the inventor and manager of
this preposterous hotel, which is the physical testimony
to his inexhaustible and wholly impracticable enthusiasm,
his exuberant high spirits, and unconquerable optimism.
Auguste is a figure of magnificent absurdity, a master of
unanswerable and ridiculous logic, a prince amongst
eccentrics. He is a character that demands more expan-
siveness, a greater sense of the enjoyment of life, than
Jouvet normally manifested, and in the end it was
Charles Dullin, and not the Jouvet company, that presented the play.

Dullin himself had a triumph as Auguste. Oddly
enough, Salacrou does not seem to have been particularly
delighted either with the success of his fervent if erratic
champion, or with the play's favourable reception.
Salacrou is the incarnation of geniality and affability, but
there is a strain of ruthlessness in his character, which is
illustrated in his relations with a distinguished French
director well known in London. There was a time when

this director and Salacrou were the closest of friends. Their thoughts on, their ambitions for, the theatre tallied exactly. They were inseparable. If one of them visited London, the other came too. They indulged in interminable discussions. Then, suddenly, their friendship ended, and for no other reason than that Salacrou became bored. "One day," says Salacrou, "these discussions utterly wearied me—and as I do not take easily to half-measures I have never seen him since." No doubt if a human relationship is losing its attractiveness, it is better to finish it off at once. Yet if all our friends cut us as soon as we bored them, how many of us would have any friends left?

Dullin's success, therefore, did not reconcile Salacrou to writing plays like *Atlas-Hôtel* and its successor, *Les Frénétiques*. About this time he became increasingly dissatisfied with the kind of work which his association with Dullin and Jouvet was leading him to do. Writing plays for a particular actor or company involves thinking in terms of character. A Dickens or a Balzac does this easily; the creation of character is their forte. It is through a Swiveller or a Grandet that they express their vision of life. Salacrou in Auguste had already shown that he too had skill in this direction. Nevertheless, it was a skill on which he resented the placing of exaggerated emphasis. Salacrou believes that critics are far too ready to discuss characters in plays as if they were real people, to wonder how many children Lady Macbeth had, and whether Othello, faced with Hamlet's problem, would not have been perfectly capable of dealing with it. Plays, he says, are not made for the characters, but characters for the plays. Characters are notes in the author's soul, and instead of examining them as if they were real people, the critic ought to seek for the play's poetic life.

To Salacrou the dramatist is not the creator of people, but of a world. What interests him in a play is not the characters, but the relationships between them. These relationships make "little closed worlds" (*petits mondes fermés*), which, so long as they are self-consistent, may have no connexion with the customary notions of time, place, and psychology. Salacrou has been enormously influenced by a remark made to him by the cubist artist Juan Gris. "People reproach me," said Gris, "with painting triangular apples. I would rather paint them round if I could, but it isn't I who am in control, but the picture." The painter uses apples as a juggler tosses balls—the balls are of no importance in themselves. "What I look at," says M. Salacrou, "is the design that the juggler draws with them."

It is a design that exists independently of the real world. Any impingement on it of that world in fact destroys it. As a young student, Salacrou saw Sarah Bernhardt when she had grown old, and had lost one of her legs. She was playing *Athalie* for the last time in her theatre opposite the Châtelet. She came to that famous point in the play where she tells her dream to Abner and Mathan. Facing full to the audience, she declaimed the celebrated passage in which Racine's heroine speaks of the paints and the pomades that are needed to repair the irreparable outrage of the years. For a moment the play, as a play, vanished. The audience thought no longer of Athalie, but of the indomitable old woman on the stage, once golden and beautiful, whom not even age and mutilation could entirely subdue. It broke, deeply moved, into a tempest of applause. But, says Salacrou, "this audience, which had, I admit it, plenty of excuse, was joining in the tragedy of a great actress struggling with death, but not in the tragedy of *Athalie*." Many Englishmen, I fancy, would regard an experience such as Salacrou here records as amongst the glories of their theatre-going, and it would be unjust to suppose that Salacrou himself was not aware how touching it was. Yet one can see that if it moved him, it moved him against his will. He resented its breaking of the unity of the play and the performance. It is

by this unity of spirit, not by the interest, the verisimilitude, or the consistency of character, nor by the
quality of plot, nor of dialogue, that the drama of Salacrou is to be judged.

Atlas-Hôtel had been produced in April 1931. Three
years passed before his next Parisian production. By the
time that *Une Femme libre* reached the stage of the
Œuvre in October 1934, in a production directed by
Paulette Pax, Salacrou's worldly position had been transformed by the success of his advertising agency, and his
ambitions as a writer had consolidated. From his early
youth Salacrou longed for theatrical success, because the
life of the theatre and everything associated with it, from
the three thumps that in France herald the rise of the
curtain, to the lining up of the players for applause at the
end of each act, passionately excited him, and he wished
to establish himself firmly in it. But by 1934 he was asking for bigger things than this.

The critics expected little from *Une Femme libre*. They
took their seats wearily, plainly showing, he says, doubtless with some exaggeration, that the name of Salacrou
at that time suggested an evening of boredom. But
during the performance their attitude was transformed.
The novelist Colette, who in 1934 formed one of them,
says she forgot the Œuvre's uncomfortable seats, its hot
auditorium, and its cold foyer in the excellence of the first
two acts. Mlle Pax rushed up to Salacrou, exclaiming,
"A triumph like this comes to an author only once in a
lifetime." *Une Femme libre* was Salacrou's first success of
the kind that brings queues to the theatre, and smiles to
the face of the cloakroom attendant.

He liked it, but he did not like it as much as Mlle Pax
expected, or as much as he himself would have expected
a few years before. The terrible mortality of the drama
weighed upon his spirits. "I did not," he writes,

    share the unbounded joy of Paulette Pax over one of those
    Parisian successes that are born in the autumn and die with

the earliest flowers. Think of the fifteen new plays that have been acted every year in Paris for three centuries. Dramatic literature is an immense, deserted cemetery. Make an anthology of French poetry, and from generation to generation, from age to age, poets speak to us still. From Rutebeuf to Reverdy, the poets stand in an unbroken line, but with their tragedies dramatists are like solitary giants in the empty centuries.

By 1934 Salacrou had already become the man who would challenge Shakespeare and Racine.

He thought the French theatre of the between-the-wars period amusing but trivial. It had no character, and no settled conception of life. His views, coupled with his own obvious desire to be the man to put things right, brought on him a certain amount of unfriendly criticism. In a phrase that has achieved some notoriety, he was accused of "trading in genius." Surely, replied Salacrou, this is better than trading in mediocrity? Were his subjects too big? But the French theatre needs big subjects. We have the right to demand that dramatists should be something more than entertainers satisfied with little successes played by little women in little theatres.

These words of Salacrou's have a brave ring, but generally speaking the greatness of a play is determined more by the mind of its creator than by the nature of its subject. If it is possible to see all heaven in a grain of sand, there are also authors who can write inconsiderably about Armageddon or the soul. *Une Femme libre*, however, showed that Salacrou was not one of them.

The first act was enormously praised. Its scene is a well-to-do house in the country, the characters a lively, attractive, irresponsible young man called Jacques, his mother Célestine, and his aunt Adrienne, a tyrannical and disappointed old woman. They are awaiting the return from Paris of Jacques's brother, Paul, a sombre, serious man who has established a flourishing publicity business. Paul, to every one's astonishment, brings with him a

young girl, Lucie Blondel, whom he clumsily announces
is his fiancée. Both Jacques and Adrienne see at once
that, with her gaiety and lightness of heart, she will not
fit into the grave, bourgeois life of the Miremont household. Adrienne is resentful, Jacques sympathetic, and the
act culminates in an impressive emotional scene in which
Jacques, in the gathering darkness, persuades her to run
away. Colette thought that the means by which Lucie
and Jacques were left alone were rather awkward, but,
like the rest of the audience at the first performance, she
surrendered entirely to the power and authority of the
scene, of which this is the climax:

JACQUES. Who are you?

LUCIE. A woman like others.

JACQUES. No. Where have you lived? Where do you come
from?

LUCIE. I come from my twenty years. Do you understand?
That is the country and family I leave behind me; my
twenty years. . . . You have to live from day to day. If
only I could cling to my young girl's life, and stop this
slipping into the unknown. One day I shall have to finish
with it, one day I shall have to say yes to a man.

JACQUES. Well, at least you are brave.

LUCIE. No, I'm not.

JACQUES. But you are. You accept, knowing what you are
doing. Here no one is deceived. You are warned on the
doorstep. Look round at all these bits and pieces. Here
is the best chair. I've seen my grandfather sitting in it.
When your sons return from military service, they will sit
in it, too.

LUCIE. My sons, soldiers?

JACQUES. You will see, in a family, how quickly the generations merge into each other, and in what way they join
in marriages, christenings, and funerals. Look at these
portraits, and the family records. Aunt Adrienne as a
baby, and Mother's wedding. Look, Aunt Adrienne at the
same age as you, and an empty place for a picture of you
in your communion-dress. You never thought that here
the picture of you at ten years old would age and grow

yellow, and that here you will hang with a little blouse
and then with your hair turned white. As for the cemetery, it is just outside, and we have a family vault.
LUCIE [*frightened and sobbing*]. Oh!
JACQUES. It is only at this moment that despair makes you sob
in front of these poor things that aren't yet there. I can
see things that others at my age perhaps can't. That
every one who is fifty was once twenty, and that we don't
believe it. And one day we shall be like them, if we live
like them. That is what I call family life. It is life in the
middle of failures and of the dead.   [*The night is falling.*
LUCIE. Put on the light, put on the light, or I shall cry. I am
afraid.   [*He puts on the light.* LUCIE *is absolutely terrified.*

This scene was one of the biggest successes in the play.
It made Colette, who never, as a dramatic critic, allowed
the Parisian managements to forget that their uncomfortable seats stretched her neck and made her thighs
ache, overlook her physical discomforts in her enthusiasm when Jacques and Lucie ran away together, and
the second act was almost equally praised. It shows
Jacques and Lucie established in a studio in Montparnasse, with Lucie more skilled in throwing off the
attentions of Jacques's friends than Jacques in recon-
ciling the claims on his time of the newspaper he works
for and the woman he is in love with. Jacques is visited
by his brother Paul, ready for the sake of propriety to forgive everything if Jacques and Lucie marry. At the end
of this scene, says Colette, Jacques Dumesnil, who played
Paul, was loudly and justly applauded.

It was at this point that the complaints of the critics
began. Jacques, on the eve of being sent for a fortnight
to Poland, asks Lucie to marry him. She is deeply,
wildly in love, but she refuses. This refusal, to Serge
Radine, seems incredible. The character of Lucie, he says,
is badly drawn. Salacrou asks us to believe that she is a
woman so resolved to lead her own independent life that
she twice rejects marriage as an unacceptable limitation

on her freedom. Such a woman should be another Nora,
a creature of vast reserves of character: Lucie is too weak
for the crusading rôle that Salacrou casts her for.

This criticism is based on a misunderstanding. *Une
Femme libre* is not the story of a feminist pioneer: Lucie is
not intended to be a leader of womanly revolt. She does
not resist marriage, like some of Hardy's heroines,
because it trammels her liberty. She refuses marriage
rather from weakness than strength. We have already
seen that it was in terror she ran away from her first
fiancé; and her rejection of Jacques is due more to futile
resentment that he is acting on his brother's suggestion
than to any determined assertion of feminine independence.

Colette's impatience with Lucie's talk of freedom to
live her own life is based on the same misreading of the
play as Radine's, but her objection to the third act is
more difficult to meet. The timid girl who, in floods of
tears, leaves Jacques at the end of the second act reappears
at the beginning of the next as a world-famous fashion
designer piloting her own aeroplane. Colette found this
difficult to accept, particularly as Lucie's striking clothes,
all black velvet and diamonds, seemed too heavy for the
girlish grace of the actress playing her, Alice Cocéa. At
this point there is a sharp break in the verisimilitude of
the play, and Salacrou himself seems to have been
conscious of it. His explanation that it is due to the
exigencies of production demanding the fusion of two
acts, a third and a fourth, into one, is, in fact, an admission of the justice of Colette's criticism.

This criticism is less damaging to Salacrou, however,
than it would be to an English dramatist. The English
school of playwriting respects consistency of plot. If
it could be shown of any play of Rattigan's or Gals-
worthy's, for example, that it contained an obvious im-
probability, that play would be seriously faulted. But
this, as we have seen, is not Salacrou's kind of drama.

His conception of the theatre is not of a place that introduces us to logically developed sequences of action, or to convincingly drawn and consistent characters. To him the function of the theatre is to reflect the moods of the author's soul, and both characters and incidents are only accessories to this end. The meaning of *Une Femme libre* does not lie in the portrayal of Lucie, nor in her desire to live her own life, nor yet in the metamorphosis that changes her into a rich and flaunting woman of the world. It is to be found rather in the mood in which Salacrou contemplates this character and these developments. *Une Femme libre* was the most complete play Salacrou had yet written: it represented more than any of its predecessors the fundamental man. From it emerged his characteristic outlook upon life, his desire to believe in the old philosophies, and his inability to do so. In the second act of this play, Salacrou for the first time struck firmly and resonantly the note that has sounded through all his subsequent work. Lucie jealously suspects that some woman has visited Jacques in their apartment.

LUCIE. You have had an idiotic flirtation. Some woman has been here.

JACQUES. Do you think that I would let a woman come here?

LUCIE. Why?

JACQUES. Here? At home? Another woman?

LUCIE. You know perfectly well that you are free.

JACQUES. And would you have a lover here?

LUCIE. Why not?

JACQUES. Why do we go on playing this farce . . . this farce of the strong woman and the man without prejudices? We've got to get rid of prejudices, that's right enough. But listen. These prejudices are the litter of profound truths that have been demolished and not replaced. They are bits of wood drifting on the sea after a shipwreck, and to-day not another boat is in sight. We have been brave enough to want to be free, yes, but in our present state, are we free to be free?

Are we free to be free? There is nothing in Salacrou's soul that can confidently answer yes.

He is not a dramatist who uses the theatre to offer a philosophy. He does not write plays in order to prove that God exists, or that God does not exist, nor even that men would be happier if they believed in His existence. But his own mind is coloured by the need for, and the want of, faith. This is what gives it its peculiar and individual quality; this is its poignant, regretful, poetic nature. And it is in so far as they reflect this that his plays succeed. After *Une Femme libre* his next work was *L'Inconnue d'Arras*, and it was very successful indeed.

The objection to Lucie Blondel's transformation from a timid girl into a suave and influential woman of the world was that it broke the realistic pattern of the play, and introduced an incident in which one could not believe. Salacrou's answer to this was to write *L'Inconnue d'Arras*, the whole of which is made credible by the fact that none of the incidents can be believed on that plane of realism on which Colette judged *Une Femme libre*. Even the revolver-shot and suicide against the background of a woman singing *Parlez-moi d'amour*, with which the play sensationally opens, were not treated realistically. For who is this servant who rushes in, and screams at his mistress bending over her husband's body, "My master has killed himself because his wife was wicked . . . selfish . . . frivolous . . . lazy . . . and a liar"? Even to-day butlers do not behave like that. Nicolas is as much a master of ceremonies at some celestial judgment-seat as a domestic in a well-to-do bourgeois household.

In other words, *L'Inconnue d'Arras* is written in that inconsecutive, Apocalyptic, Expressionistic style in which Priestley composed *Johnson over Jordan*, and Guthrie *Top of the Ladder*. It is a style that in general I find tiresome, tiring, and pretentious; arbitrarily overthrowing the integrity of time and space, it usually results in a jumble of small scenes, each of which individually is too brief to build up much of an effect; and instinctively I sympathize with the critic who wistfully wondered why some authors try so hard to be original when it would be simple to write good things by following the old rules, forgetting for the moment how often following the old rules has resulted in plays so abominably dull that those who have seen them wake up in the middle of the night for years afterwards and feel like screaming with boredom.

The narrative line of a realistic play imposes some sort of rough unity on even the most amateurishly used material, but the especial danger of Expressionism is confusion. Because the easily apprehended logical connexion between scenes is dispensed with in an Expressionistic play, these scenes have to be bound together with particularly strong emotional bonds. In such a play the author allows himself to bring in apparently anything and everything, introducing characters who are long since dead or even who are not yet born, and transposing incidents so that causes follow effects, and the order of the entire universe is disarranged. In *L'Inconnue d'Arras*, for example, M. Salacrou brings in Maxime, the hero's friend and his wife's lover, at the ages of thirty-seven and of twenty; and these two incarnations of the same man, played by different actors, meet and talk to each other, holding some of the most important conversations in the play. Further, the hero's father and grandfather appear: but because the grandfather was killed in the Franco-Prussian War early in life, and the father lived to a ripe age, the father is grave and white-bearded, and the grandfather has the fresh face of a youth. Further still, Salacrou accepts the assumption that a man dying by some sort of violence sees in an instant of time, in this case in the infinitesimal moment between the pulling of the trigger and the lodging of the bullet in the brain, the whole of his past life, the entire circle of his friends and acquaintances, and hears everything that he has said, or that has been said to him since the day he was born. Proceeding from this, he actually asks the producer to show the audience a procession of all the words that Ulysses has spoken in his thirty-five years' existence, finishing with the last he uttered on earth, "Where," addressed to his wife. He even requires a couple of these words, "Thank you," to separate themselves from the rest, and to turn round, and look back at Ulysses. And this is not all. For the first procession is succeeded by a second, that of all the words that Ulysses had ever heard spoken to him. No wonder that Ulysses' wife, Yolande, exclaims she had no idea a man's death was so lively an affair.

Now, if a dramatist adopts a convention of writing which lets him make parents half a century younger than their children, subdivide his characters by psychic surgery, and solidify sound by a chemical process not yet discovered, it would seem that anything is permitted to him. But if the dramatist truly takes this view, if he puts into his play, helter-skelter, hugger-mugger, whatever pops into his head, all he will produce is a shapeless, unmeaning, theatrical Lancashire hot-pot.

An Expressionistic play, like any other, is under the æsthetic necessity of creating unity of effect. Every part of it must contribute to the final emotional impression the author wishes to produce, or it will turn out to be an affair of spreadeagled dramatic incompetence. It is because the connexion between the separate incidents and the total impression is less direct than in a realistic play, less controlled by obvious laws of logic, time, and place, that a good Expressionistic play is hard to write. But if the play is not controlled by other, no less imperious laws, it will be a failure. A failure, of course, it usually is. Expressionistic writing has not given much of value to the theatre. The more reason, therefore, for welcoming *L'Inconnue d'Arras*.

The play begins, as I have said, with the suicide of Ulysses, who no longer wishes to live when he finds in his wife's pocket a love-letter to his friend Maxime. The stage then becomes peopled with the men and women who, out of his memory, file before his dimming eyes. Those still alive are as they were when Ulysses knew them, or at their moment of greatest happiness: the dead appear as they were at the time of their dying. All of them, living or dead, mingle with each other, talk, laugh, and cry together. There is a rush of memories: a red-plush arm-chair, with a splash of green ink on the left arm: Ulysses as a little boy burying his pet cat, or answering the call of nature: Ulysses as a young man during the First World War putting his cloak over an unknown shivering girl in the ruins of Arras: and in his maturer years with his mistresses, both those whom he loved and those who only loved him: always ill at ease, unhappy, searching for something that would make life worth while, and coming near to it only in his solitary unselfish action to the woman of Arras, whose name even he never knew. And through these shifting, troubled memories the dying man, in the splinter of a second left to him, which Salacrou stretches over three whole acts, finds time to return again and again to the rankling, tormenting agonizing question of his wife's infidelity.

Already in *Patchouli* Salacrou has hinted at his extraordinarily vivid horror of female unfaithfulness. (Unfaithfulness in men he appears to take more calmly.) Here he explains his repugnance to it on purely physical grounds. Yolande has uttered her surprise that so much should happen round what is in effect a death-bed, and Nicolas replies, "Why do you expect a man's death to be quieter than his life? Both are different aspects of the same misery."

Then follows a scene which strikingly illustrates, in recoil, the fierceness of Salacrou's Puritanism.

YOLANDE. Misery?
NICOLAS. When a man like him meets a woman like you!
YOLANDE. Listen, Ulysses! I admit, I am guilty. I wish I

could say I wasn't, because I love you, and you are in pain, but how can I deny it? You know I am guilty. . . . I have been weak, imprudent, foolish. But is it a crime? Who knows whether you have never deceived me?

ULYSSES. Yes, I have deceived you.

YOLANDE [*astounded*]. What do you say?

ULYSSES. Oh, this wretched life of mine has been complicated enough!

YOLANDE [*angrily*]. You have deceived me?

ULYSSES [*simply*]. You didn't know?

YOLANDE. And you have the nerve to . . . [*To* NICOLAS] You knew it, of course, all the time?

NICOLAS. Don't play this scene now. Keep to the chronological order. Begin at the beginning.

ULYSSES. Perhaps, Yolande, it is the memory I have kept of these trivial adventures that has killed me.

NICOLAS. What is going to kill you, sir, is the shot from the revolver.

ULYSSES. I stored up in my mind exact memories of all these women.

YOLANDE. All these women? How very charming!

ULYSSES. Memories without love, in which these women appeared in ridiculous positions.

YOLANDE. Oh, I beg, no details, please!

ULYSSES. And I couldn't bear that another man should carry in his head and body a memory so humiliating of a woman who belonged to me.

YOLANDE. Nicolas, leave us!

ULYSSES. In his rooms you took off your dress—while he was looking at you, and he saw your skin, rather cold and pale, show above your stocking.

YOLANDE. Are you mad? Don't lift up my dress in front of Nicolas.

NICOLAS. Don't be so modest. Soon God will see you naked—and with disgust.

ULYSSES. And you took off everything, and he stretched himself on you, heavily.

YOLANDE. Be quiet!

ULYSSES. He was your first lover?

YOLANDE. Yes, I swear he was.

ULYSSES. There you were, with your legs apart, beneath him.
YOLANDE. For pity's sake, calm yourself.
ULYSSES. Calm myself? Does a calm man take a revolver and
shoot himself? And what absurd endearments did your
lips breathe over him? Calm myself? How can you say
such things with a mouth that has slobbered over another man's flesh? . . . I ought to have cut off your lips
before I killed myself.

This intense and bitter anger at the breach of the
marriage vow is not, in *L'Inconnue d'Arras*, specifically
linked to that sense of separation from God which Salacrou thinks is a capital mark of the present age. The connexion in this play between the two is below the surface.
It is only in a subsequent work, *Histoire de rire*, that it is
brought into the forefront, and emphasized and under-
scored.

L'Inconnue d'Arras, produced by Lugné Poë at the
Comédie des Champs-Élysées in November 1935, ran for
more than a hundred performances. It sharply divided
opinion. People either liked it enormously, or could not
stand it at all. One evening Salacrou, on his way backstage, passed through the long and spacious room in
which the bar is installed. It is a very different bar from
those fetid little overcrowded horrors which I sometimes catch sight of on my way to my seat in a London
theatre. It is wide and clean and civilized. At one end
is a table bearing the latest books on the drama. The
barman is white-coated, attentive, and courteous even to
those who are not customers. Outside the windows are
some noble trees. Here, in this delightful and healthy
room, Salacrou during one performance saw an agitated
man walking hurriedly up and down. The barman
explained to him: "This gentleman came to the theatre
with his wife. After the first act he was furious, and
wanted to go. But his wife was enjoying herself, and
wouldn't. Rather than see the rest of the play, he prefers
to stay in the bar. You can see he really means what he

says, because he isn't even drinking." Salacrou thought
of this man throughout the third act. His wife apparently
was enthusiastic, but he would not return into the auditorium. When the play finished he had already recovered
his overcoat from the cloak-room, and his wife's mantle
was on his arm.

The critics also differed from each other. Robert
Kemp, in *La Liberté*, thought that *L'Inconnue d'Arras*
belonged to a dying tradition. "It is," he wrote, "a
survival. It is the result of one of the drama's little ill-
nesses." On the other hand, Edmond Sée said that if it
had come from a foreign country, it would be hailed as a
work of genius.

One can see why the play was criticized. An Englishman, brought up in the English tradition of the drama,
can hardly accept as satisfactory in themselves the characters of Ulysses and Yolande. There is no indication why
so many women found Ulysses so attractive; there is no
indication why anyone at all should have wished to marry
Yolande, who is cold, selfish, frivolous, and stupid.
Salacrou would reject this criticism of his play as Gris
rejected the criticism that he painted triangular apples.
The apples are to be looked at, not in themselves, as
individual edible fruit, but in relation to the scheme of
the entire canvas. They form part of a pattern. So do
Ulysses and Yolande, and it is in relation to this pattern
that Salacrou would ask for them to be judged, not as
independent beings with lives that began before the curtain went up, and will continue, at any rate with Yolande,
after it has come down.

Whatever the theoretic objections to Salacrou's Expressionistic method of drawing his pattern, it gave him
certain dramatic advantages he could not have derived
from realism. No realistic technique would have permitted him the sharp juxtaposition of Maxime at twenty
with what he was at thirty-seven, or have allowed him so
vivid a presentation of the disillusioned and arrogant

scorn of idealistic youth for what idealism too often becomes. Realism could not have shown the fear that may interpose itself between the firing of the bullet and its reaching its mark: that is possible only in Salacrou's elongation of time. His Expressionism in *L'Inconnue d'Arras* is handled with mastery, the only scene not entirely justifying itself in its contribution to the total impression being a brief episode between Ulysses and a beggar. In short, the play has passion, anguish, humour, poetry, and one tremendous burst of rhetoric which was immediately recognized as, until that time, Salacrou's finest piece of sustained prose. It is an invocation to Ulysses's ancestors to help him at the moment of death, and is worth contrasting with the brief, factual, unimaginative speeches with which English plays of the same period, like Dodie Smith's *Service* and Priestley's *Eden End*, nevertheless managed to release their considerable emotional potentialities.

ULYSSES. Who can make me forget this love-letter that has left that spot of ink on your finger?

YOLANDE. A letter for your best friend. You will not be able to bear it, proud as you are.

YETTE. Perhaps he will not be able to bear it because he has loved you.

MADELEINE. Be careful, Ulysses, she wants to make you suffer, to be alone in your suffering, to drive us all away.

ULYSSES. All the same, she is right. I have been terribly proud—with the sort of pride, I must admit, grandfather, that has sometimes led me to despise you.

THE GRANDFATHER [*astonished*]. What do you say?

ULYSSES. Forgive me. First of all you were a picture in my mind, the young hero of Gravelotte, that I was proud of during the history lessons at school. Then you became a tormenting question——

YOLANDE. Ulysses, you are not going to forget me——

ULYSSES. Do not interrupt so much, wife of my thoughts. My friends, with you, I do not, alas, escape from myself, and if sometimes you seem rather absurd, that is because

I am enough in love to make fun of myself. But the moment that I leave you, I shall perhaps find, on the other shore and beyond all tears and breathing, the real truth about those who have during many ages loved each other so that one day a child might be born and grow up and become Ulysses. Where are you, my grandparents and the parents of my grandparents, who, in every generation, four by four, stretch out in order to surround me with a whole horizon of ancestors? What kind of people have they been, what thoughts have they thought, these two people who every twenty years, at each renewal of the generations, since Adam and Eve, have brought into the world a little girl that a little boy was waiting for, so that one day might be born this last and final child? How I long to question them, in order to discover, somewhere in this sad procession, the shape of a finger in some hand, in some face an obvious resemblance, in the anger of an old chief the memory of one of my childish rages, and in the terror of a violated peasant, this jealousy . . . which is strangling me. . . .

YOLANDE. Ulysses!

ULYSSES. Ah, all the fathers and mothers of my life, all you who have been twenty years old, every twenty years, during the centuries, who spoke languages I do not understand, who all, without doubt, knew every sorrow and every joy, receive me on this last day, and help me, as I enter into the ground, leaving no one behind me.

In 1939, when Armand Salacrou wrote *Histoire de rire*, he was still preoccupied with the same question of unfaithfulness to the marriage vow that precipitated the tragedy of *L'Inconnue d'Arras*. Adé, the heroine of *Histoire de rire*, betrays her husband, Gérard, as Yolande betrayed Ulysses. Adé is younger than Yolande, more frivolous, more mischievous, less responsible, warmer and more impulsive, and far less unattractive. She also had greater provocation than Yolande, though Gérard was not unfaithful to her. Since their marriage he had not looked at another woman, but he prided himself on not letting Adé guess this. So is masculine authority maintained in the home.

Gérard piled upon Adé a heap of petty irritations. He was careful about money. He treated her as an engaging but often tiresome child. This Adé resented. She resented also being called Adé. She flared up about it on the very night that she left Gérard, the unsuspecting and fatally self-satisfied Gérard. "Adé, your little Adé. Always Adé. I am not, I don't want any more to be, little Adé. Don't forget my name is Adélaide."

But more annoying than Gérard's choice of diminutives was his habit of completely cutting his wife out of his life for an hour between six and seven every evening. The office closed, the day's work done, this young man would retire with his friend Jean-Louis Deshayes to a playroom at the top of the house, where Gérard had lodged all the lumber of his bachelor days. There they would forget the cares of business in a game of Russian billiards, or in recalling the pleasures of their boyhood.

A generation versed in psychiatry would suspect the nature of the friendship between Gérard and Jean-Louis, as such a generation has been conditioned into suspecting the foundation of friendship between women, or the most ordinary manifestations of family affection. Adé, however, being no psychiatrist, had no suspicions of this sort, and so was spared a good deal of ill-directed anxiety. Nevertheless, she was angered by the playroom. She resented being kept out of it; and when, at the beginning of the play, she with trepidation took her lover into it, his somewhat alarmed caresses (Achille Bellorson was a timid young man) seemed the more piquant for being enjoyed on forbidden ground.

This is a titillating and amusing scene. It starts the play off with a Coward glitter. The glitter remains to the end, and Salacrou was even a little afraid of it. By the time *Histoire de rire* was ready for production, the War of 1939–45 had begun, and Salacrou wondered whether the

play would not seem out of tune with the seriousness of
the times. Might it not appear to be just a gay farce
about adultery? He was reassured, however, by the
Genevan critic Lucien Dubech, who read the manuscript, and saw that there were other levels in it besides
its surface frivolity. *Histoire de rire* was presented at the
Théâtre de la Madeleine in December 1939, with Alice
Cocéa as Adé, André Luguet as Gérard, and Fernand
Gravey as Jean-Louis. It attained and retained great
popularity until the fall of France carried away, temporarily, the prosperity of the Parisian theatres. Had not
the theatrical life of London at this time been dislocated
it is probable that *Histoire de rire* would have been seen in
England. Noël Coward spoke of translating it, and
Henry Sherek considered its production.

It is regrettable that these projects came to nothing, for
Histoire de rire is an extremely amusing comedy, and a
satisfactory refutation of the depressing theory that a
serious play must necessarily be solemn. There is
nothing portentous about it. Its characters are people of
wealth and wit. Its settings are a comfortable house in
Paris, and a suite in a luxury hotel on the Côte d'Azur.
There are seven people in the play, and five are under
thirty. Only one of them is described as an old man: he
turns out to be forty-six. The sun shines. The young
people wear bathing-dresses. They are in love. The
dialogue is gay.

Nevertheless, *Histoire de rire*, though its subject is
adultery, and its form farcical, is certainly not just
another farce about adultery. It might seem so in the
first act, with its artificial heightening of the piquancy of
Adé's behaviour, and Gérard's response when Jean-
Louis tells him that he has a mistress, Hélène, who is intending to run away from her husband, Jules Donaldo.
"Why not?" exclaims Gérard. He shows no moral uneasiness. "A woman," he says, "who no longer loves her
husband not only has the right, she positively ought, to

leave her husband in order to be with the man she really loves."

Adé, who has been turning some such thoughts over in her own head, is not quite so undisturbed, and Gérard gaily reassures her. "Don't you remember," he asks,

> how often in the evenings we have said to each other "One day Jean-Louis will marry. What sort of a woman will she be?" You know Hélène Donaldo by reputation as well as I do. Aren't you happy, first for Jean-Louis's good luck, and then that it is this ravishing Hélène Donaldo that he has chosen for his wife?
>
> ADÉ [*to* JEAN-LOUIS]. Mme Donaldo is your mistress?
>
> GÉRARD. Call her Hélène. It isn't necessary to add a commentary.
>
> ADÉ. Hélène Donaldo is abandoning her husband to-night for you!
>
> GÉRARD. "Abandoning her husband." You dramatize everything. To-night Hélène, instead of returning to her husband's, will return to Jean-Louis's. That's all.
>
> ADÉ. That's all!
>
> GÉRARD. That's all! And afterwards the lawyers will arrange everything.

So far adultery is treated as merely a jest. As a matter of principle, Gérard has not the least objection to it in the world. Nor has Jean-Louis, nor Hélène, nor Adé. Adé's apparent hesitations and misgivings are due entirely to her desire to get her unsuspecting husband to commit himself so deeply that he will be left with no rational objection to her own behaviour. That does not prevent Gérard, of course, when he later discovers Adé's unfaithfulness, from flying into the grimmest and gloomiest rages. He goes to the South of France with Jean-Louis and his mistress, and mopes and pines on the sunny terrace of their hotel. They try to distract his attention with a pretty girl, and fail; they cannot entice him into bathing; he will not accompany them to their favourite restaurants. He is thoroughly miserable. But Salacrou has no sympathy with him. He might not go so far as to say that Gérard has got what he deserves, but decidedly he has got what modern philosophy, or the lack of it, sooner or later makes inevitable.

This is the feeling that unites *Une Femme libre*, *L'Inconnue d'Arras*, and *Histoire de rire*. In the first play Jacques is uneasily aware that the convictions and certainties of the past have been destroyed, and that nothing has taken their place. In the second Salacrou presents the effects of this emancipation. In *L'Inconnue d'Arras*, however, he does not relate these effects to what he, in the light of his general philosophy, considers to be their causes. It is in *Histoire de rire* that this connexion is drawn.

While his friends are vainly attempting to solace him, Gérard impatiently exclaims that they have understood nothing. There is only one thing that could comfort him for the loss of Adé, and that is the sight of a woman who is loyal, a woman who can refuse. "But," he cries bitterly, "are there any faithful women left?" This is the moment at which Gérard uncovers himself to attack. For the entire point of the second, and crucial, act of *Histoire de rire* lies in the response the author himself implicitly makes—why should there be?

Shortly afterwards there follows a scene that is the most vital in the play. Hélène's middle-aged husband has come after her, and calls on Gérard in his hotel. Jules Donaldo says:

> May I sit down? Thank you. So you see Hélène every day, sir? [GÉRARD *gasps*.
> JULES. An adorable woman, isn't she?
> GÉRARD. Has Adé decided to come back to me?
> JULES. But wives always come back, my dear fellow. How young you are! A piece of advice: when she returns, give her children. Women would have fewer lovers if they had more children. I tell you this because I find you rather sympathetic. Tell me, is Hélène happy?
> GÉRARD. I don't know.

JULES. And your friend? I'm told he is a handsome young chap?

GÉRARD. Your wife's escapade doesn't seem to upset you? You find her behaviour almost normal?

JULES. Normal? I am twenty years older than my wife. Is that normal? If I were a romantic poet or a great explorer ... things might be all right, but I am a contractor.

GÉRARD. And because you are a contractor, you accept these lies, these betrayals?

JULES. You are using old-fashioned words to judge a new situation. These are precisely the mistakes that at a board meeting brings a business undertaking into bankruptcy. You talk of betrayal. You can't betray what doesn't exist any more. It was only in days gone by that people married to found a family, that they took their wives for eternity. To-day, my dear fellow, our wives are no longer religious. And whose fault is it? Do we go to Mass? No. Well, then? The only scrap of morality left to them is 'love.' And it is the least certain word, the worst defined, the vaguest in our vocabulary. At different times, and often the same day, we use it in contradictory senses. Have you tried to explain to your wife why she should love you for always, and only you, and no one else, and by what right?

GÉRARD. But——

JULES. Only because you find it pleasant? You cannot found a philosophy of life on an egotism as narrow as that.

Here I am perhaps in danger of making Salacrou appear a more didactic writer than he is. It is no part of his purpose to urge men and women to return to the Christian faith. It is a faith that he cannot himself believe in. But he perceives in the world around him certain consequences of the abandonment of faith, and they produce in his mind a wistful and poetic, and at times agonized, regret for the stay and comfort that are now beyond his reach. This is the state of mind which he projects into the theatre in nearly all his plays, though sometimes he reflects it in a tragic and sometimes in a comic mirror.

To this statement there is, in Salacrou's work, one out-standing exception. During the War Salacrou wrote little for the theatre. First he exiled himself to Lyons, and then came back and lived in solitude in the heart of Paris. During this time the theatre occupied much of his thought, and he wrote several valuable items of auto-biography which he added as postscripts to the plays to which they referred. But he. produced no new dramas until after the Liberation of Paris. Then he became like a man new inspired. I do not mean a man new inspired in his work, but rather in his life. The return of freedom to France was like a new dawn, and it was bliss to be alive. Salacrou looked upon his fellow-creatures, not, as hitherto, as feeble people wandering through a confused maze without a guide, but as gods walking. There rose in him the exhilarating thought that man might be able to gain salvation through his own efforts alone. Man has banished God from the universe. Salacrou ceased, about the middle of the nineteen-forties, to regret this fact. Perhaps, after all—so the hope leapt in him—God may be unnecessary.

In this mood of exalted humanism he wrote *Les Nuits de la colère*. *Les Nuits de la colère* is, I believe, the only one of Salacrou's plays that has been translated into English or seen in this country. Roger Livesey appeared in a television production here, and M. Barrault included the play in his memorable St James's season. It is a surrealist tragedy of the Resistance, set in Chartres, under the shadow of the great cathedral. The living and the dead meet in it, and talk, the absent and present commingle, time moves backward and forward and one place merges into another, but throughout the essential unity of the piece remains, a unity founded in the betrayal of a brave and compassionate Resistance saboteur by a weak, well-meaning friend whose only fault was that he found him-self unequal to the heroic demands of the age. This friend was played by Jean Desailly with bewildered, heart-rending perplexity, while Barrault, as the deceived and blinded saboteur, gave one of the finest and most unusual performances of his life, a performance of un-expected serenity, that showed a man with the smoke of conflict behind him, knowing only the peace of a task well discharged, and of duty done. One of the most moving moments of the St James's season—a moment to which I have already referred—was the conclusion of *Les Nuits de la colère*, when Barrault stepped forward to the front of the stage and spoke the last words of the play, in which, with restrained and simple nobility, M. Salacrou affirmed his new faith in mankind: "And you who will survive us for a few years, tell your children growing up around you, that they must never despair of life, since, in the confusion of these times, we have been able to live honourably." Before the final word—*honorablement*—M. Barrault paused slightly, and then spoke it so that it seemed to linger in the air and to pro-long itself in our memories like a note of music.

Les Nuits de la colère was presented by M. Barrault at the Marigny Theatre in December 1946, and its recep-tion was more than friendly. Jean-Jacques Gautier, of *Le Figaro*, greeted it as the first play of the Resistance to have "style, the first to be written by an author who thinks and creates theatre." This was the opening sen-tence of M. Gautier's notice, and it was particularly pointed in that Sartre's *Morts sans sépulture* (the one-act play about torture under the Gestapo which was seen at the Lyric, Hammersmith, in 1947, under the title of *Men without Shadows*) had been produced a few weeks pre-viously. Francis Ambrière, in *Opéra*, specifically com-pared *Morts sans sépulture* with *Les Nuits de la colère*, and brought Gautier's veiled comparison out into the open by plainly declaring that Salacrou had succeeded where Sartre had run aground.

We have seen that Salacrou had misgivings about *Histoire de rire*, fearing that its superficial gaiety might cause it to be misunderstood. Exceedingly interested in, but diffident about, his own work, *Les Nuits de la colère* also made him uneasy. The continuing classical tradition of the French theatre, and the repute and policy of the Comédie-Française, still gives to the words of Racine immense influence, and, in the preface to *Bajazet*, Racine had written: "I would not advise an author to take for a subject a story as modern as this, if it had taken place in the country where he wished his play to be performed, nor to put characters upon the stage whom the greater part of the audience have known." This rule does not, of course, prevent the French stage from dealing with contemporary problems. On the contrary, the Paris theatre is far more closely involved in present-day social and political discussions than either the London or the New York. What it does result in is that these problems are set against a background of ancient myth, as in *Les Mouches* and *Antigone*, or, as in *Les Mains sales*, they are situated in some Ruritanian invented country. This is not the English fashion. Our Ruritanian stories are purely tales of adventure, and we eschew the classical altogether. When Mr Rattigan wishes to discuss personal freedom he does not hesitate to put on the stage, in *The Winslow Boy*, a well-known incident of modern public life in the very city where his play was presented. When a Frenchman, like M. Pol Quentin, has a similar desire, he creates, in *La Liberté est un dimanche* (in which Edwige Feuillère gave a performance like the advancing tide of a tropic sea, irresistible and warm), an imaginary police state on an imaginary island in an imaginary ocean. In either case, the result is admirable, since it is in conformity with the national taste.

The scene of *Les Nuits de la colère* was a city within an hour and a half's drive of Paris, its period was barely two and half years before the actual date of production, and its characters had parallels within the experience of every one in Paris. It was in flat contradiction to the rule

laid down by Racine, or, rather, to the rule in which
Racine summed up the dramatic experience of the ages.
Nevertheless, it succeeded, but, in some opinions, at a
price. "The people and the conflict that M. Salacrou
puts into his play," wrote M. Ambrière,

> have that quality of *présence* which is the mark of the born
> dramatist. But the price paid is this, that the characters
> withdraw behind the conflict and the rival ideologies which
> confront them. Certainly, Jean and his friends, who,
> through love of liberty and the desire to cut an honourable
> figure before their children, throw themselves into the
> magnificent adventure of the Resistance; Bernard, whom the
> bourgeois wish for tranquillity and anxiety for his family
> urge towards base submission and the moral complicity
> which it entails; Pisançon, a thief who has turned inevitably
> into a collaborator; Pierrette, who wishes at all cost to be
> happy; and the sad and courageous Louise, who will count
> as one of the most moving characters created by M. Sala-
> crou—these are true and living people. But their truth as
> individuals is never the main thing about them: it is their
> value as symbols that dominates our attention. Thus we
> are invited less to a play than to a debate between opposite
> ideas and natures, but the outstanding merit of M. Salacrou
> is that he has so conceived his work that he neven turns to
> mere philosophical demonstration. . . . These characters
> remain people of flesh and blood.

I fancy that M. Salacrou would consider this paragraph,
in which M. Ambrière intended to introduce a few reservations of praise, as among the highest compliments he
has received. For it is a plain admission that, in *Les Nuits
de la colère*, he achieved his ideal of the drama, which
involves the characters being created for the play, and
not the play for the characters.

Les Nuits de la colère showed a fine sympathy for human
nature, and confidence in it; and, in the excitement and
exhilaration of the Liberation, an expectation of the
future happiness of the whole race. Salacrou in this play
forgot that men no longer believe in God; forgot they

have no religion to sustain them; he forgot the depression and misgiving which these realizations entail. Despite its tragedy, *Les Nuits de la colère* is his first and, so far, his only optimistic play.

It is based on an admiration of men sufficiently strong to suggest that they can achieve salvation through their own efforts alone. Salacrou's next play was *L'Archipel Lenoir*, produced by Charles Dullin at the Théâtre Montparnasse in November 1947. The admiration so evident in *Les Nuits de la colère* has now entirely vanished. *L'Archipel Lenoir* is a conversation-piece in which all the characters give themselves away each time they open their mouths. The Lenoirs manufacture a famous wine, and are extremely rich; unfortunately, the head of the family, Paul-Albert Lenoir, an old man of seventy-three, has assaulted a young peasant girl. Prosecution, imprisonment, and ruin threaten the family. Lenoir's children, grandchildren, nephews, nieces, and relatives by marriage are called together to discuss what can be done to avoid exposure and disgrace. The ensuing conclave is hysterical, passionate, cynical, exceedingly funny, and not at all complimentary to human nature. Out of it there results only one practical proposal, whose macabre nature indicates the sharp descent into pessimism that Salacrou's spirits were now taking. One of Lenoir's relatives by marriage is a Rumanian prince, and it is he who sees a way out of the difficulty.

THE PRINCE. To sum up: the trial is inevitable, and you wish to avoid it?

THE GRANDFATHER. Yes.

THE PRINCE. Then, the solution is simple.

THE GRANDFATHER. Simple?

THE PRINCE. It avoids the trial and M. Lenoir can be saved from prison.

THE GRANDFATHER. You are magnificent. [*To the others*] Bobo is magnificent.

VICTOR. What is your solution?

THE PRINCE [*icily*]. The death of M. Paul-Albert Lenoir.
THE PRINCESS [*in a silence*]. Bobo!
THE GRANDFATHER [*tries to laugh, then, shouting*]. Valentine!
Valentine!
THE PRINCE. No, Monsieur Lenoir, you are not in a nightmare. Unless you think that life, the whole of our existence, the passage of man over the earth, is a nightmare.
If you do, then we are all in a nightmare from the first
moment we understand we are alive. Do you remember,
Monsieur Lenoir, the exact moment when, a little boy,
this thought struck you: I am a living being, I could have
not existed, and I am going to die. No? But I do. I
nearly fainted. It was an intolerable weight to be borne
by the shoulders of a little boy.

Despite its sombre theme—the thought of death hangs
over its most farcical episodes—*L'Archipel Lenoir* is a
wildly diverting play, and an agile counsel could argue
that it does not necessarily take a poor view of humanity, a view inconsistent with that in *Les Nuits de la colère*.
Certainly no salvation is to be expected from these
degenerate, selfish, incompetent bourgeois. But the
bourgeoisie does not extend over all humanity. May
there not be hope beyond its limits?

Dieu le savait, which was presented at the Théâtre
Saint-Georges, on December 2, 1950, answers no. This
play, whose scene is among the ruins of Le Havre in
September 1944, is an echo of the Resistance. The
heroine, Aziza, is a middle-aged woman whose husband
has been murdered by the Germans. She is filled with
bitterness, not grief, or pride at the thought of him. Had
he loved her, she thinks, he would not have sacrificed his
life in the Maquis. In *Les Nuits de la colère* the thought of
the Resistance had exalted Salacrou. The heroism of men
made him feel ten feet high. This poetic view turns the
stomach of his heroine in *Dieu le savait*. She looks upon
her husband's courage as a betrayal of his home, his love
of country as a desertion of his family. The Liberation,
which fired the blood of the people in *Les Nuits de la*

colère, means to Aziza only ruined lives and broken buildings. "Have you walked through the town?" she asks. "Everything is razed to the ground. We have nothing left. My husband is dead. And our house, the place I was born in, which my father built, if the English hadn't destroyed it two years ago, just before my husband was arrested, the Americans would be bombing it to pieces now." This is not the degeneracy of the higher bourgeoisie. In *Dieu le savait* humanity itself has lost hope, and, from the long quotation from Luther which he makes on his title-page, Salacrou would seem to hold God responsible, and misery inevitable. "For if God has foreseen everything from all eternity . . . and if he is actually in control of things, who can possibly imagine that we have free will, or that anything can happen which he has not foreseen and ordained?"

Does this mean that Salacrou now believes in God? Hardly. Throughout his illustrious dramatic career the great source of his philosophic distress has been his inability to accept the existence of God. Were mankind now able to believe in religion, the unhappinesses and the betrayals of *L'Inconnue d'Arras* and *Histoire de rire* would never happen. That, at any rate, was his view up to the beginning of the War. But now the thought of religion, at least of orthodox religion, could not comfort him, even were he able to believe it. What hope can there be, he cries, in a God who creates or permits evil? If M. Salacrou ever should find God (and there is no evidence that he ever will) He will not be the God of conventional faith.

6

Henry de Montherlant

HENRY DE MONTHERLANT has been described
by an American journalist as "the ideal type of
Association football player." I cannot imagine either
Sartre or Salacrou turning out for the Arsenal or Sheffield
Wednesday. In engaging English sympathies M. de
Montherlant, therefore, starts with a certain advantage.
A people that sets as much store as the Anglo-Saxon
upon physical prowess in competitive sport may not be
much impressed by Montherlant's plays, but they cannot
altogether, in their insular prejudice, despise a man who
got into a street fight with a coachman the day after his
arrival on holiday in Rome, and can (or could) do the
hundred metres in eleven and four-fifths seconds. For
these feats they might even forgive Montherlant for
having once in Tangier adopted the deplorable Continental habit of duelling, and for having at the age of
fifteen killed a bull in a *corrida* in Spain.

But there are other points about Montherlant that may
be more difficult to overlook. Most of the leading
French dramatists to-day are middle-class people: the
parents of Sartre, Salacrou, Marcel Aymé, Jean Anouilh,
Marcel Achard, André Roussin, earned their living in a
profession or a trade. But Montherlant is an aristocrat.
Born in Paris on April 21, 1896, Montherlant comes of a
family that he traces back to the nobility of Catalonia. I
use the active form of the verb intentionally, for Montherlant is continually conscious of his aristocratic
origin. He is prone to think himself different from other

members of the Republic. He has a pride and a realization of his own merit that recall Landor and the great
eighteenth-century lords. Salacrou is distressed because
he believes that happiness is not attainable by mankind:
Sartre is happy because he believes that mankind soon
will achieve happiness by changes in the social structure.
Both of them think that the happiness of mankind is
important. Montherlant does not. The happiness of
Montherlant, the opportunity for Montherlant to live a
full and satisfying life, to fulfil untrammelled all the
Montherlant potentialities—this is what Montherlant
considers the mark of a well-ordered universe.

It is something quite different from ordinary selfish-
ness. Montherlant believes that every man should get
what he deserves; and he is convinced that the deserts of
Montherlant are great. "I have known," he says, "prac-
tically everything that is exquisite in life: but I expect
better things still." This is not optimism: it is the
consciousness of merit. He recognizes and salutes this
same consciousness in others. A friend told him that
D'Annunzio, at a rehearsal of one of his own plays,
turned to him and exclaimed, "Isn't this sublime?" The
incident might have seemed naïve to others, but not to
Montherlant. He saw a kindred spirit. D'Annunzio's
remark did not make him smile. When others don't
praise you, praise yourself (preferably in a loud voice).

Montherlant, therefore, excels in the portraiture of
pride. Only one play of his has, I think, been produced
professionally in Britain. It is among the most famous,
La Reine morte, created at the Comédie-Française on
December 8, 1942, and introduced into this country at
the Dundee Repertory Theatre in the summer of 1952. It
opens with a scene in which the young Infanta of
Navarre, brought to Portugal to marry the Prince, Don
Pedro, the son of the King, Ferrante, is rejected by him,
and pours out before his father all the passion and anger
and pride of her insulted soul.

I have been made to come here, like a servant, to be told that I am despised, and thrown back across the sea. My mouth dries when I think of it. Sire, do you know that in Navarre we die of humiliation? Don Guzman Blanco, reproved by my grandfather, King Sancho, fell into a fever, took to his bed, and died within a month. Father Mortorell, my father's confessor, when he was suspended, had an eruption of boils all over his body, and died in three days. Were I not young and vigorous, Sire, this affront I have received from the Prince would already have killed me.

"If God himself wished to send me to heaven," goes on this high-spirited young lady, "but delayed doing so, I would prefer to fling myself into hell, rather than wait on his good pleasure." These are sentiments one feels sure that Montherlant approves, as he approves the Infanta's eloquent method of expressing them.

He is a backward-looking man. A friend once asked him what countries he would wish to see before he died, and he replied, "Egypt, Greece, Jerusalem, and Rome, in that order." His thoughts are moulded to an antique time, and his style belongs to a richer, a more magnificent age than ours. It is an Imperial style, inflated with pomp, purple with rhetoric, and its great danger is that it can degenerate into monotony. Montherlant is always ready to assume the grand manner. Urging murder on Ferrante, his adviser, Egas Coelho, exclaims, "One gesture frees you from this abasement. You strike terror and respect into the realm. The rumour of it swells and crosses the sea. The desert is amazed by it." This readiness of Montherlant to exaggerate, to raise his voice, to use resounding metaphors, irritates some of his critics. They think he tries too hard to make the welkin ring: and claim that often he makes it ring false. But there are others who regard him as the greatest stylist of the contemporary French stage.

The countries that most stimulate Montherlant's imagination are, as we have seen, those whose history chiefly is in the past. Though he has written several fine novels of twentieth-century life, it is significant that, for *La Reine morte*, his first major play, Montherlant chose a Renaissance story, for it is in the Renaissance that he is most at home. The splendour of Renaissance life, the wealth of the fortunate, the unrestricted tasting of curious pleasures, the sensuous delight in human beauty and the workmanship of artists, the fighting and the amorality, are things that please the Montherlant soul.

But though the action of *La Reine morte* takes place five hundred years ago, its speeches echo with the troubles and problems of our own day. Coelho, urging Ferrante not too much to annoy Navarre, argues:

> Your Majesty, Portugal at the present moment not only on certain points is genuinely weak, but on others must simulate weakness, the better to deceive its enemies. Therefore, partly justly, and partly unjustly, the kingdom is thought feeble, and this situation will continue a long time still. . . . Look at the facts: it cannot be denied that everywhere Portugal is on the retreat.

As the first French audience, at Christmas 1942, listened to these words, could it avoid substituting France for Portugal. And, again, could it prevent its thoughts from turning to Hitler as it heard Coelho, later in the same scene, exclaim:

> Is it not incredible that men are content to suffer, only because some one is living whose death would solve everything? While thousands of people die whose death is useless, and even deplorable? Really, it is amazing that so many people continue to defile the world by their existence, when murder is relatively so easy and safe a thing.

Is not our present world of suspicion and terror the same world as Don Pedro's? "The whole universe lives in the throttle of fear. . . . Many times have I seen my father's face at the moment he was scoring a point against an adversary. What then was on his face was never a look of triumph, but a look of fear: fear of the reply."

Montherlant's plays are full of carefully elaborated reflexions like these. His characters always have leisure to embody in a flow of impressive words the thoughts and the beliefs that anger, depress, or sustain them. He is indifferent to the charge, which an English playgoer would press with relish, that these speeches hold up the external action of his dramas. Of external action his dramas contain little. His aim in the theatre is quite other than that of his contemporaries. He does not try, like Marcel Aymé, to construct an ingenious story; nor to be witty, like Roussin; nor to build a coherent poetic universe, like Salacrou; still less, like Sartre, to establish a new philosophy of existence. As Jacques de Laprade says in *Le Théâtre de Montherlant*, he attempts by means of a story of the greatest simplicity to expose, "with the maximum intensity and depth, a certain number of movements of the human soul." "The tragedies of the Ancients," says Montherlant himself, "are not only those of members of the same family, but also of the various people there are in the same person."

Don Pedro, in *La Reine morte*, cannot marry the Infanta of Navarre, because he is already married to a lady of the Portuguese Court, Inès de Castro, whose death is necessary before the safety of the realm can be assured. Other dramatists than Montherlant would have made of *La Reine morte* a piece of melodrama, or a play of true lovers faithful to death. These elements do in fact enter into the play, but they are pushed into the background. The central point is the soul of Ferrante, his vacillations and hesitations, his inner contradictions, and his inconsistent impulses: *La Reine morte* is a study of a man driven hither and thither by fear. It is, like *Hamlet*, a drama of indecision. Ferrante cannot make up his mind to murder Inès any more than Hamlet could bring himself to kill his uncle. But, whereas in *Hamlet* there is an abundance of changing and exciting action varying from ghosts in the basement to a duel with poisoned swords, passing by

shipwreck, war, funerals, and domestic theatricals to a
general holocaust, *La Reine morte* is a play almost entirely
devoid of incident. It belongs to a country where the
classical tradition is still powerful, and audiences do not
require their attention to be titillated by the liberal provision of minor, enticing kickshaws. It is as if Shakespeare had cut out the street fights, the midnight ball, the
lover's serenade, the potion and the suicide, and had
concentrated the whole force of *Romeo and Juliet* into what
happened in the soul of old Capulet.

In some ways Ferrante is a strange character for Montherlant to choose to analyse. He has lost his zest for the
banquet of life. Montherlant's usual preference is for
men whose appetite is strong and eager. Some of them,
like Alban de Bricoule, the hero of his novel *Les Bestiaires*,
are young, almost boys. In the opening words of this
lyrical novel the enthusiasm of Alban for life waves like
a great banner.

> A bullfight was announced in the arena at Bayonne. It
> was decided to go there, simply because the word arena had
> on Alban an electric power. When he was preparing for his
> first communion Mme de Coantré had given her grand-
> son a child's edition of *Quo Vadis?* and since that time Alban
> had seen himself as a Roman. He had skipped the pages
> devoted to the apostle Peter. . . .
>
> He watched the fight with passion. . . . Knowing nothing
> of the technique of the *corrida*, he shouted louder than any-
> one else, without understanding them, the Spanish words
> that better informed people shouted round about him with-
> out understanding them either. And yet, completely
> ignorant, he was annoyed to be sitting between two women:
> what they knew, he felt, must be worse than nothing.
> When the public let itself go against a clumsy matador,
> Alban rolled the fine programme he had intended to keep as
> a souvenir into a ball, and hurled it at the head of the
> wretched fellow. It missed him. But he had thrown furi-
> ously, with all his strength, genuinely intending to do
> harm.

The critic Maurice Bruézière says that the aim of Montherlant in *Les Bestiaires* is the same as in *La Reine morte*, to reveal, not an exciting and ingenious story, but the 'interior adventure' of a soul. That may be so, but if it is, *Les Bestiaires* is only another example of the familiar truth that authors often accomplish something different from, or in excess of, or less than, their aim. *Les Bestiaires* may delineate Alban de Bricoule's soul; but in doing so it tells, as *La Reine morte* does not, a story of varied interest and excitement. There are excellent descriptions of Madrid and Seville, and of the great bull-breeding grounds outside the latter city. There are huge parties on the plains, fights in the arena, scenes in the city streets after darkness has fallen. The tone is sometimes of lyric poetry, sometimes of malicious irony, always the impression is of a young man in a wondrous and magic land. There are the hot sun, the hard light, the roving and savage animals of Southern Spain. But the main thing, which is never lost sight of, is Alban's passion for the *corrida*. This is carried to extravagant and inordinate lengths, to lengths that in an Anglo-Saxon would seem either pathological or absurd, for, when it comes to the point, Alban loves a bull more than he does the heroine.

The love of characters who push some particular feeling to excess is typical of Montherlant. Michel Mohrt, in *Montherlant, 'Homme Libre,'* draws this moral from the story of the philosopher Peregrinus. Peregrinus stupefied his contemporaries by his extravagances; sometimes he proclaimed himself a Christian, sometimes a pagan; he loved women, and young boys. But at the end he decided he had not done enough to make himself famous. So, in a last effort for notoriety, he flung himself into the fire at the Olympic Games. Peregrinus is a man after Montherlant's heart. Montherlant likes to see himself as a man of antique mould, but nothing is more antipathetic to him than the Greek doctrine of the golden mean. He loves extremes.

Far more congenial to him, therefore, than the indecisive and policy-balancing Ferrante is Don Alvaro Dabo, the hero of *Le Maître de Santiago*. Don Alvaro, a knight of the Order of Santiago, is not a rich man. The sheets on his bed have more holes than substance in them, and the chickens peck about in the hall of his house in Old Castile. His friends wish him to go to the New World, where in a short while he can become wealthy in the great new Spanish colonies, and find a dowry for his daughter Mariana, who is in love with a young knight who does not appear in the play. These suggestions are made to him with tact, and Mariana herself prompts the most subtly persuasive of them. Don Alvaro rejects them with scorn. He desires neither comfort, nor action, nor splendour, nor fame, nor money. He wishes only to sit, day after day, year after year, in his own bleak and draughty home, watching through uncurtained windows the recurring prospect of burning sun and drifting snow, and contemplating the gaunt and magnificent spectacle of his own immense pride. There is nothing in the world which he does not regard with contempt. He addresses his only friend as "Torrent of uselessness." He has no tender feelings, no human weakness for his daughter, no desire for her happiness. The thought of compromise, in any direction, on any subject, fills him with repulsion. The world is a place of fetid wickedness and evil, of self-seeking, and of dishonour. He renounces and denounces it, and spits in its face.

Le Maître de Santiago is a very short play, consisting of hardly more than a few conversations, richly adorned with insults, between Don Alvaro and his friends. Its single dramatic point is the sudden conversion, at the end, of Mariana to her father's point of view. In the last moments of the play she sacrifices herself utterly to his ascetic scorn of human joys and impulses, and in an ecstasy of self-mortification she, like him, dedicates herself to a life of devotion and stoicism.

Jacques de Laprade says that in reading *Le Maître de Santiago* one encounters nothing to suggest that it could successfully hold the stage. It has no theatrical seductions, and what would seem to be the big scene of the play—the conversion of Mariana at the foot of the cross —takes place off-stage. Yet at the Hébertot it ran in 1948 for more than 500 performances, an astonishing proof, says Laprade, of Montherlant's prodigious theatrical power.

This theatrical power was widely recognized by the Parisian critics, but Montherlant's sense of values was brought sharply into question, especially by Jean-Jacques Gautier. Gautier assumed that Montherlant admired his hero, that he presented Don Alvaro as a genuinely strong character, and then proceeded to give reasons for thinking that in reality the Master of Santiago was weak. To isolate oneself, to refuse contact, to retire from the heat and dust of the conflict, to indulge only a secluded virtue, to avoid all temptation, to wallow in pride, to show no sign of affection—these, said Gautier, are not the marks of strength, but of feebleness.

> There is more true elevation in accepting without agreement, in facing and risking contamination, in living among one's fellows without deterioration, in skirting the abyss and trying to overcome vertigo....
>
> There is, in any case, more strength, merit, and nobility in loving than in hating, in forcing oneself to understand than in curling one's lip in scorn....
>
> There is more grandeur in this single thought of Pascal's than in all the precepts of *Le Maître de Santiago*:
>
> "I try to be just, true, sincere, and faithful to all men, and I have a special kindness for those to whom God has united me most closely!"

Yes, yes, yes: but does Montherlant in fact admire Don Alvaro as blindly as M. Gautier supposes?

That the play is founded in some sort of admiration cannot be doubted. That is evident from Montherlant's account of the origin of the piece. The background of the play is the rich gold-mines of South America, which had recently come into the possession of Spain. Some time in 1933 Montherlant read in the works of a historian whose name he has forgotten these words: "A few years after the discovery of America, there were old Spaniards who considered this discovery to be one of Spain's misfortunes." Ten years later he visited Barcelona for the first time, and, standing in front of the statue of Columbus, he reflected, "Here is a statue the Spaniards would do well to destroy, on one of their days of revolution."

Montherlant once said to an interviewer that he is in some ways a Left Wing writer, and it was out of this hatred of colonialism that *Le Maître de Santiago* was born. Of that hatred Don Alvaro is the unwavering champion. When his friends urge him that by going to the New World he will acquire glory, he says that he has no desire for such a thing, and the following dialogue takes place:

OLMEDA. If your personal glory distresses you, there is that of the Order, which is there engaged in a holy war.

ALVARO. A holy war? In a war of this sort, the cause that is holy is the natives'. Chivalry is fundamentally the defence of the oppressed. If I went to the Indies it would be to protect the Indians, which, according to you, is betrayal. I suppose you know the story of that Spanish soldier who was hanged as a traitor, because he cared for a wounded Indian. That is worse than the worst cruelties.

OLMEDA. There are many knights of the Order in the Indies —Hernando Cortez and Pizarro among them—who do not think like you.

LETAMENDI. And it is well known that in a certain battle our patron saint himself, St James, appeared to the Spaniards, riding his white horse.

ALVARO. Yes, I know that it is to the cry of "Santiago" that the most odious infamies are committed. I know that when Ovando led into a trap the innocent and trusting Queen of the Indians of Xaragua, who wished us nothing but good, the signal for action was that he put his hand

on his decoration as a knight of Alcantara, which represented God the Father: the Queen was hanged, and her
caciques burned alive. For what our chivalry covers in
the New World, there are no words to say how much I
scorn it.

These are the opinions of Montherlant himself. So that
we may be left in no doubt that Alvaro is speaking for his
author, Montherlant notes, in the printed edition of *Le
Maître de Santiago*, that the incidents of the Indian Queen
and of the Spanish soldier who was hanged as a traitor
are historically true. Now, a dramatist does not choose
as his mouthpiece a character for whom he has no sympathy. But to assume that because Montherlant has sympathy for Don Alvaro he has nothing else but sympathy,
that he sees no defect in him, and endorses everything he
says and does, that Don Alvaro is in fact his ideal of a
sure-founded Christian gentleman, is, I think, going farther than the facts warrant.

Montherlant specifically declares that he does not
advance Don Alvaro as a model Christian. At times, he
says, he is the opposite of a Christian, almost a Pharisee.
Even at his best he is only half a Christian, not because he
is insincere in his application of Christianity, but because
the Christianity which he has to apply is incomplete. He
is not a hypocrite, but he is a man of limited sight and
understanding. There are certain aspects of Christianity
which he incorporates in his very being; there are others
of which he knows nothing. He feels with great force
the first constituent of Christianity, its unworldliness, its
scorn of earthly comforts and riches, its renunciation;
but of the sense it gives of union with God he is wholly
ignorant. Montherlant notes that at the period of *Le
Maître de Santiago* Islam still exerted in Spain a powerful
influence. Now the religion of Alvaro consists almost
entirely, like that of the Moors and of the Old Testament, in a consciousness of the infinite grandeur and
distance of God: Allah is great. But the Incarnation?

The tender union with Christ on the Cross? Immanuel
(God with us)? These things remain outside Alvaro's
experience.

Montherlant not only recognizes all this, but categori-
cally states it in the very terms I have used. He is as well
aware as M. Gautier that Alvaro is not a perfect Christian.
But before we can conclude anything from this another
question has to be answered. When Sir Winston Chur-
chill says that a man is not a perfect Socialist, when Mr
Attlee says that another is not a perfect Conservative,
before we can know whether the remarks are intended as
praise or blame, we have to satisfy ourselves as to what
these gentlemen think of Conservatism and Socialism,
which is not perhaps as simple a matter as it might seem.
And, in determining Montherlant's attitude towards Don
Alvaro, it is necessary to know whether Montherlant
himself is a Christian, and, if he is not, whether he would
desire to be.

I have spoken at length of the attitude towards religion
of Armand Salacrou. In the second number of *Recherches
et Débats*, which is devoted to *Le Théâtre contemporain*,
José van den Esch says specifically that to Salacrou the
doctrine of the revelation is unintelligible, the dogma of
final ends unthinkable, the Redemption unimaginable.
Montherlant was educated in a Roman Catholic college,
and the pageantry of the Roman Church colours all his
outlook, but I doubt if he has any more belief to-day
than Salacrou in specific religious conceptions. Nor does
he share Salacrou's desire for the faith he has not got.
He is a philosophically happy and contented man.

It seems from his work that M. Salacrou would wish to
preserve the Christian rules of behaviour and the Christian attitude of love and compassion, even if the Christian
faith were abandoned. One does not get at all this
impression from the novels and plays of M. Montherlant.
The ideal—the Renaissance ideal of the arrogant, cul-
tured ruler, of the man conversant with all the civilized

pleasures—that emerges from his books is not in the least
the Christian ideal of self-abnegation and devotion. Yet
Montherlant himself describes *Le Maître de Santiago* as
belonging to the Christian side of him, and the conclusion
is at any rate plausible that he is more aware of the defects
of Don Alvaro than some of his critics, including M.
Gautier, suppose.

The truly Christian character in *Le Maître de Santiago*,
however, is not Alvaro, but his daughter Mariana, who
eventually sacrifices herself in order to share his renunciation of the world. Mariana is an affectionate and unselfish
girl who has captured the admiration of many critics.
Jeanne Sandelion calls her "the most ideal figure of the
contemporary theatre," and Thierry Maulnier says that
she is Montherlant's reparation to women for the picture
he has painted of them elsewhere.

That such a reparation is needed would be generally
admitted, for in some of his works, especially in the four
novels *Les Jeunes Filles*, Montherlant speaks of women
more bitterly and contemptuously than any other contemporary writer. In a nation of men of honour and of
cavaliers he is the least chivalrous of authors. Even as a
boy he took a remarkably unromantic view of the relations between men and women in love. When he was
fifteen he wrote a story of a young honeymoon couple
who were chased through the winter snows of Russia by
a pack of wolves. The wolves gained on the fugitives,
and it became necessary to lighten the sleigh. What did
Montherlant's hero do? Without hesitation he flung his
bride into the snow, and made off at an accelerated speed
to safety.

Montherlant rarely loses an opportunity to make
women behave badly. Alban in *Les Bestiaires* offers to
kill a bull in honour of the young Spanish girl Soledad
with whom he is in love. They go down to the breeding
grounds of Seville to choose an animal for the next day's
corrida. There is one particularly vicious beast which it

would be unreasonably dangerous for the inexperienced Alban to match himself against, and, in spite of his manifest alarm, it is this bull that Soledad selects. She does it out of sheer perversity. Montherlant nearly always sees women as cruel, light-minded, and irresponsible, and he frequently compares them, often to their disadvantage, with animals. Simone de Beauvoir, in *Le Deuxième Sexe*, is made very angry by this disagreeable habit, and recalls with justifiable indignation a particularly flagrant passage in *Les Jeunes Filles*.

The natural consequence of this attitude is that Montherlant is more heartily detested by many women than any other living French author. Mlle de Beauvoir considers him a very poor fellow indeed, and thinks that his bravado and bravura mask an essential cowardice. Less eminent ladies than the author of *Le Deuxième Sexe* do not worry about psychological analysis, but content themselves with rejoicing whenever anything particularly unpleasant happens to Montherlant. In November 1925 Montherlant was wounded by a bull, and an ecstatic letter appeared in the correspondence columns of *La Femme de France*. "What luck!" it read. "Montherlant, this poseur, has just had his loins ripped by a bull's horn. That's exactly what I wanted for him. Brave little bull!"

But, by the saintly and Christian Mariana, does Montherlant put himself right with women, as Mlle Sandelion and M. Maulnier too readily suppose? One of the salient features of the contemporary French theatre is that it attempts to change the bases of morality. Montherlant does not accept the traditional standards any more than does Sartre, and I should take a great deal of convincing that he really admires the qualities he ascribes to Mariana.

The next play of Montherlant's to be produced was *Malatesta*, the only one of his that I have seen upon the stage. It was written between March 1943 and February 1944, and was produced by Jean-Louis Barrault towards the end of 1950 at the Marigny, where I saw it in the spring of the following year. It is an extraordinary contrast with *Le Maître de Santiago*. *Le Maître* is cold, classical, austere, almost Puritanical in its æsthetic severity. Its hero is withdrawn from the world, despising its pleasures and comforts, whereas the note of *Malatesta* is hot-blooded sensuousness, the lust of the body, the pride of the eye, and the soaring, thirsting spirit of the Renaissance. It is written, and its plot is developed, with magnificent spread and amplitude, decorated with rich ornaments of speech and thought; it is a princely and purple play.

Malatesta, the lord of the Italian city of Rimini, is fond of fighting, of play, of foul play, of men of learning, of his wife, of young girls, of splendid food and wine, of gorgeous and glorious words. He plunges his arms to the elbows into the bowl of life, and bathes his forehead in its warm and exciting waters. The bright sun of the Renaissance is on all he does, and gilds both his virtues and his crimes.

When the curtain rises two men roll on to the stage, writhing and struggling in each other's arms. One of them is Malatesta, the other his fencing master. By means of a foul stroke, which seems to him only legitimate high spirits and amiable irresponsibility, Malatesta kills his opponent, after attacking him with wild, coarse, and eloquent words. At one moment he cries, "Cette fois, je te les coupe! Je te les coupe et les mange à dîner!"(the "them" being something I had better not particularize), and the next breaks into one of his best speeches, "Then was my glory youthful. It sang and made its wings shine in the first sun of the morning."

The best English realistic drama makes its effects through the management of theatrical situation and the development of character. When these things are done with outstanding skill deep emotions can be released, as in *The Deep Blue Sea*, by words of the utmost banality.

Only rarely in modern English prose drama is there a passage eloquent and striking enough in itself to be taken from its context and put into an anthology. There was one such passage—that on the railroads of America —in Noël Coward's *Quadrille*, but such things are rare in the contemporary English theatre.

But in France the tradition of rhetoric handed down from the seventeenth century is still potent even in the boulevard playhouses. In Montherlant it is particularly strong, and in *Malatesta* particularly strong even for Montherlant. One of the speeches of the play has become especially famous, and is generally taken as representative of Montherlant, in his Imperial mood, at his best. Malatesta's son-in-law, Camerino, has come to offer him from the Pope the cities of Spoleto and Foligno, in return for the right of placing Papal troops in his own city of Rimini. "Take Spoleto and Foligno," breaks out Malatesta in anguish and rage,

> and abandon Rimini to the Pope! That is what it comes to, isn't it? Very well, then, say it, wretch! Is this the monstrosity the Pope wishes? Rimini of my entrails! Rimini of my birth and my youth, Rimini of my loves and my spirit, Rimini of my eternal life! Give up Rimini when I wished to put upon her head a crown! Rimini that shakes my heart when I think of her.

In England we prefer something simpler than this, something more restrained. English players feel embarrassed by this emotional eloquence. But out of its torment and its passion and its affection Barrault drew magnificence.

His performance, however, was not universally praised. Some critics said that he was too small for this grandiose Renaissance tyrant, others that he looked too young, but every one praised his fire and spirit. He was at his best in the big scenes of the play, as in his interview with the Pope whom he has determined to murder, in the second act.

I have doubted whether Montherlant is a Christian

writer, yet between the third act of *Malatesta* and the theme of *Partage de midi* there is a remarkable resemblance. Claudel is one of the most deeply religious of French authors, and the climax of *Partage de midi* comes when Mesa is brought to realize through the measure of his own human anguish the intensity of suffering of Jesus upon the Cross. In the very fine third act of *Malatesta* the Pope pardons Malatesta's crimes, when, because of the pleading of Malatesta's wife Isotta, he momentarily catches in her love for her husband a glimpse of the meaning of the love of God. In *Partage de midi* this love is perceived through betrayal, in *Malatesta* through devotion, but in both it is the human that leads to an understanding of the divine.

This, to Montherlant, is a non-essential. *Malatesta* is primarily a pagan play. But it is splendidly alive, and holds the stage well, though it was not one of the Marigny's greatest successes.

Malatesta was followed by *Celles qu'on prend dans ses bras*, which was presented, without much success, at the Théâtre de la Madeleine in October 1950. I never saw this play on the stage, and I came to the reading of it with distaste. French critics when they find it necessary to flay an actor or an author alive usually do so with an endearment on their lips. "Never," they will remark, "have we seen our dear Jean-Louis give so poor a performance as in this play," or, "I cannot think what our good friend Anouilh is coming to." *Celles qu'on prend dans ses bras* was treated somewhat after this fashion. Francis Ambrière, for example, pleaded, almost tearfully, with Montherlant that he should cease writing plays like this, assuring him that, in spite of such a work, he still preserved his confidence in Montherlant's integrity and honour. Running through nearly all the reviews could be found the implication that the play was a disgraceful act. Gabriel Marcel called it a "venomous postscript" to *Les Jeunes Filles*.

In reading the play did not make on me this painful
impression. Its theme is similar to that of *The Deep Blue
Sea*. It is a study of sexual obsession—indeed, a double
study of obsession; for if Ravier, the wealthy antiquary, is
obsessed with the young Christine Villancy, so his friend,
Mlle Andriot, who, at sixty, is two years older than he, is
obsessed with Ravier. There are, says Ravier, two kinds
of women: those whom men embrace and those whom
they don't. Mlle Andriot belongs to the latter class; and
from the tone of the reviews I imagined that Montherlant
treated her with the contemptuous callousness that has
been the lot, in life and in fiction, of generations of unattractive women.

But the picture that Montherlant draws of Mlle
Andriot is not unsympathetic. Her efforts to represent
herself to Christine as a woman who has in her time had
adventures are less absurd than pathetic. Though she is
so dominated by her passion for Ravier that she will do
anything to please him, even on occasion acting as his
procuress, or discussing with him his physical needs in
terms surprisingly frank to English ears, she preserves
his respect, and her courage and self-control are considerably greater than his. He, indeed, repelled by
Christine, whines and complains abominably, and at the
end totally fails to maintain the attitude of magnanimity
he at first assumes when chance at last throws her into
his power. Yet, though he is cowed and made half mad
by passion, one is aware all the time that he is a man of
culture, of intellect, and of force of character. Both these
people, like the heroine of *The Deep Blue Sea*, rendered
weak as they are by the ravaging of their obsessive
instincts and desires, are far from despicable. And plays
in which human nature is not despicable may sadden, but
they do not pain us.

Nevertheless, there are considerations that account for
the comparative failure of the play. Alan Dent remarked
of a 1952 pantomime, *Jack and Jill* at the Casino, that it

revealed "an undeniable dearth of incident." The same phrase might certainly be applied to *Celles qu'on prend dans ses bras*. There were many people who found even *The Deep Blue Sea*, for all its probing of character, despite even the magnificent performances of Peggy Ashcroft, Roland Culver, and Kenneth More, monotonous. These critics said that the play moved in too narrow an emotional groove. Yet in Rattigan's play there was always something happening. It had two attempts at suicide, the return of a deserted husband, the intervention of a doctor who had been struck off the medical register. Even so there were people—I emphatically was not one of them—who felt that its surface was too little varied.

Such a criticism offered against *Celles qu'on prend dans ses bras* is immensely more valid. For in Montherlant's play almost nothing happens at all, apart from the central crisis of Ravier's pursuit of Christine. Almost the only subsidiary incident is the arrival of a customer to buy a doubtful antique in Ravier's shop. French audiences will stand a great deal in order to get the sort of obsessed analysis of physical passion that Montherlant gives in this play, but even so he seems here to have carried his deprivation of incident too far for popularity.

Writing soon after the production of *Celles qu'on prend dans ses bras*, A. A. Hartley, in *Mandrake*, remarked that much of Montherlant's work, despite its genius, leaves an unpleasant impression. Montherlant, says Hartley, approves actions that seem "atrocious to most of us." But that this can be said of nearly all the leading French dramatists is one of the principal arguments of this book. French morality never has been the same as English. The heroines of Anouilh, without losing their author's esteem, indulge in conduct which Birmingham and Sheffield decidedly would not condone. There are not many French playwrights who, like Salacrou, adopt the English attitude towards marital fidelity. In consequence of this difference in sexual philosophy, most French plays when seen by an English audience require a considerable mental adjustment.

With some of the dramatists discussed in this book, that adjustment is very great; and it is called for from French audiences as well as British. In Roussin's *Nina* the middle-aged heroine has a lover, and the plot of the comedy is concerned with her efforts to prevent him from straying to younger and more attractive folds. In England, even in London, it is still necessary for an audience to make an effort of the imagination, to forget generations of Protestant upbringing, before it can regard Roussin's attitude towards his heroine as normal, for, from that attitude, any spirit of social or moral criticism is absent. But in France, where the wife with a lover is not looked upon as an alarming phenomenon, this initial difficulty of acceptance clearly is not encountered.

Yet some of the plays we have been considering shock French audiences as profoundly as they would shock Liverpool or Lichfield. The blasphemies of *Le Diable et le Bon Dieu* have created quite as big a critical commotion in Paris as they would in London. In the contemporary breakdown of Western philosophic values, we have seen that Sartre is attempting to develop a new scheme of life, and in accordance with this scheme the behaviour which he presents and approves instinctively arouses the mental opposition of the majority of his audiences in France as well as in England. Whereas the behaviour of Nina can be squared more or less easily with French conventions, Sartre's justification of Orestes is as revolutionary in the Parisian theatre as in the British.

It is impossible, therefore, for a play by Sartre or by Genet to be fully enjoyed at the present time. Every audience contains more or less people who sympathize with and even share the moralities of these authors. But every audience also contains large numbers of people to whom their philosophic and personal ethics are strange if not abhorrent. At a performance of a Sartre play either in London or in Paris there is never that unquestioning acceptance of the author's spiritual premises which is necessary to a complete æsthetic experience. There is always a partial difficulty of communication and acceptance.

To some extent this is true also of Montherlant. The influence of the Christian religion is much more powerful on Montherlant than on Genet, Anouilh, or Sartre. His education in a Catholic school at Neuilly has left deep traces on him, and his nature is such that the rituals and ceremonies to which he was accustomed as a child have aspects of impressiveness and grandeur to which he cannot be indifferent. Though he does not believe the Christian religion, he believes that the Christian religion has qualities of truth in it, and he has felt impelled to vary Christian with un-Christian plays and books so that, in a method of alternance, his conflicting attitude towards Christianity might be fairly represented in his work.

Not every one, however, who cries "Lo here" and "Lo there" is a follower of Christ, and Montherlant's intention to make certain of his writings Christian does not necessarily mean that they are so. His co-religionists have long regarded him with mistrust. He himself has recalled that when he inscribed his *Aux Fontaines du désir* "to a priest of an illustrious order who had known him for many years," the book was returned to him immediately, with the inscription angrily removed.

Montherlant has always had an intellectual grasp of Christianity. He knows that it is a religion of love as well as of renunciation of material things. He has himself explained this in his comments on *Le Maître de Santiago*. But because love, in the larger sense of compassion, is a feeling to which Montherlant is a stranger, those pages of his which are designedly Christian have always been incomplete. His Christian characters, like Don Alvaro, either have not known love, or, if they have been acquainted with it, one has never been sure that Montherlant did not intend it to be in them a sign of weakness.

Hitherto, at any rate, Montherlant has not accepted the Christian compulsions of behaviour. I do not, of course, mean to imply by this that he has not led an honourable and upright life: I mean only that he has not accepted the theoretical Christian standards. His rules of conduct are altogether different from those of a conventional Christian society. His morality, says Michel Mohrt, is a morality of pride which looks for no retribution in this world or in any other. It is not a morality of self-abnegation nor of compassion nor of mercy nor of righteousness. With Montherlant, says M. Mohrt,

> there is no question of doing or not doing a thing because it is considered morally good or evil, but because it either increases or diminishes us in our own eyes: we ought so to live as to do ourselves honour. The only law is a natural law, hidden deep down in ourselves. This is not the voice of conscience: its imperative is æsthetic, a noble and lofty idea of ourselves. The morality of Montherlant, therefore, finds its basis in art, in poetry. Perhaps the word that gives the most complete idea of it is stateliness. . . . Stateliness is consciousness of one's dignity, self-respect. A man can kill or rob without in this sense losing his self-respect. . . . But time-serving and cowardice disgrace a man, because these are the signs of a vulgar and debased soul.[1]

These exalted notions are not foreign to the European tradition, as the notions of Sartre and Genet are foreign to it. Many a king, many a Pope, even many a private individual, has felt the force of them. Louis XIV understood them when he declared, "L'État, c'est moi"; so did Rob Roy, crying, "My foot is on my native heath, and my name is MacGregor." They play their part in ruling the actions of all Christians: self-respect is no pagan prerogative. Where Montherlant differs from the European tradition is in the exclusive stress he places upon

[1] Michel Mohrt, *Montherlant, 'Homme Libre,'* p. 213.

them, in making them the whole rule of life. It is this exclusive sense of value, leading him to despise everything that is gentle and merciful, that causes Mr Hartley and some other critics to consider the conduct of his heroes unsympathetic.

But Mr Hartley goes farther than this. He regards Montherlant's moral attitude as also an æsthetic defect. Montherlant, he says,

> appears to approve actions that seem atrocious to most of us. . . . The result is that when seeing these plays we are liable to find ourselves in opposition to the spirit of them. And this is an artistic flaw. . . . For myself, I should say that Montherlant's great error is, while asking admiration for his heroes, to have introduced any fact, of whatever nature, which might counter that impression. Moral feelings, after all, exist, and if the writer affronts them he must reckon with the effect he is producing. I regard Montherlant's failure to do so as the outstanding flaw in an otherwise highly interesting and successful series of works.

This seems a doubtful doctrine. It is even more extreme than the doctrine by which Clement Scott condemned Ibsen. Scott disliked Ibsen's morality so much that he said that the evil of this morality outweighed the theatrical merits of Ibsen's plays. If I understand him aright, Mr Hartley maintains that his dislike of Montherlant's morality means that Montherlant's plays are technically defective. He seems to assume that no dramatist should adopt a spiritual attitude different from that of a conventional audience. This would not only deprive us to-day of most of Sartre, but it would have deprived us in the past of *A Doll's House*, *Ghosts*, and *Hindle Wakes*.

We have no right to resent in the theatre an author's philosophy merely because it is different from our own. We no longer accept the moral premises of Greek tragedy, but we can and do adjust ourselves to them sufficiently to enjoy *Œdipus*. The effort is worth making, because the Greek conception of inexorable destiny, though it is profoundly incompatible with Christianity, is nevertheless an impressive and, on its own plane, satisfying thing. It makes it possible for us imaginatively to reconcile ourselves with actions and attitudes that would normally seem to us, in Mr Hartley's phrase, "atrocious." Montherlant is æsthetically defective, not because he makes his heroes behave in ways that revolt us, but because he fails to secure, for the philosophy that justifies this behaviour, the same willing suspension of disbelief that we accord so readily to classical tragedy.

Nothing will ever again make us believe in the religion of Sophocles, but when *Œdipus* is performed we cease our active disbelief because, after all, that religion, though mistaken, is in itself grand and complete. If we do not cease our disbelief in the religion of Montherlant it is because Montherlant's religion is only a partial reflexion of another religion of altogether wider scope and more impressive pattern.

The attitude of Montherlant in *Le Maître de Santiago*, *La Reine morte*, and *Malatesta* is merely that of an incomplete Christian. There is nothing in Montherlant that cannot be found in Christianity, but there is an enormous amount in Christianity that cannot be found in Montherlant, or at least in the Montherlant of these particular plays. Montherlant is a proud man, but he never said anything so proud as "Heaven and earth shall pass away, but my words shall not pass away." The Master of Santiago is an ascetic; but he did not wander through the world penniless, as the disciples were told to do. Malatesta loved his native city; but his "Rimini de mes entrailles" is less passionate than Christ's "O Jerusalem, Jerusalem, thou that killest the prophets . . . how often would I have gathered thy children together, even as a hen gathereth her chickens under her wings, and ye would not!" Ferrante is ruthless; but less ruthless than he who said, "The children of the kingdom shall be cast forth into outer darkness: there shall be weeping and gnashing of teeth." Malatesta loved fine and beautiful things; but not more so than many a successor of St Peter. Montherlant's is an exalted style; but not so exalted as "I am the resurrection and the life." All these things—the pride, the renunciation, the splendour, the severity—which are in Montherlant are also in Christianity; and in Christianity they are fused and reconciled with something that is not in Montherlant, but which is found in admonitions like "Suffer the little children to come unto me, and forbid them not," and in verses like "Though I have all faith, so that I could remove mountains, and have not charity, I am nothing." This is Montherlant's weakness: his philosophy is not a whole thing: it is merely a piece broken off from another and more comprehensive religion.

That is true of the Montherlant of the most famous plays and novels. It is not, however, altogether true of the Montherlant who wrote the last act of *Celles qu'on prend dans ses bras*, nor of the Montherlant who is the author of *La Ville dont le prince est un enfant*. This is Montherlant's latest work, and in my opinion his best. For throughout it breathes what his writings, for all their splendour, have hitherto lacked—the spirit of compassion.

It is probable that it is the most tinged with autobiography of any of his plays. Montherlant passed his early schooldays at the École Saint-Pierre at Neuilly, and at the age of thirteen wrote a thirty-six-page essay on bullfighting. Over one phrase that he used in this juvenile production quite a little storm arose. Speaking of the matador Bombita, the young Montherlant observed coolly, "It is much to be admired that his legs were so steady after what he had done that night." The head of the school, a priest, wrote to Montherlant's family, but nothing worse happened than that the bold author was invited to alter the offending words to "what he had drunk."

The incident, however, suggested that Montherlant's

schooldays were not going to pass without excitements. A much more important episode occurred after Montherlant had left Saint-Pierre for the École Sainte-Croix, which was also at Neuilly, close to the Bois de Boulogne. One day Montherlant was named before all the other boys of the school as the centre of a turbulent group of students, and his parents were told to remove him. The same priest who had objected to part of his essay on bull-fighting told him that he would laugh at all this when he was twenty. But when he was twenty Montherlant did not laugh at it; nor at forty; nor does he laugh at it to this day. Its memory has never burned itself out in his soul. It influenced his first book, *La Relève du matin*, which he wrote in 1920. It influenced his *Fils des autres* in 1939; and it is at the centre of *La Ville dont le prince est un enfant*, which is the work of 1951.

The theme of this play is not dissimilar to that of *The Hidden Years* and *Children in Uniform*, and it is directly stated in the first words of the opening speech. To a young boy, Sandrier, who is a pupil in a religious school, his form master, the Abbé de Pradts, says sternly, "No, you understand? I will no longer permit this association between you and Sevrais. Friendship between boys of different years is absolutely forbidden." Sevrais, at sixteen, is two years older than Sandrier, and genuinely anxious for his welfare, and the Abbé decides to trust them. There is, however, an incident in a gymnasium, indiscreet but harmless, that goads the Abbé to fury. His own motives, which he is far from himself either understanding or suspecting, are complicated; certainly his zeal for and interest in Sandrier pass the bounds of normality. At Sainte-Croix unreasoning trust had been arbitrarily followed by unreasoning severity. The same thing happens in this play, and Sevrais is expelled. In the impressive last act the Superior of the college, in a scene in which anger, sorrow, and compassion are brilliantly combined, exposes to the Abbé his real

motives, and leaves him apparently broken and yet with
a possibility of true redemption, the redemption that can
come only through love. There is an affection of the
flesh, says the Superior.

> But there is another affection, Monsieur de Pradts, even
> towards the creature. When it reaches a certain measure of
> intensity, through endurance and forgetfulness of self, it is
> so close to the love of God that you might say that the
> creature has been made only to lead us to the Creator: I have
> good reason for saying that. May such a love come to you.
> And may it lead you to that last and tremendous Love com-
> pared with which all the rest is nothing.

This is a new note in Montherlant; or, rather, it is new
to hear it so strongly and so confidently sounded. Since
it is so unexpected, and yet so magistral, one might be
inclined to overpraise the play in which it appears. I have
in fact read *La Ville dont le prince est un enfant* with more
appreciative excitement and warmth of feeling than any
other of Montherlant's plays. Some of it—particularly
the scene in the gymnasium—is unconvincing, but it has
about it a strength combined with sweetness which is
most remarkable. It would probably be very impressive
upon the stage, where Montherlant, feeling that Sandrier
and Sevrais are called on to experience emotions which
it is undesirable for boy-actors to simulate, has not yet
allowed it to appear. The final scene especially, in which,
after his last and magnificent speech, the Superior stands
motionless at the door of the Abbé's room, watching
sternly and compassionately his stricken and sob-shaken
figure, while the voice of a child is heard outside practising the leitmotiv of *Qui Lazarum ressuscitasti*, is extremely
moving.

I do not think, however, that to admire *La Ville dont
le prince est un enfant* is like admiring, for example, *A Tale
of Two Cities*, a work, that is, quite uncharacteristic of its
author. *A Tale of Two Cities* is different from the rest of
Dickens, whereas *La Ville dont le prince est un enfant* is less

different from the rest of Montherlant than more complete. Its suffusion with the spirit of compassion does not hinder it from possessing the qualities which are usually associated with Montherlant. It has his customary exaltation of style. Though the picture it draws of conditions in a Catholic school is disturbing, Montherlant did not intend it as an attack on the religion in which he was brought up. Rather, in fact, the reverse. "For me," he says in his preface, "wherever there is elevation, there is grace." "There is grace," he goes on,

> in the Superior of the college, who acts as he must, and speaks as he must, in this delicate situation in which he is involved. There is grace in André Sevrais, who sacrifices his pleasure, and then his affection. . . . There is even grace in the little Serge Sandrier, who passes through it all without quite understanding it. . . . I will say, that, in spite of appearances, there is grace also in the Abbé de Pradts, a dark grace, and this grace is only because he loves, and continues to love: his night is not deeper than is normal in passion.

There is nothing degrading in this play, as there is nothing degrading in *The Deep Blue Sea*: for the characters, whatever their weaknesses and their distresses, are not contemptible.

Nor is the place contemptible in which these distresses are endured. The Abbé and the Superior never lose consciousness of the fact that they are summoned to a higher calling than other men, whatever their imperfections. "Whatever happens among us," says the Abbé, "even when it seems to be on a lower plane, is infinitely higher than what happens outside." For all his agony of spirit and his self-deceptions, the Abbé in this matter has the pride of the Master of Santiago.

The substance of the play is the substance of a great part of Montherlant's work. He is irresistibly attracted by the spectacle of sacrifice. Montherlant's imagination is drenched in the atmosphere of the bullfight, and the sacrifice of the bull is the culmination of the *corrida*. Montherlant's sentiment towards the bull is one neither of pity nor of hatred, neither of scorn nor of indifference. So that the æsthetic catharsis may take place in its proper atmosphere of magnificence and doom it is necessary that the bull should die, necessary, indeed, that it should die well, in such a manner as to deserve and extort admiration and a kind of sympathy, but not regret. Such sacrifices have been the basis of a high proportion of Montherlant's imaginative writing. He himself gave to *La Reine morte* the sub-title of "How to kill Women." *Les Célibataires*, it has been observed, might easily have been called "How to kill Nobles," and *Le Maître de Santiago* "How to kill Lovers." In that sense *La Ville dont le prince est un enfant* is a play on the theme of "How to kill Priests."

But for the first time there is here the hope of resurrection. It is not a certain hope. One cannot tell, at the end of this piece, whether the Abbé de Pradts will eventually rise out of his despair, a man newmade and purified. But at least one cannot say either that he will not. Montherlant here for the first time regards his characters with true compassion, the compassion that sees clearly, that does not despise, and does not lose hope.

7

Jean Anouilh

OF all the playwrights of modern France, or of any other country with whose drama I am acquainted, Jean Anouilh possesses the most sure sense of the stage. Many years ago, one Sunday afternoon in Sheffield, I listened to a broadcast of *Much Ado about Nothing*, in which the Beatrice and Benedick were Marie Ney and Henry Ainley. I had small knowledge of the play at the time, and the church scene came to me as a complete surprise. When, in answer to Benedick's offer to help her, Beatrice made the totally unexpected reply, "Kill Claudio," the effect was overwhelming: the words leapt out of the loud-speaker like an arrow. In an instant, by one brief masterful stroke, the entire emotional atmosphere of the scene was changed; what had been a gay, romantic interlude, a playing at wit and sentiment, became, in the twinkling of an eye, in the time required to utter only four syllables, a deadly conspiracy.

Now, in his fine play *The River Line* Charles Morgan, at the end of the second act, has an effect which is superficially very similar. The English major, hiding with his companions in flight in a hayloft in France during the War, is suspected—nay, more than suspected—of being a traitor. The news is given to the French girl who is in love with him; and while he and his friends, or those he thinks to be his friends, play cards by the flickering light of a candle, she is left a few moments in which to accommodate herself to the dreadful truth. Suddenly her voice rings out, "Kill that man," and in an instant a sword has gone through his heart, and he falls to the ground.

The effect of this at the first performance at the Edinburgh Festival of 1952 was, it cannot be denied, very great. It came as a tremendous and unforeseen climax, and it recalled irresistibly the words of Beatrice to the stricken Benedick. Yet it is an effect less rich and subtle than Shakespeare's, for it lacks one aspect which is the most remarkable dramatic feature of the scene in *Much Ado about Nothing*. As I have said, the words of Beatrice are astounding because they instantaneously reverse the emotional atmosphere. But in *The River Line* the emotional atmosphere is unchanged except in so far as it is intensified. The intensification is, of course, in itself a sufficiently exciting thing. But to get, at the same time as the intensification, a complete overturning is a miracle.

Many years after hearing *Much Ado about Nothing* I was reading, on another Sunday afternoon, Anouilh's *Ardèle*. I still vividly remember, as vividly as I remember that broadcast of *Much Ado about Nothing*, a scene in which, with hardly more words than Shakespeare used, Anouilh instantly darkens and overclouds an atmosphere that till then had been light and easy. To the fantastic, farcically tormented house, raddled with passion and lust, in which the action of the play is situated, a young soldier returns from his service in the East, and is met by the girl with whom he had been in love. They greet each other shyly, and, as he gathers confidence, Nicolas recognizes, with a thrill of pleasure, that everything is just the same as he had left it. "Nothing here has changed," he says, "for two years. Everything is in its place. Even you," and Nathalie replies gently, "Even me." They look at each other in long silences charged with all the affection they had felt in their youth, two slim figures of infinite tenderness; and then Nicolas suddenly asks: "Nathalie, why did you marry my brother?" Nathalie, motionless, does not reply, and the stage is—again suddenly—black. The serpent did not more dramatically raise his head from behind the flowers in the Garden of Eden than on this scene of young affection treachery impinges. For once, in a modern play, we get the sharp reversal of *Much Ado*.

The work of Anouilh is perhaps richer than that of any other writer in this exploitation of theatrical effect. The scene I have mentioned is laconic; indeed, it is mainly composed of silences. Rattigan is equally a master with Anouilh of the dramatic effect of the brief, commonplace phrase. But Anouilh, though he is not technically a poet, though his mind does not, like Fry's, overflow with curious and glittering metaphors, is at home also with eloquence and rhetoric. The speech of the disreputable old harpist in *Eurydice*, based on the proposition so much disliked by the rich, that the best things in life aren't free, that life with plenty of money means comfort, and big meals, and women of all shapes, nationalities, and colours, and a succulent cigar at the end of the evening, a speech in which this incompetent and vulgar, but indomitable, old man maintains with an unbroken spirit the magnificent adventurousness of existence, is surely, in its humour, its truth of character, and its picturesqueness, a piece of rhetoric worthy of the great traditions in this matter of the French theatre. Certainly, as Hugh Griffith delivered it, with such delighted relish, in the London production of the play, it is not an experience to be forgotten. And it is a refutation too of the conviction which is by no means confined to Britain and the United States, that Anouilh perversely shuts his eyes to the joy of life. Not often in the theatre has existence been savoured so rapturously as in this speech.

Eurydice was written in 1941, when, by incessant practice, Anouilh had attained mastery of his art. But in the first of his *pièces noires*, *L'Hermine*, dating from ten years earlier, he already showed skill in the management of long speeches. The speech in which Monime offers herself to the young man who thinks he cannot marry her without money is not so fine as that of the old father in *Eurydice*; but its tenderness and power to hold the stage are remarkable in a dramatist who was then only a little more than twenty years of age. Since *Eurydice* Anouilh's command of rhetoric has not declined. If the third-rate harpist's statement of the hedonistic view of life can hardly be bettered, where can one find a more harrowing lamentation than in the terrible outburst of the General's wife in *Ardèle*, a play that belongs to the later phase of Anouilh's development? But there is no point in indefinitely prolonging a list of this kind. It is sufficient to establish the fact that Anouilh is a master both of the dramatic situation that can be precipitated by half a dozen words, and of the rhetorical effect that is the result of the bravura of a rich and picturesque imagination.

This, however, is to say things that no one has ever denied. Anouilh's mastery of theatrical technique is generally admitted. The objection that is brought against Anouilh in France has nothing to do with his dramatic skill. It is not an æsthetic objection at all. It is a feeling that his view of life is horrible and degrading, that he takes something which is fine and honourable, like love, and makes it foul and disgusting. Serge Radine, in *Anouilh, Lenormand, Salacrou*, maintains that Anouilh has sunk into a black and terrible despair which causes him to sully and insult all the highest values of mankind. The world shown in *Ardèle*, for example, says M. Radine, "is a veritable sepulchre." And Jean-Jacques Gautier protests against the filthiness of language in *La Valse des toréadors*. Where, he asks, will Anouilh's despair finally lead him? "After excess comes the excess of excess, and after that . . . what?"

In Britain there has been not only an objection to Anouilh's pessimism, but an uneasiness, often felt in relation to the French drama, with his morality. When

Christopher Fry adapted *L'Invitation au château* into *Ring round the Moon* it was a sound instinct that made him conceal the fact that the shy Isabel whom Claire Bloom played with such pathetic delicacy was really the mistress of the man who called himself her uncle. I remember the horror that John Gielgud expressed to me over the scene in *Ardèle* in which the apparently pure young Nathalie confessed to Nicolas her powerlessness to resist the impulses of the flesh; and over many a luncheon Henry Sherek has described as revolting the ending of the same play, where two children are made to ape the sexual desires of their parents. I myself did not find it easy to accept the promiscuity of the young Eurydice. The heroines of Anouilh have all kinds of virtue. They are kind, they have the air of an enchanting innocence, they are simple and sincere, but they do not behave like well-brought-up young English ladies.

Of course, the same can be said of many theatrical heroines. Deceived maidens are stock characters of the stage. But Anouilh's heroines are not deceived maidens. Eurydice knew perfectly well what she was doing with her gross and fleshly impresario. When Monime demanded to become the mistress of her lover in the first of Anouilh's major plays, she acted entirely of her own volition, without the slightest encouragement from the impecunious Frantz. Isabel shows no disgust nor resentment with her absurd but concupiscent lepidopterist.

Now, it may be said, there is nothing odd about all this. Such behaviour might be thought reprehensible in the Victorian drama, but the right of women to have experiences, as Wells calls it in *Christina Alberta's Father*, is a fundamental attitude of the twentieth-century literature and drama, at least since John Tanner eloquently preached the desirability of defying the tyranny of the wedding ring, and Sue Bridehead shrank from the respectability of the registry office. It is true that the lady to whom Mr Tanner addressed his advice did not take it, but the heroine of *Jude the Obscure* paid as little attention as Eurydice herself to the marriage ceremony.

Yet Christina Alberta and Sue Bridehead, the "New Woman" that Shaw talked of, the emancipated female of the Fabian Society, were not in the least like the young girls of Anouilh's plays. Isabel, Monime, Nathalie, Eurydice, are frail, simple, gentle creatures, quite different from the strong-minded characters of Wells and Hardy. In their shy quietness they resemble Scott's Rose Bradwardine, or Trollope's Lily Dale. In their behaviour they come near to nymphomania, but they have the innocent face of a saint. And the curious, the disturbing thing is that Anouilh perceives no incongruity in this. He does not, like Hardy, defy morality. He does not seem to know that it exists. He has a passion for purity, and he finds it in people who have no more sensitiveness over the sexual act than if they had been brought up in a brothel. To English audiences this seems the height of unreason. It is depriving words of their meaning. It is reducing the dictionary to absurdity. Anouilh takes up the exasperating position of a man who wants to have it both on the swings *and* the roundabouts.

Is he aware that he takes up this position? I do not think so. I do not believe that with Anouilh this question arises. His plays are not made out of moral categories. He is an instinctive writer, for whom feeling replaces reflexion and thought. Reading and seeing such pieces as *Eurydice*, *L'Hermine*, and *L'Invitation au château*, watching the constant recurrence of such heroines as Monime, Isabel, Eurydice, Nathalie, all simple, all kind, all frail, all with a curious stamp of soiled purity, it would almost seem to Anouilh's audience that in his youth he must have encountered some girl who is the model for them all, a girl who seemed to him to be, from her appearance and her nature, the incarnation of purity, and whose behaviour it has never occurred to him to question. This conception—which is pure fantasy, for there

is no important living French playwright of whom bio-
graphical details are so scarce—would go far towards
explaining the basis of Anouilh's attitude to the conduct
of his characters. His heroines are pure, and they behave
as they behave. It is extremely unlikely that he has
consciously accepted Genet's theory that what makes a
man a criminal is not his criminal acts but his criminal
nature, yet he does write as if purity were in being and
not in doing. If there is a paradox here, it is one that
Anouilh has not perceived.

This being so, is he an immoral writer? He is certainly outspoken. Such speeches as the mad old Général-
ale's in the last act of *Ardèle*, in which her crazed and
morbidly acute ears hear everywhere around her the
sound of animals and people and even flowers coupling,
or the frank phrases of sensual enjoyment over which the
touring harpist of *Eurydice* smacks his lips, or the free
physical references of *Colombe* and *Le Voyageur sans
bagage* are apt to make English audiences uncomfortable.
None of these speeches is introduced in order to shock or
to titillate. They are all in character, they are all dramatically justifiable. But they do not produce the honest,
Rabelaisian laughter provoked, for example, by the out-
rageous activities of the Crazy Gang. They raise the
temperature. They excite the senses. If to heat the
imagination is immoral Anouilh, though it may be harsh
to call him an immoral writer, undoubtedly has immoral
moments. And these immoral moments are even
numerous.

Again, if immorality be identified with sexual irregu-
larity viewed without condemnation it is obvious from
what has already been said that Anouilh must be an
immoral writer. When Monime offers herself in the
night to Frantz in *L'Hermine*, Anouilh does everything
he can, by putting on her lips words of a golden tenderness, to represent her action, not as an attempted seduction,
but as something extremely moving and beautiful. And

in *Eurydice* he is wholly on the side of his heroine, plainly believing that sexual promiscuity is an admirable thing if only it proceeds from kindness of heart, unselfishness, and the desire not to give pain.

When he introduces a character who, like Julien in *Colombe*, is moved by conceptions of right and wrong, he makes him utterly savage and revolting. Before Julien, about to depart on his military service, leaves his young wife, he makes her, simple, incredulous, natural creature that she is, swear to forgo the most trifling and innocent pleasures. She must not even look at dresses in the shop windows, at rings or at flowers. She must not accept compliments. She must not smile. She must distrust every one. She must live a life of absolute spiritual and mental seclusion, thinking only of her absent husband, waiting only for his return. She must not exist except in her thought of him. All else is unimaginable and unforgivable wickedness. In this odious character Anouilh expresses his instinctive reaction to people who conduct their lives, not according to feeling, but to ideas of what is good and what is evil.

Yet if an immoral writer is one who encourages immorality by portraying it as the road to prosperity and happiness, by representing it as gaiety, freedom, and joy, Anouilh is among the least immoral of dramatists. His characters may, in the eyes of the moralists, commit evil, and Anouilh may refrain from censuring them. He may even be unaware that what they are doing is wrong; he may plainly love them with his heart's blood. But what he does not do, what he never comes within a million miles of doing, is to suggest that their wrong-doing brings them happiness. With Anouilh the wages of sin (though he does not see it as sin) always is death.

His plays show an extraordinary range of exuberant and witty characters; grotesque old dowagers, tyrannical old men, young men about town, shy young men, sly waiters, dignified waiters, shabby touring players, wildly successful and temperamental old actresses, rich provincials, charming and amenable girls. They are all amusing. Anouilh's farcical invention is inexhaustible. It is more extravagant than Ben Travers's. Even his most anguished plays are acted to irresistible shouts of laughter. But behind all the laughter can be heard continuously the moan, and at times the scream, of pain.

His characters desire only happiness. They act always so as to bring themselves pleasure; and this pleasure, this happiness, they never attain. Eurydice taking her midnight bus out of Marseilles: Monime finding herself in love with a murderer: the General Saint-Pé fumbling the skirts of the maids: the Count in *Ardèle* telephoning his mistress: the Count in *La Répétition* flirting with the pretty governess: Héro trying to seduce her: these people have in them not a scrap of morality, but neither have they a scrap of happiness, either. If a moral writer is one who shows that sin breeds misery then Anouilh is among the most moral of dramatists.

But his morality, of course, is quite unintentional. It is the product of a wider, and desperate, pessimism. I have said that in Anouilh the wages of sin is death. But in Anouilh the wages of everything is death. Immorality does not bring happiness; but then, in this fascinating, terrible world of his, nothing brings happiness. In the face of this horrible conviction Anouilh, left with no other resource, with no belief in religion, with no faith in politics, with no trust in human nature, laughs his head off.

Will it always be so? French critics are inclined to say yes. They think that Anouilh will go on tightening the same screw play after play, year after year. They see the farce getting wilder, the anguish keener, but no fundamental change. Yet a change there is.

It is simply this, that in his latest plays, for the first time, Anouilh introduces a conscience. In *Colombe* the conscience is Julien, and Anouilh hates it. But in *La*

Valse des toréadors the conscience, far more intermittent than in Julien, is in the old, lascivious, maid-chasing General, who has stayed with his demented wife, despite his affection for the girl with whom he had danced seventeen years before at the military ball in Saumur. This conscience Anouilh pities, but he does not hate. In the third act of *La Valse des toréadors* the Générale's doctor asks her husband why he had not left his wife, or made the girl who had danced with him his mistress. And the answer simply is that inside the General was something that made it impossible for him to do either. For the first time a sympathetic character in Anouilh has a soul. It brings him the harrowing misery that is the usual lot of Anouilh characters. But its presence is of huge significance. No one can tell what may in the end come of it.

8

Some Books

THE French theatre is much better documented than
the English or the American. The number of theatrical books published in Paris not only exceeds the number
of those issued in London and New York; but also the
proportion of serious works among them is greater than
in those of either of the English-speaking cities.

There are at least three bookshops in Paris which exist
wholly for the purpose of buying and selling theatrical
publications. Two of them are in the Rue Marivaux, in
the second arrondissement, near the Opéra-Comique.
These two shops sell only new books. On the Left Bank,
in the Rue Bonaparte, close to the church of Saint-
Germain-des-Près, is the excellent Librairie Bonaparte,
which sells theatre books both new and second-hand.
This charming establishment is almost a club for those
who are seriously interested in the theatre. I know of few
pleasanter ways of passing a Parisian morning than to
drink a cup of chocolate in the near-by Café de Flore,
and then to stroll round to the Librairie Bonaparte and to
chat with its highly informative and enthusiastic pro-
prietress and her friends about the latest plays.

Of the books about the modern French theatre and its
authors which I have found most interesting and helpful,
the following is a representative, but by no means complete, selection. (Most of them are fairly easy to obtain
in Paris, and there are several London shops which will
get them within a month or two of ordering. Not many
cost over thirty shillings.)

Les Enfances de Montherlant, by J.N. Faure-Biguet (Henri Lefebvre). This excellent book, which is written with sharp intelligence, no sentimentality, and an unforced sense of humour, is the work of a childhood friend of Montherlant's. It is very informative about Montherlant's excessively romantic upbringing. His childhood was passed in an atmosphere of Edgar Allan Poe and Mrs Radcliffe. As a girl his grandmother, when her mother died in an isolated house, put the dead body beside her in the carriage and drove it into the village. At the age of nine Montherlant's keen appreciation of physical beauty was already manifesting itself. He held a beauty competition, with prizes, for little boys and girls. As a child Montherlant wrote stories which he carefully copied into elaborately decorated albums. Nowadays his books are written on the backs of envelopes and circulars. As the author says, he has transferred his care from the paper the words are written on to the words themselves.

Montherlant, ' *Homme Libre*,' by Michel Mohrt (Gallimard). A book written in an admirably clear and seductive style, with every capacity to please, but without desire to dazzle. M. Mohrt believes that the heroes of Montherlant's plays and novels are different aspects of himself; and this leads him to attempt to discern the real figure that is behind Alban de Bricoule, Costals, and Ferrante. It is a questionable aim, for the most significant thing about an artist is his art; and to M. Mohrt the art of Montherlant is secondary to his personality. This might easily result in a vulgar sensationalizing of Montherlant's biography. Happily, it does not, for in practice what the book offers is a series of sensitive studies of *Les Jeunes Filles*, *Les Bestiaires*, and *La Reine morte*.

Le Théâtre de Montherlant, by Jacques de Laprade (La Jeune Parque). M. de Laprade's short book is in high repute in France. It contains essays on most of Montherlant's plays, and is mainly concerned with the religious aspect of Montherlant's work. Laprade is less afraid that Montherlant is not a Christian than that he is the wrong kind of Christian. In Montherlant's preoccupation with severity, asceticism, self-denial, and withdrawal from the world, shown chiefly in *Le Maître de Santiago*,

Laprade discerns a streak of Puritanism that causes him much
disquiet. He identifies it with Jansenism, whose similarities
with Calvinism make him regard it as incontestably a reason for
the decline of religion in France. His views being what they
are, Laprade seems justified in his alarm about Montherlant.
For Montherlant says that Laprade's view of Jansenism makes
"his hair stand on end." He quotes Nietzsche as saying that
Pascal's imaginary conversation with Jesus is finer than anything in the New Testament. Laprade retorts that Nietzsche
was a notorious unbeliever.

Montherlant et les femmes, by Jeanne Sandelion (Librairie
Plon). This is primarily a study of Montherlant's attitude
towards women, and it analyses the heroines of most of his
plays and novels. Its scope, however, is really wider than this,
and it makes many useful critical observations of a general
nature on Montherlant's work. It begins with a chapter describing a dinner with him in his house on one of the quays of the
Seine, overlooking the book-boxes on the Left Bank. Montherlant lives in a low-ceilinged house, and his love of physical
beauty is apparent in the room in which he receives Mlle
Sandelion. It has several exquisite statuettes, antiques and
torsos, with here a Dionysos, there an Artemis. Mlle Sandelion calls it "a hymn to the splendour of the human body.
You could almost say that it is one of its possessor's creations."
The book is completed by forty-five letters from Montherlant
to the author. The tone of some of these is rather theatrical,
as when Montherlant makes an appointment to meet Mlle
Sandelion at four o'clock one Saturday "opposite the Santé
prison, along its wall in the Boulevard Aragon, at the point
where the execution of murderers is carried out."

Notes sur mon théâtre, by Henry de Montherlant (L'Arche).
Here are aphorisms on *La Reine morte*, *Malatesta*, and on the
general theory of drama. The aim of the theatre, says Montherlant, is to attain the universal through the most tremendous or
the most ordinary particular. There are two moments in
dramatic creation. Creation through emotion, which gives the
substance of the play; then, creation through art, which judges,
chooses, combines, and constructs. "In my plays I have

shouted those high secrets which can only be murmured." In proportion as actors are bad, the public likes them. "A bad actor attracts the public as bad meat attracts flies."

Taurinus furor, by Henry de Montherlant. This is an essay published in Number Forty-eight of *Les Œuvres libres* (May 1950). It is the story of how the passion for bullfighting, which has greatly influenced the development and imagery of his plays and novels, was born in Montherlant. In September 1909 Montherlant wrote to M. Faure-Biguet, "I have just come from the *corridas* at Bayonne. Some day I shall certainly make something of it. It is one of the most magnificent and exciting things in the world." That "something," M. Faure-Biguet remarks, was to be *Les Bestiaires*, one of the world's great lyrical novels, which translates into unmatched prose the exalted imagination of youth, drunk in the sunshine of a hot and romantic land.

In Taurinus furor Montherlant gives a detailed account of the incident mentioned in the letter to Faure-Biguet. It was on the nineteenth of September, when he was thirteen years and five months old, that Montherlant with his grandmother, the Comtesse de Riancey, went to the *corrida* at Bayonne. Both he and Mme de Riancey returned from this, their first *corrida*, which they had visited purely from curiosity, "touched with grace." These are Montherlant's own words, as he recalls the experience forty years later. The bulls fought on that day had been bred by the Duke of Veragua: the matadors were Bombita and Concherito. This was the beginning of Montherlant's passion for the *corrida*. On returning to his home in Paris, he opened subscriptions to three Spanish bullfighting papers, and covered the walls of his room with photographs of bulls. His grandmother preferred pictures of matadors, which she mixed with family photographs and objects of piety. The comtesse found herself much attracted by Bombita, to whom she wrote a letter, for which in return he sent her a signed photograph. She gave up her regular confessor for another whose pale face and blue chin reminded her of Bombita. Mme de Riancey was then sixty years and seven months old, but, says Montherlant, young for her age.

I have tried to find out something about the career of the

matador who lit this flame of enthusiasm in the young
Montherlant. He can be traced in *Los Toros*, by José María de
Cossío (Espasa-Calpe, S.A., Madrid). This tremendous work,
which must be the most comprehensive study ever devoted
to any form of athletic activity whatever, is in three volumes
of a thousand pages each, and contains hundreds of illustrations
to its two and a half million words. It treats exhaustively of
the history of bullfighting and its technique, bullfighting in
literature and poetry, bullfighting authors, bullfighting in art,
the great bullfighting arenas, and winds up with 900,000 words
on matadors famous and obscure, illustrated with pictures of
matadors blinking into the sun, warily waiting for the bull to
attack, smiling amiably in their finery, or being savagely
tossed into the air.

This is an experience that often happened to Bombita. His
real name was Ricardo Torres Reina, and he was born near
Seville in February 1879. He was therefore thirty years old
when Montherlant saw him, and had been fighting for twelve
years. Two of these years had been passed as a *novillero*, when
he fought only bulls of medium strength. Nevertheless, in
these two years he received the prodigious number of forty-
five wounds. He seemed to attract misfortune out of the bull-
ring as well as in it. In Madrid he ran a nail into an arm wound;
and in Dax a piece of wood fixed in the ground pierced a
wound in his foot. There must have been a certain amount of
clumsiness about this Bombita. Señor de Cossío agrees that,
but for his determination of will and courage, Bombita would
quickly have abandoned the career of bullfighting. He did not,
however, retire until 1913, and he continued being gored until
his last appearances in the bullring. Señor de Cossío says that
no other matador has ever had so many serious wounds. Yet a
high proportion of matadors get themselves killed, and Bombita did not die until 1936. In his sixteen years of active fighting he fought in 91 *corridas* as a *novillero*, and in 692 as a full
matador. He killed 1800 bulls. This is a very big number,
though it is not a record. Rafael Guerra, called Guerrita
(1862–1941), the first matador to abandon the traditional
reckless extravagance of his profession, and conduct his career
like a hardheaded business-man, killed 2333 bulls in the course
of 887 *corridas*, and Marcial Lalanda, who retired in 1942,

accounted for 2271. On the other hand, the two greatest matadors of modern times, Juan Belmonte and Manolete, both killed some hundreds of bulls fewer than Bombita in the course of his career.

Bombita, at the time that Montherlant saw him, was at the height of his powers. For some five years he had been at the head of his profession during a period when it numbered several first-class men, though no one of outstanding repute. Yet during 1909 Bombita was fighting under great strain. Public opinion in Spain had been exacerbated by his demand for extra pay when meeting bulls of the Miura breed, which were celebrated for their ferocity. The simplest, least charitable, and most generally accepted explanation of Bombita's attitude was fear. But, as Señor de Cossío points out, Bombita could easily have reduced to a minimum his encounters with the Miura bulls (Guerrita, for example, always chose carefully the animals he was to fight), but he preferred to make common cause with his colleagues. Altogether it was a troubled man that Montherlant saw fight that September afternoon.

Jean Cocteau (*Empreintes*, Mai-Juin-Juillet, 1950). An interesting jumble of documents, photographs, and critical essays connected with Jean Cocteau, the whole being intended (designed is too strong a word) to give a favourable picture of this deliberately unusual author. There is a facsimile letter from Colette, as well as an essay by Jean Marais, and another facsimile (family) letter describing Cocteau's birth. Roger Lannes contributes an account of Cocteau's first meeting as a young man of twenty with Diaghilev. At this meeting Diaghilev exclaimed to Cocteau, "Surprise me." This advice has been almost as influential, and as dangerous, as that given by his mother to the young George III, "George, be a king." Cocteau has been trying to surprise the world ever since. Robert Goffin considers him as a poet, breaking other people's rules and making his own out of his peculiar compulsive temperament. Georges Sion, of Cocteau as dramatist, says that properly speaking he has invented nothing. "Like Shakespeare, he borrows with a prince's prodigality." Jean Genet sums him up in the word "Greek." Claude Mauriac thinks the best thing Cocteau has ever done, in all his multifarious excursions into different arts, is his film *Orphée*.

Edwige Feuillère, by Robert Kemp (Calmann-Lévy). This biography of an actress whom it is no secret that I regard as the greatest in the world is by the dramatic critic of *Le Monde*. Mme Feuillère was born at Vesoul, in the Haute-Saône. As a child her name was Vigette Cunati, her father being an Italian who, after the First World War, became a naturalized Frenchman. It was her grandmother who earliest called her Edwige. She went to school in Dijon. The Cunatis—Mme Feuillère's mother was a Protestant—looked upon the theatre with horror, associating it with Babylon and Gomorrah. M. Cunati became involved in a lawsuit, and one day the Mayor of Dijon, Gaston Gérard, her father's counsel, heard the young Edwige imitate the witnesses in the case so skilfully that he proposed she should study at the local Conservatoire. Her parents' opposition was overcome, and later she took a first prize in comedy, a prize in tragedy, and another in comic opera. But her parents' misgivings continued.

Edwige's father's affairs did not go well, and it looked as if she would have to become a typist. Instead she took the train to Paris, with an introduction given to her by a clergyman in Dijon to the manageress of the Union of Christian Young Women at 22 Rue de Naples. At this address she passed her early days in Paris. She studied at the Conservatoire, met another student, Pierre Feuillère, whom she later married, and made her first appearance on the stage at the Bouffes-Parisiens, in *Le Roi Pausole*, under the name of Cora Lynn. Her subsequent career, both on the stage and in the cinema, is well-known.

On another occasion I wrote of her dignity at a big reception given at the French Embassy in London. What I did not describe there, because I had not yet met her, was the quite extraordinary grace, friendliness, and charm of her bearing in private life.

Louis Jouvet, 1887–1951 (Revue de la Société d'Histoire du Théâtre; quatrième année; Olivier Perrin). This superb documentation of the career of one of the greatest figures in the modern French theatre should be a model of its kind in all countries where dramatic art is considered seriously. It begins with an essay by Pierre Brisson on "Les Deux Jouvet." There are two kinds of producers, says M. Brisson. Those who seek to inspire, and those who seek to be inspired. It is the latter kind to whom the French give their admiration, and Jouvet was one of the most illustrious of them. This essay is followed by a year-by-year biography, the main events being given in ordinary print, with illustrative anecdotes, reminiscences from friends, and quotations from letters and the Press in smaller type. Newspaper references to the famous men, like Giraudoux and Christian Bérard, with whom Jouvet worked are included. This part of the book is extremely detailed, I open it absolutely at random, and find, under the heading of November 1, 1941, to September 21, 1942, this entry:

> The company presents eight productions during this season. The stagehands build 22 sets, of which two require complicated machinery. There are 200 costumes to be manufactured. The work is carried on under the supervision of Louis Jouvet. He has got into touch with Darius Milhaud, Vittorio Rieti, Pavel Tchelitchew, Barbara Karinska, who are now in the United States [Jouvet was then on a South American tour]. He calls in the help of Brazilian, Portuguese, and Argentinian theatre designers: Eduardo Anahory, Joas-Maria de Santos, Enrique Liberal, Ana-Inès Carcano, and two musicians: Paul Misraki and Renzo Massarani.
>
> February 6. Louis Jouvet is officially informed by a note from the French Embassy that he is considered to be dismissed from his Chair at the Conservatoire. He becomes Professor Emeritus from January 1, 1942.
>
> May 13, 1942. Louis Jouvet receives *L'Apollon de* . . . Giraudoux has sent it from Switzerland. He writes upon the manuscript:
>
> DEAR JOUVET, DEAR LOUIS,
> Find the name for Apollyon yourself. May we meet soon. I am working well for you. *Sodome et Gomorrhe* is finished. *La Folle de Chaillot* [*The Madwoman of Chaillot*] will be ready on your return. We all think of you, of all of you, with affection, and we are waiting for you.
> JEAN
>
> June 16. Creation of *L'Apollon de Marsac*, which later in Paris will be *L'Apollon de Bellac*.

In spite of the success of this second season, the company had to run into debt. It counted on the performances at São-Paulo to put things right.

July 21 to August 2. Municipal Theatre at São-Paulo. Performances under very adverse conditions. Transport strike, mass illness, very cold. Receipts reduced.

August 21 to September 20. Théâtre Ateneo at Buenos Aires.

If only we could have the careers of men like Cochran, Olivier, Gielgud, and Richardson analysed like this, how much easier would be the task of recording the history of the English theatre!

This part of the book is followed by a list of all the productions in which Jouvet appeared, with dates, the name of his part, and the number of performances. Then comes a list of his tours. From 1923 onward there is an annual roll-call of the players in his company. There are notes on Jouvet at the Comédie-Française, and as a teacher at the Conservatoire. There is a record of his appearances on the screen and in radio. There is a bibliography. Finally, there is a résumé of the books, studies, and articles written about Jouvet. There are numerous photographs.

Mannequin de Paris, by Praline (Éditions du Seuil). This is the autobiography of the most celebrated mannequin in Paris, who was killed in a motor accident near Limoges during 1952. I had seen her the previous year on her only stage appearance. This was with Edith Piaf in a play by Marcel Achard, a gangster musical set in Montmartre and a fashionable couturier's. Praline's single scene was in the showroom of this establishment, in which, a slim, tall, graceful figure, she tried on a white silk dress bought for her by an admirer. She had a few lines to speak, and, when a dark handsome stranger peered round the door and fired a shot at her lover, she had to duck. That was the end of her dramatic obligations in this particular piece.

The interest of her autobiography lies chiefly in the picture it draws of France during the Occupation. This should be compared and contrasted with that given in previous pages. There is a famous passage in Carlyle's *French Revolution* in which young lovers are shown strolling along the banks of the Seine even at the height of the Terror, oblivious to the dreadful events happening around them. War and revolution have become more obsessive since then, but the world of Parisian *haute couture* seems to have preserved its attractive, trivial values through Pearl Harbour and Stalingrad.

Praline did not enter it until the middle of the War. She passed her childhood at Le Bourget, watching the aerodrome there rapidly grow. After leaving school before she was fourteen, she became a bank messenger, then an apprentice in a fashion house near the Gare de l'Est, and later a salesgirl in a shop in the Rue Tronchet, not far from the Madeleine. She was evacuated from Paris at the beginning of the War, but soon afterwards came back to take up her old job, which she found had in the meantime been given to some one else. A chance meeting with a photographer in the Place de l'Étoile resulted in the suggestion that she should become a mannequin. The next morning she applied at Balenciaga's in person, and was kindly received, but did not secure a job. She went on to Schiaparelli's, where she hardly got through the entrance. She then answered an advertisement of Lelong's, and on February 6, 1942, was engaged as a mannequin. Until they were momentarily interrupted at the Liberation, the great fashion houses of Paris held their displays in an atmosphere apparently untouched by the War. There were still large numbers of women whose only concern in life was to make themselves elegant, and these thronged the half-yearly Collections. At these Collections there was hardly a uniform to be seen, though now and again they were visited by a group of young German officers, who would sit seriously, as if in class. It was at the Collection which Lelong displayed about the time of the battle of El Alamein that Praline made her debut. It was attended by about 2000 people, with artists making sketches and photographers clicking cameras. She had incurred the enmity of important people in the House, and she was allowed to wear clothes designed only by a couple of unknown young employees. She obtained an enormous success. As she walked from room to room, applause broke out, there were exclamations of "Beautiful!" "What an excellent figure!" and M. Lelong himself winked at her in satisfaction. The names of the inexperienced young men who designed the dresses which she wore with such gratifying results were Balmain and Dior.

Le Style au microscope, by "Criticus" (Calmann-Lévy). This book seems rather pettifogging. It takes a dozen authors, of whom Montherlant, Sartre, Salacrou, and Aymé are the only ones who much concern us, reprints the opening paragraph of one of their characteristic works, and proceeds to examine it from a literary, dramatic, and grammatical point of view. Each separate phrase is made the subject of copious comments, and at the end of the examination the author is summed up in a brief judgment. The method which Criticus adopts is somewhat similar to that of the man who tries to assess the architectural merit of Chartres by tapping and weighing a single brick. But in his final judgments Criticus allows himself to be influenced by a wider knowledge of his author's work than is permitted by the deliberately restricted technique he adopts elsewhere. This leads to favourable judgments on Salacrou, Sartre, and Aymé, but not on Montherlant, who seems to have a singular capacity for antagonizing people.

Le Théâtre contemporain (*Recherches et Débats*, 2; Librairie Arthème Fayard). This publication contains studies of Salacrou, Anouilh, and Montherlant. The book's basic purpose is to discuss the relations between religion and the theatre in contemporary Europe. Religion, since this is a French book, is identified with the Roman Catholic faith, though there is an examination of T. S. Eliot's Anglicanism in connexion with *The Family Reunion*. (Eliot has an immense reputation in France. His *Murder in the Cathedral*, along with Charles Morgan's *The Flashing Stream*, is considered the highest achievement of the Anglo-Saxon world in the contemporary theatre. R. P. Carré dates the entry of religion as an important force in the modern theatre "from the unforgettable performances of *Le Soulier de satin* in the dark hours of the Occupation. Suddenly, the walls of our spiritual prison burst for an evening, and we became citizens of that universe which enlarged the stage of the Comédie-Française to the dimensions of eternity." *Le Soulier de satin* was followed by *Le Maître de Santiago*, whose third act, in M. Carré's opinion, failed to approach Christianity, though its earlier portions came nearer the mark.

Then came the atheistic counter-attack, chiefly in Sartre's *Le Diable et le Bon Dieu*, and many a play was agitated by the question of whether God exists or not. Mlle Simone de Beauvoir attempted to dispose of the problem by declaring airily, "The question of this presence or this absence in the depth of the sky is no concern of man's." But, in spite of this talented author, it has continued to be a concern of the stage. *Le Théâtre contemporain* also has a long discussion, in the form of a debate, on atheism in the theatre.

Notes de théâtre, by Béatrix Dussane (Lardanchet). Mme Dussane gives, in the form of a continuous narrative, an account of the main events in the Paris theatre between 1940 and 1950. The book is much more than its modest title suggests. It is not a series of disconnected observations, but a well-organized and thoughtful study. It is divided into three principal sections: the vicissitudes of the Comédie-Française, which has had its ups and downs, but nothing comparable with the vertiginous post-war experiences of the Old Vic; the serious commercial theatre, which means chiefly Sartre, Anouilh, Montherlant, and Salacrou; and the theatre of sheer entertainment, dominated by Roussin. This last is the briefest part of the book, which shows good judgment and sense of values. It is excellent on Jean-Louis Barrault.

Paris sur scène, by Jean-Jacques Gautier (Éditions Jacques Vautrain). Ten years of the Paris theatre, 1941 to 1951, covered in reviews which M. Gautier contributed to *Le Figaro*. The earlier notices vividly describe the physical and mental conditions of theatre-going in Paris in the first days of the German Occupation. In his novels, for one of which, *Histoire d'un fait divers*, he was awarded the Prix Goncourt, Gautier can organize a plot with impressive logic, building carefully, as in his story of Parisian theatrical life, *La Demoiselle du Pont-aux-Anes*, to a climax of shattering completeness. But in his criticisms he seems to prefer a series of passionate exclamations to a reasoned exposition. In these notices he writes in a succession of short, sharp stabs. Stabs in the back, some might call them, for Gautier is the most savage of French critics, though on occasion his enthusiasm can also be boundless. He first wrote under a pseudonym, "Le Boulevardier," and did not sign his reviews until after the Liberation. Authors and managers at that time accused him of being the critic who dare not give his name. *Paris sur scène*, illustrated amusingly by the caricaturist Sennep, has notices of many of the plays mentioned earlier, among them being *Ardèle*, *Dieu le savait*, *L'Archipel Lenoir*, *Le Diable et le Bon Dieu*, *Le Maître de Santiago*, *Les Mains sales*, *Malatesta*, and *Partage de midi*.

La Galerie dramatique, by Francis Ambrière (Corréa). A collection of M. Ambrière's reviews of productions in Paris between 1945 and 1948, giving much attention to authors mentioned in the foregoing pages. Ambrière is a serious, well-informed, and judicious critic, feeling deeply about the theatre, but not inclined either to wild enthusiasms or sudden rages. He notes the financial prosperity of the theatre during the Occupation, but, with Georges Pitoeff dead, his wife Ludmilla in Switzerland, Jouvet and his company in South America, and Armand Salacrou and some other leading dramatists withdrawn from the stage, he sees its only distinction at that time in *Antigone*, *Eurydice*, *Le Soulier de satin*, *La Reine morte*, and *Les Mouches*. London towards the end of the War had the Old Vic triumphs of Olivier and Richardson, and John Gielgud's brilliant Haymarket season, but its good new plays were certainly not more numerous than these. There is an introductory chapter·discussing the condition of the theatre since the War, with special reference to such subjects as the assistance it has received from the State, decentralization, and the problems of the Comédie-Française. A second chapter examines contemporary authors and their works. *Les Nuits de la colère* and *L'Archipel Lenoir* cause M. Ambrière to place Salacrou at the head of French dramatic authors, followed by Anouilh, whom he finds, on what I consider to be insufficient grounds, to be passing through a severe internal crisis.

Théâtre (*Troisième Cahier: Aspects du théâtre contemporain en France* (*1930–45*)), edited by Paul Arnold. M. Arnold denies that the unsettlement and confusion of the age is unfavourable to the drama. The Elizabethan Age, he recalls, was unparalleled in its mental and doctrinal disarray. M. Arnold is one of those who stress the importance of society in developing great drama. He reminds his readers that Matthew Arnold said that every age has roughly the same number of talented actors, and adds (rather airily, it seems to me) that the same is true about the supply of great dramatists. What matters is whether the society in which they live encourages or stifles their talent. This sort of thing would seem suitable as an introduction to a work examining the theatrical implications of contemporary social organization. But in practice it forms a preface to a series of quotations from and essays on individual authors, including Anouilh and Roussin.

There are interesting details on Anouilh. It is said that at the time of the *répétition générale* of *L'Hermine* (April 26, 1932) little was known of him except that he was about twenty-two years of age, had been born at Bordeaux, but had passed most of his life in Paris. He had already written nearly twenty plays, and been Louis Jouvet's secretary. Yet in his early years he had not much frequented theatres, apart from the Casino at Arcachon during the holidays. The first performance of *L'Hermine*, it is said, with its apparent sympathy for murder in the cause of young love, its eloquent claim that only money can preserve love's purity, made a sensation. The critics were mostly agreed that Anouilh lacked everything except the essential, the capacity to excite an audience passionately. They exclaimed, with immense relief, not "Here is a well-constructed play," but "This is a dramatist!"

Entretiens, by Paul Léautaud, with Robert Mallet (Gallimard). These radio interviews, conducted with great skill, consideration, and strength of mind by Robert Mallet, were transmitted between November 1950 and July 1951. They were an enormous success, and made M. Léautaud, then over eighty, one of the most famous literary figures in France. The French public found irresistible this extraordinary revelation of character. M. Léautaud exposed his mordant dislike of his fellowmen and women, his bitterness of tongue, his uncompromising views on art, his absolute lack of tenderness or respect for his parents, his total indifference to poverty and privation, and his lifelong and indefatigable devotion to starving animals abandoned by their owners, with a complete frankness and simplicity which the most careful art could not have bettered, giving, in the process, an amusing and sardonic picture of the world of Parisian literature, theatre, and journalism of the last seventy years, accompanied by some positively astounding social reminiscences.

Interviews impubliables, by Gilbert Ganne (Éditions André Bonne). This young journalist, M. Ganne, has suddenly, on the strength of this book, become known as one of the best interviewers in France. His work is lively and generous, but every now and then he says something unexpected that makes the well-known people he is interviewing—among them Montherlant, Cocteau, and Jean-Jacques Gautier—realize that they have to do with a man of spirit. He says he was made nervous by Montherlant's reputedly ferocious insistence on punctuality, and hung about a long time on the Quai Voltaire, calculating the exact number of seconds it would take him to arrive at Montherlant's front door precisely at four o'clock, which he managed to do. Montherlant told him that no one could write well before he was twenty-seven, and Ganne pointed out that Montherlant had himself written *L'Exil* before reaching that age. "Inexplicable. An exception," said Montherlant. He maintains to M. Ganne that he is not a Christian. "I have had," he says, "an exceptionally happy life." Cocteau M. Ganne found in a particularly ebullient mood. He had just returned from a tour in Germany, on which he had been received like a king. Every time he entered a theatre people cheered him. Coming back to Paris was like returning to a provincial city.

"Nevertheless," he adds, "I prefer living at home, even if people do put me away in a corner."

Réflexions du comédien, by Louis Jouvet (Librairie Théâtrale). This volume contains Jouvet's essay on Victor Hugo, his estimate of Beaumarchais, a review of Becque's *La Parisienne*, and an interesting paper on "Where is the theatre going?" The actor Pierre Renoir reminded Jouvet that, though it is not always possible to say where one is going, it is easy enough to decide where one has come from. This set Jouvet considering the point of origin of the modern French theatre, which he found in Antoine's Théâtre Libre. "A curious epoch," he calls this period in the history of the drama, enamoured of the exact sciences, anxious for demonstrable and verifiable truths, which, along with the bicycle and the phonograph, discovered the play of social significance, and gave birth to the theatre of ideas. Strange was the liberty of this Théâtre Libre, which itself was conquered by décors that aimed at being genuine, ornamented with real doors and real windows, and with real animals walking about, where art consisted in dousing the stage in real rain, in showing a butcher's with the bodies of real animals, and real grates with real coal . . . where every play had genuine flora and fauna sharing in the dramatic ceremonies whose principal themes were industrial disputes, strikes, the family, divorce, syphilis, and feminism.

"Ah, yes," exclaimed the theatre manager earnestly, "I recognize that your criticism of this play is well founded. The hero's psychology is not perhaps very convincing. Yes. But in the third act, in the third act—ah, he sleeps with the maid!"

It was the period of the slice of life.

This era has its echo in the naturalism we still often find in the London theatre, where, at the end of 1952, there was in *The Man* a real kitchen-sink with a real tap, and in *For Better, For Worse* . . . real water dripped into a real bucket through a real hole in the ceiling. Then came the period of the fourth wall. "To be able to act a piece as if it was really taking place, as if the spectator were there by accident or surprise, this was the highest ambition of a dramatic art in which the actor had to do no more than let the public imagine that it had the soul of an eavesdropper." Jouvet's contempt for realism is so widely shared in the French theatre to-day that characters in modern comedies press bell-pushes that are not there, and make speeches to the audience instead of to each other. It is one of the reasons why casual visitors to Parisian theatres often conclude that French acting is bad, by which they mean that it fails to keep to the English rules. It is not, of course, trying to keep to the English rules, about which it is inclined to be either ignorant or scornful.

Critiques d'un autre temps, by Jacques Copeau (*Nouvelle Revue Française*). Jacques Copeau was the director of the Vieux-Colombier, which with its Shakespearean productions did much to reinvigorate the French theatre. One of his principal pupils was Michel Saint-Denis, who worked for a long time in London. These reviews and articles belong to the eve of the First World War, and are an invaluable background to the modern French theatre. Copeau in these pages reveals himself as that rare phenomenon, a theatre worker who considered that dramatic critics are too kind. He demands savagery and fire, not indulgent praise for the mediocre. One has, however, the suspicion that the plays he wanted the critics to denounce and tear to pieces were the sort of play which did not get on to the stage of the Vieux-Colombier.

Lectures dramatiques, by Robert Kemp (La Renaissance du Livre). These reflective essays were written by Robert Kemp, the dramatic critic of *Le Monde*, mainly between 1940 and 1942. They are not reviews of actual productions, but reassessments of French and Greek classical tragedy, supplemented with a few considerations of modern work.

Le Théâtre des années folles, by Pierre Brisson (Éditions du Milieu du Monde). During the early years of the German Occupation, Lyons became a place of exile for Parisian intellectuals. It was there that M. Kemp wrote the articles in *Lectures dramatiques*, and that several Paris newspapers set up their publishing offices. Among these was *Le Figaro*, of which M. Brisson is director. Here, in exile, cut off from active participation in the War, far more sheltered from its impact than it was possible for London to be, this group of leading metropolitan figures had leisure to ponder Æschylus and to immerse themselves in Molière. M. Brisson plunged into the world of Harpagon and Alceste, and, under the chestnut-trees of the Place Bellecour, meditated and discussed this history of the French theatre between the wars.

It is a brilliant and forceful book, written in the light of the War of 1939–45. It is filled with sparkling, and sometimes acid, sketches of leading people in the theatre world like Sacha Guitry, who, M. Brisson says, during the First World War, "resolutely preferred the fires of the footlights to those of Verdun." He evokes many an exciting evening, like that of Henry Bernstein's introduction to the Comédie-Française, when flocks of pigeons were released in the auditorium. In these pages can be seen the beginnings of Salacrou and Anouilh.

L'Amateur du théâtre, by Pierre-Aimé Touchard (Éditions du Seuil). The author was for some years after the War Administrator of the Comédie-Française, a job he found as invidious as that of being a leading actor or a director at the Old Vic. Nowadays, says M. Touchard, people understand the art of football, but not of the theatre. They must learn to read plays, and the first thing they must do is to ask themselves what they would do if they were called on actually to produce them. Unless they know how to produce a given play they cannot understand it. M. Touchard then gives an illuminating account of what the production of a play demands. Then follow stimulating discussions of the Théâtre Libre, the theatre's double necessity of having both emotion and technique, and the difference between character in the novel and in the drama. Character in the theatre, according to M. Touchard, does not exist in itself; "it lives in the centre of an action, and its chief task is to preserve the vigour, meaning, and rhythm of this action." *L'Amateur du théâtre* is a book that will deepen anyone's appreciation of the drama.

Dionysos: Apologie pour le théâtre, by Pierre-Aimé Touchard (Éditions du Seuil). There are chapters on tragedy, comedy, the public, morality, and style. M. Touchard makes much of the unhealthiness of the actor's profession, based principally on the length of time and the intensity with which the actor must inhabit another character than his own. The actor is a man who half his time is away from home. M. Touchard believes that since the seventeenth century the French theatre has been in a state of decline. It has given itself to every casual influence and development, and in consequence has had no controlling style. "The so-called revolutions that have taken place on the stage during these 200 years, including those of Romanticism, and the Théâtre Libre, have been only domestic quarrels in a middle-class house devoid of grandeur." But he thinks that the theatre to-day is on the eve of a new era of tragic splendour.

Le Plaisir du théâtre, by André Bellessort (Librairie Académique Perrin). Bellessort was probably the most gracious of modern French dramatic critics. His essays are pleasantly discursive. His best reviews are of classical revivals. They seem to be based equally upon his own personal reaction to the performance in question, and on a detailed knowledge of the stage history of previous performances. They are as well turned and urbane as an Addison essay. Contemporary dramatists are not prominent in this book, but it is possible in it to follow the work of Jouvet as a producer. Some of Jouvet's innovations, such as accompanying certain speeches in Molière with music, arouse Bellessort's gentle disapprobation. On the other hand, he does not mind when a *metteur en scène* has a little fun with an English classic. He raises his elegant eyebrows when Shakespeare, in *Troilus and Cressida*, sends into the Grecian camp Hector's challenge about the beauty and fidelity of his wife. This is introducing into antiquity the feudal customs of the middle ages, which is a grievous sin; and Bellessort approves a production at the Odéon which parodies Shakespeare by putting the challenge against an air from *La Belle Hélène*.

Le Théâtre et son histoire, by André Boll (Sequana). A brief handbook in the series "Arts pour tous." It includes chapters on theatre buildings, contemporary authors, production, décor, and ancient comedy and tragedy. M. Boll approximates to the English rather than the French view of the importance of the producer. His theory is that the play as written is nothing beside the play as performed. This leads to high praise of the work of Jouvet, though it is a proposition that Jouvet would have found horrifying. Its implications are close to the feeling of Jean Vilar, who was prevented from appearing in London as Œdipus during the Jean-Louis Barrault season of 1951 by his appointment as director of the Théâtre National Populaire, for which he has presented a very fine *Le Cid* and a less satisfactory *Mère courage*. At the end of 1952 M. Vilar caused much animated, not to say angry, discussion in French theatrical circles by saying that between 1920 and 1940 the most important work in the French theatre had been done, not by authors, but by producers.

Au Hasard des soirées, by Pierre Brisson (Gallimard). A collection of theatrical notices of productions between 1929 and

1935—that is, of the years immediately preceding those considered in this book. It contains reviews of the early plays of Marcel Achard and Jean Cocteau. Brisson's method is to take each play that comes under his notice step by step, and to subject it to a light, but penetrating, criticism. The author has a civilized and attractive but not showy style. He has more grace than epigrams, more elegance than fireworks.

Le Théâtre en France depuis 1900, by René Lalou (Presses Universitaires de France). It is rare that a book whose aim is to give a summary of a subject to readers not well informed about it has the depth and liveliness of this admirable study. M. Lalou views the last half-century of the French theatre in an excellent and balanced perspective, but every now and then he selects a moment from this half-century, and enlarges upon it vividly. Like the *Cahiers*, he brings back the excitement provoked by Anouilh's *L'Hermine*. "Coming away from the *générale* of *L'Hermine*," he says, "we were all of one mind. This young secretary of Louis Jouvet had just brought us something which recalled the effect of a purge that might have been concocted by the Dumas of *Antony*, the Dostoevsky of *Crime and Punishment*, and the best melodrama specialists. But this evening had revealed to us incontestably a dramatic mind, and we took to the Métro with joyous hearts." Of Sartre's *Huis Clos* he says that for an hour and twenty minutes its dialogue, without recourse to action, enthralled the audience "with a poignant debate in which ideas were felt as emotions." On the other hand, though I share his admiration of Salacrou's *Les Nuits de la colère*, his reference to its "complete absence of declamation" disturbs me a little. Certainly this play has no bombast or rodomontade. But I cannot help feeling that its final speech, which I have referred to at length on a previous page, is one of the finest examples of controlled rhetoric, or, if you like, of declamation, in modern French drama.

Index